Creo Parametric 4.0 Basics

Basics

Tutorial Books

Contents

Introduction

Welcome to the *Creo Parametric 4.0 Basics* book. This book is written to assist students, designers, and engineering professionals. It covers the important features and functionalities of Creo Parametric using relevant examples and exercises.

This book is written for new users, who can use it as a self-study resource to learn Creo Parametric. In addition, it can also be used as a reference for experienced users. The focus of this book is part modeling, assembly modeling, drawings, sheet metal, and surface design.

Topics covered in this Book

Chapter 1, "Getting Started with Creo Parametric 4.0", introduces Creo Parametric. The user interface and terminology are discussed in this chapter.

Chapter 2, "Sketching", explores the sketching commands in Creo Parametric. You will learn to create parametric sketches.

Chapter 3, "Basic features", teaches you to create basic 3D geometry using the Extrude and Revolve commands. You will also learn to create datum features, which will act as supporting geometry.

Chapter 4, "Holes and Placed Features", covers the features, which can be created without using sketches.

Chapter 5, "Patterned Geometry", explores the commands to create patterned and mirrored geometry.

Chapter 6, "Sweep Features", teaches you to create basic and complex features by sweeping a profile along a path.

Chapter 7, "Blend Features", teaches you to create features by using different cross-sections.

Chapter 8, "Modifying Parts", explores the commands and techniques to modify the part geometry.

Chapter 9, "Assemblies", explains you to create assemblies using the bottom-up and top-down design approaches.

Chapter 10, "Drawings", covers how to create 2D drawings from 3D parts and assemblies.

Chapter 11, "Sheet Metal Design", covers how to create sheet metal parts and flat patterns.

Chapter 12, "Surface Design", covers how to create complex shapes using surface design commands.

Chapter 1: Getting Started with Creo Parametric 4.0

Introduction to Creo Parametric 4.0

Creo Parametric 4.0 is a parametric and feature-based system that allows you to create 3D parts, assemblies, and 2D drawings. The design process in Creo Parametric is shown below.

Environments in Creo Parametric 4.0

Creo Parametric offers many environments to carry out different types of operations. For example, Creo Parametric provides you with the **Part** environment to design a part. Likewise, there are many environments to perform advanced operations such are manufacturing process, process diagrams, assemblies, and so on. However, in this book we cover the basic environments such as **Part**, **Assembly**, and **Drawing**. A brief introduction to these environments is given next.

Part environment

The **Part** environment provides you with commands to create parametric solid models. You can start a document in this environment by clicking the **New** icon and selecting **Type > Part** on the **New** dialog. To create solid models, you must draw parametric sketches in the **Sketch** environment, and then convert them into solids.

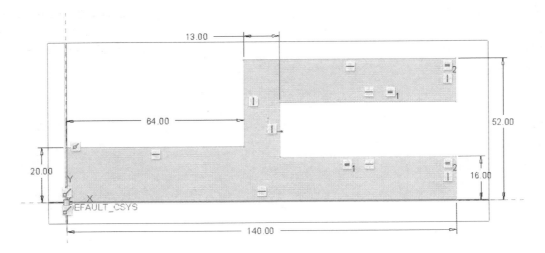

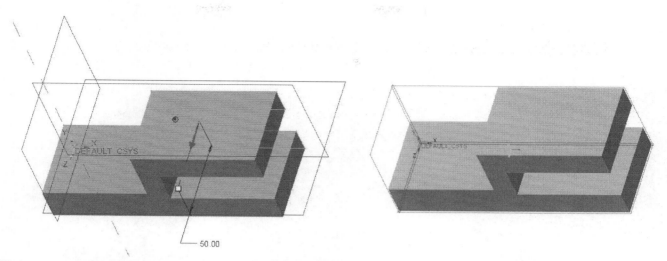

However, you can add some additional features to the solid models, which do not require sketches.

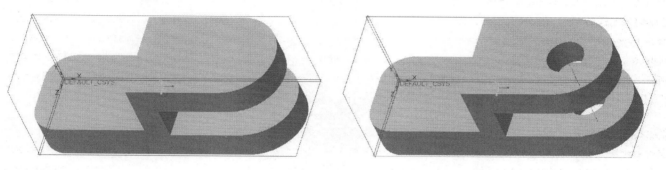

Assembly

The **Assembly** environment (click **Type > Assembly** on the **New** dialog) has commands to combine individual parts in an assembly. There are two ways to create an assembly. The first way is to create individual parts and assemble them in the **Assembly** environment (Bottom-up assembly design). The second way is to start an assembly file and create individual parts in it (Top-down assembly design).

Drawing

The **Drawing** environment (click **Type > Drawing** on the **New** dialog) has commands to create 2D drawings, which can be used for the manufacturing process. There are two ways to create drawings. The first way is to generate the standard views of a 3D component or assembly. The second way is to sketch the drawings, manually.

Sheetmetal

The **Sheetmetal** environment (click **Type > Part** and click **Subtype > Sheetmetal** on the **New** dialog) has commands to create sheet metal models. You can create a sheet metal model either by building features in a systematic manner or by converting a part geometry in to sheet metal.

Parametric Modeling

In Creo Parametric, parameters, dimensions, or constraints control everything. For example, if you want to change the position of the hole shown in figure, you need to change the dimension or constraint that controls its position.

Associativity

The other big advantage of Creo Parametric is the associativity between parts, assemblies and drawings. When you make changes to the design of a part, the changes will take place in any assembly that it is a part of. In addition, the 2D drawing will update automatically.

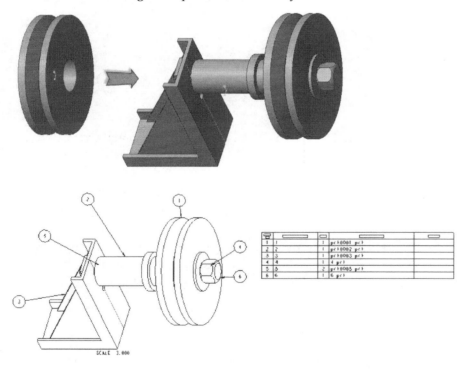

Modified Part

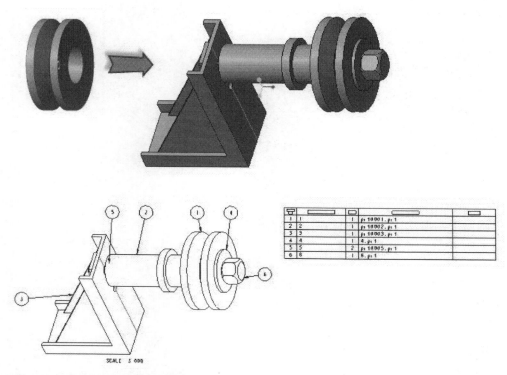

File Types in Creo Parametric

Creo Parametric offers three main file types:

.prt: This type of file has a geometry of individual part. The files created in **Part** and **Sheetmetal** environments will have this extension.

.asm: This type of file is an assembly of one or more parts. In fact, it is a link of one or more parts.

.drw: The files created in the Drawing environment have this extension.

Starting Creo Parametric 4.0

To start **PTC Creo Parametric 4.0**, click the **PTC Creo Parametric 4.0** icon on your computer screen (or) click **Start > PTC > Creo Parametric 4.0**.

User Interface

The following image shows the **PTC Creo Parametric 4.0** application window.

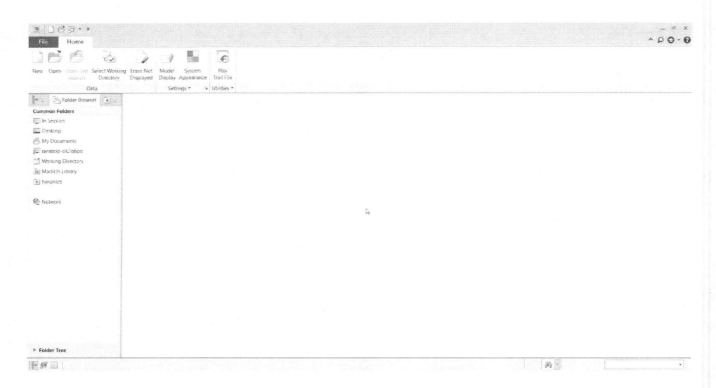

1. On the **Home** tab of the ribbon, click the **New** icon.
2. On the **New** dialog, select **Type > Part**.
3. Type-in the name of the part file in the **Name** box.
4. Click **OK**.

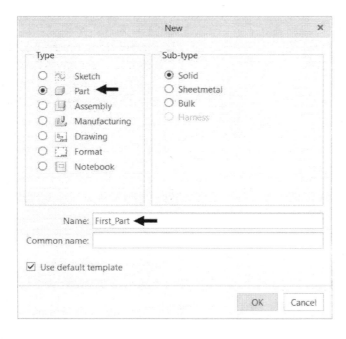

The Creo Parametric part window appears, as shown.

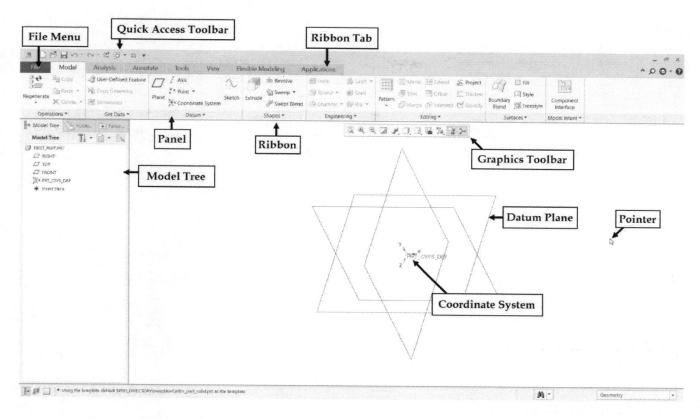

Various components of the user interface are:

Quick Access Toolbar

The **Quick Access Toolbar** has some commonly used commands such as **New, Open, Save, Undo, Redo, Regenerate,** and so on. You can add more commands to the **Quick Access Toolbar** by clicking on the down-arrow next to it, and then selecting commands from the drop-down menu. If the required command is not available in the drop-down menu, then select the **More Commands** options; the **Creo Parametric Options** dialog pops up on the screen. On this dialog, select the required command from the commands list available on the left side, and the click **Add selected item to ribbon** ➡ icon. Next, click **OK.**

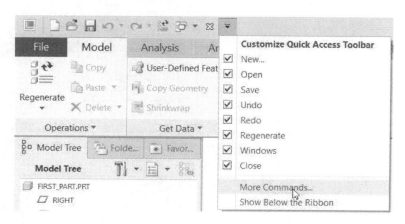

File Menu

The **File Menu** appears when you click on the **File** button located at the top left corner of the window. The **File Menu** has a list of self-explanatory menus. You can see a list of recently opened documents in the **Recent Files** menu.

Ribbon

Ribbon is located at the top of the window. It has various tabs. When you click on a tab, various panels appear. These panels have commands.

Various ribbons available in different environments are given next.

Part environment

Sketch tab

The **Sketch** tab has commands to create and edit sketches. This tab is activated while creating sketches.

Model tab

This tab has commands to create and edit solid/surface geometry.

Analysis tab

This tab has commands to measure the physical properties of the geometry.

View tab

This tab has commands to zoom, pan, rotate, or change the view of a 3D model.

Assembly environment

The **Model** tab has commands to create components or insert existing components into an assembly.

Sheetmetal environment

The **Model** tab has commands to create sheet metal parts.

Drawing environment

Layout tab

This tab has commands to generate and edit standard views of a 3D geometry.

Table tab

This tab commands to insert tables, balloons and other data into the drawing.

Annotate tab

This tab has commands to add dimensions and other annotations to the drawing.

Status bar

This is available below the graphics window. It shows the prompts while using the commands.

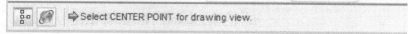

Command Search

The **Command Search** bar is used to search for any command. On the top right corner of the window, click the **Command Search** icon to display the **Command Search** bar. You can type any keyword in the **Command Search** bar and find a list of commands related to it.

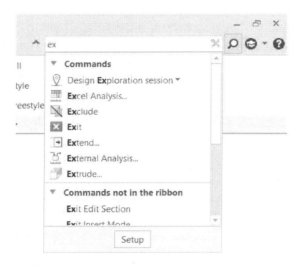

Model Tree

It contains the list of operations carried while constructing a part.

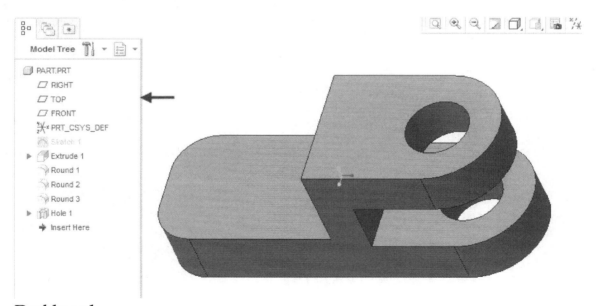

Dashboard

When you execute any command in Creo Parametric, the dashboard related to it appears. A dashboard has various options. The following figure shows various components of a dashboard.

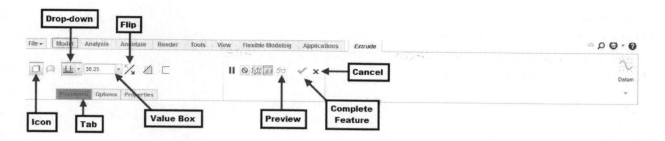

This textbook uses the default options on the dashboard.

Mouse Functions

Various functions of the mouse buttons are:

Left Mouse button (MB1)

When you double-click the left mouse button (MB1) on a feature, the dimensions related it would appear. You can edit the parameters of the feature.

Middle Mouse button (MB2)

Press the middle mouse and drag the mouse to rotate the view.

Right Mouse button (MB3)

Select an object and click this button to open the shortcut menu related to it.

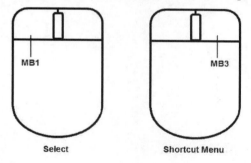

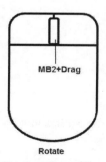

Background

To change the background color of the window, click **File > Options**. On the **PTC Creo Parametric Options** dialog, click **System Appearance** on the left side. Set the **System Colors** and click **OK**.

Shortcut Keys

CTRL+Z	Undo
CTRL+Y	Redo
CTRL+S	Save
F1	Creo Parametric Help
CTRL+N	New File
CTRL+O	Open File
CTRL+P	Print
Ctrl+F	Search
Ctrl+C	Copy
Ctrl+V	Paste
Delete	Delete
Ctrl+R	Repaint
Ctrl+D	Switch to the default view orientation

Chapter 2: Sketching

This chapter covers the methods and commands to create sketches used in the Part environment. In Creo Parametric, you can create sketches in the Sketch environment. You will learn to create sketches in this environment.

In Creo Parametric, you create a rough sketch, and then apply dimensional and geometric constraints that define its shape and size. The dimensions define the length, size, and angle of a sketch element, whereas geometric constraints define the relations between sketch elements.

The topics covered in this chapter are:

- Sketching in Sketch environment
- Using constraints and dimensions
- Learn sketching commands
- Learn commands and options that help you to create sketches easily

Sketching in the Sketch environment

Creating sketches in the Sketch environment is very easy. You have to activate the **Sketch** command, and then define a plane on which you want to create the sketch.

1. On the ribbon, click **Model** tab > **Datum** panel > **Sketch** icon.

2. Click on the top datum plane located at the center in the graphics window.

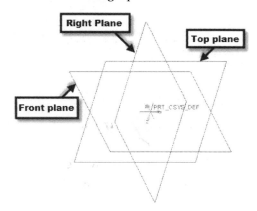

Now, you need to define the reference plane. The sketch will be constrained with respect to the reference plane. When, you select the top datum plane, the right and top planes are selected as reference. However, you change the reference as per your requirement.

3. On the **Sketch** dialog, click in the **Reference** box and select a reference plane.

Now, you can define the viewing direction of the sketch. By default, the view direction is from the top. You can reverse it by clicking the **Flip** button.

4. On the **Sketch** dialog, click the **Properties** tab and type-in the name of the sketch.
5. Click the **Sketch** button to start the sketch.
6. On the ribbon, click **Sketch** tab > **Setup** panel > **Sketch View** icon. This changes the view orientation parallel to the screen.

7. You can now start drawing sketches on the selected plane.

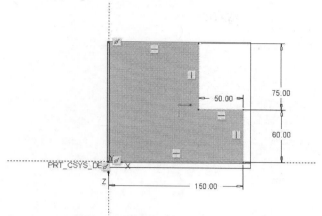

8. After creating the sketch, click **Sketch** tab > **Close** panel > **OK** icon to exit the sketch.

Sketching Commands

Creo Parametric provides you with a set of commands to create sketches. These commands are located on the **Sketch** ribbon tab.

The Line Chain command

This is the most commonly used command while creating a sketch.

1. To activate this command, click **Sketch** tab > **Sketching** panel > **Line** icon on the ribbon.
2. To create a line, click in the graphics window, move the pointer and click again. After clicking for the second time, you can see that an end point is added and another line segment is started. This is a convenient way to create a chain of lines.

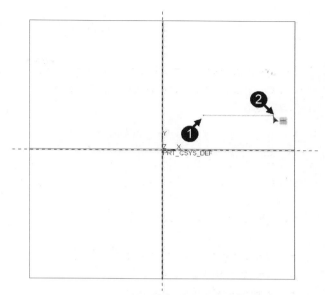

3. Continue to click to add more line segments.

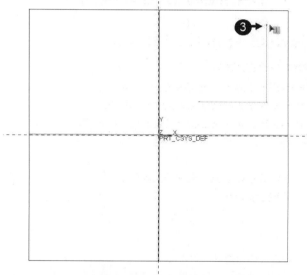

While creating lines, you will notice some symbols. For example, when you click and move the pointer horizontally, the Horizontal symbol appears. This indicates that you are drawing a horizontal line. Now, when you click the right mouse button, the constraint will be locked.

When you move the pointer vertically, the Vertical symbol appears. This indicates a vertical line.

If the Equal symbol appears on two different lines, the lengths of the two lines will be equal.

If the endpoint of the line is collinear with another point, the vertical symbol appears. Also, a vertical dotted line appears between the points. This indicates that the points are aligned vertically.

If you want to draw a line parallel to another line, then move the pointer until the parallel symbol appears.

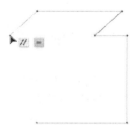

Likewise, you can draw perpendicular lines using the perpendicular symbol.

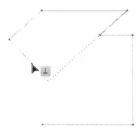

If you want to click on the midpoint of a line, move the pointer until the midpoint symbol ⊿ appears.

Likewise, select the start point of the sketch to close it.

You will notice that another line is attached to the pointer even after closing the sketch loop. On the ribbon, click **Sketch** tab > **Operations** panel > **Select** icon to deactivate any sketch command.

After creating the sketch, you will notice that the dimensions are added to it, automatically. However, these dimensions will not constrain the sketch fully. When you drag the elements of the sketch, the dimension values will change automatically. In addition, some dimensions may not be required. You will learn more about how to add and modify dimensions later in this chapter.

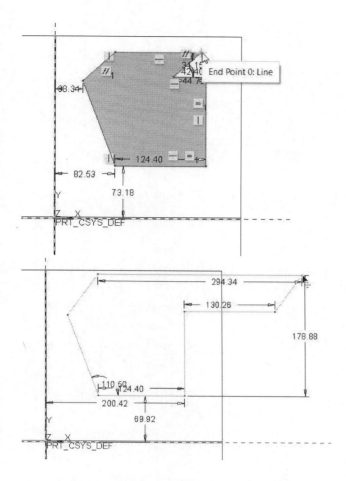

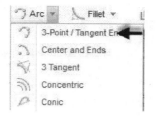

2. Click to define the start point of the arc.
3. Move the pointer and click to define the endpoint of the arc.
4. Move the pointer and click to define a point on the periphery of the arc.

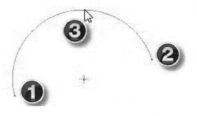

To create an arc tangent to a sketch element, activate the **3-Point/Tangent End** command and select the endpoint of the sketch element.

You will notice that a tangent arc appears along with a four-segment circle at the selected endpoint.

To delete a line, select it and press the **Delete** key. To select more than one line, press the Ctrl key and click on multiple line segments; the lines will be highlighted. You can also select multiple lines by dragging a box from left to right. Press and hold the left mouse button and drag a box from left to right; the lines inside the box boundary will be selected.

3-Point/Tangent End

This command creates an arc by clicking three points in the graphic window. You can also use this command to create an arc tangent to another sketch element.

1. On the ribbon, click **Sketch** tab > **Sketching** panel > **Arc** drop-down > **3-Point/Tangent End**.

If you do not want to create a tangent arc, take the pointer to the endpoint of the sketch element and move it in the direction perpendicular to it.

Define the endpoint and limiting point.

Center and Ends

This command creates an arc by defining its center, start and end.

1. On the ribbon, click **Sketch** tab > **Sketching** panel > **Arc** drop-down > **Center and Ends**.
2. Click to define the center point.
3. Next, move the pointer and you will notice that a circle appears attached to the pointer. This defines the radius of the arc.
4. Now, click to define the start point of the arc and move the pointer; you will notice that an arc is drawn from the start point.
5. Once the arc appears the way you want, click to define its endpoint.

3 Tangent

This command creates an arc tangent to three lines.

1. On the ribbon, click **Sketch** tab > **Sketching** panel > **Arc** drop-down > **3 Tangent**.
2. Select three lines, arcs or circles. This creates an arc tangent to selected lines.

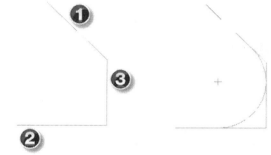

Concentric

This command creates an arc concentric to another arc or circle.

1. On the ribbon, click **Sketch** tab > **Sketching** panel > **Arc** drop-down > **Concentric**.
2. Click on an arc/circle or its center point.
3. Move the pointer and click to define the radius and start point of the arc.
4. Move the pointer and click to define the endpoint.

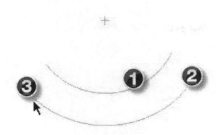

5. Likewise, you can create multiple concentric arcs.
6. On the ribbon, click **Sketch** tab > **Operations** panel > **Select** icon to deactivate the command.

⊙ Center and Point

This is the most common way to draw a circle.

1. On the ribbon, click **Sketch** tab > **Sketching** panel > **Circle** drop-down > **Center and Point**.

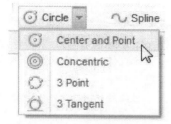

2. Click to define the center point of the circle.
3. Drag the pointer, and then click again to define the diameter of the circle.

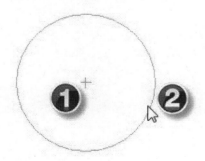

◯ 3 Point

This command creates a circle by using three points.

1. On the ribbon, click **Sketch** tab > **Sketching** panel > **Circle** drop-down > **3 Point**.

2. Select three points from the graphics window. You can also select existing points from the sketch geometry. The first two points define the location of the circle and the third point defines its diameter.

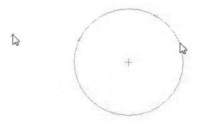

⊙ 3 Tangent

This command creates a circle tangent to three lines, arcs or circles.

1. On the ribbon, click **Sketch** tab > **Sketching** panel > **Circle** drop-down > **3 Tangent**.
2. Select three lines, arcs or circles. This creates a circle tangent to the selected elements.

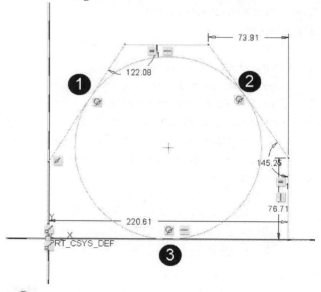

◎ Concentric

This command creates a circle concentric to another circle or arc.

1. On the ribbon, click **Sketch** tab > **Sketching** panel > **Circle** drop-down > **Concentric**.
2. Select the circle of center point of the circle.

3. Move the pointer and click to create the circle.

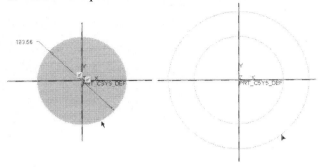

Corner Rectangle

This command creates a rectangle by defining its diagonal corners.

1. On the ribbon, click **Sketch** tab > **Sketching** panel > **Rectangle** drop-down > **Corner Rectangle**.

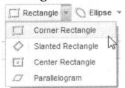

2. Click to define the first corner.
3. Drag the pointer and click to define the second corner.

Slanted Rectangle

This command creates a slanted rectangle. The first two points define the width and inclination angle of the rectangle. The third point defines its height. You can activate this command by clicking **Sketch** tab > **Sketching** panel > **Rectangle** drop-down > **Slanted Rectangle**.

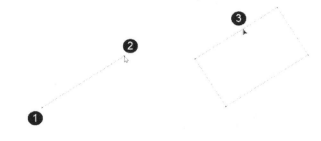

Center Rectangle

This command creates a rectangle by defining two points: center of the rectangle and its corner.

1. On the ribbon, click **Sketch** tab > **Sketching** panel > **Rectangle** drop-down > **Center Rectangle**.
2. Click to define the center of the rectangle.
3. Move the pointer and click again to define the corner point.

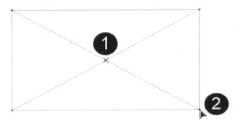

Parallelogram

This command creates a parallelogram by using three points that you specify.

1. On the ribbon, click **Sketch** tab > **Sketching** panel > **Rectangle** drop-down > **Parallelogram**.
2. Select two points to define the width of the parallelogram.
3. Drag the pointer and click to define the height of parallelogram.

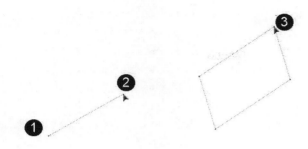

✕ Line Tangent

This command creates a line tangent to two circles or arcs.

1. On the ribbon, click **Sketch** tab > **Sketching** panel > **Line** drop-down > **Line Tangent**.
2. Select two circles or arcs. A line tangent to the selected elements is created.

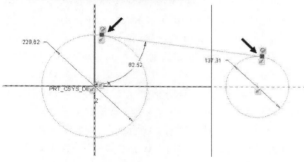

⋮ Centerline

This command creates a centerline, which can be used while creating the revolved feature.

1. On the ribbon, click **Sketch** tab > **Sketching** panel > **Centerline**.
2. Click to define the start point.
3. Move the pointer and click to define the endpoint of the centerline.

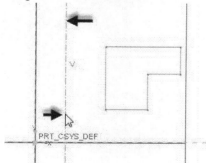

◯ Axis Ends Ellipse

This command creates an ellipse using the endpoints of the major and minor axes.

1. On the ribbon, click **Sketch** tab > **Sketching** panel > **Ellipse** drop-down > **Axis Ends Ellipse**.
2. Define the endpoints of the first axis.
3. Drag the pointer and click to define the second axis.

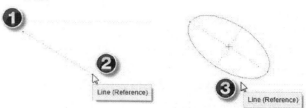

◎ Center and Axis Ellipse

This command creates an ellipse using a center point, and major and minor axes.

1. On the ribbon, click **Sketch** tab > **Sketching** panel > **Ellipse** drop-down > **Center and Axis Ellipse**.
2. Click to define the center of the ellipse.
3. Drag the pointer and click to define the major axis and orientation of the ellipse.
4. Drag the pointer and click again to define the minor axis.

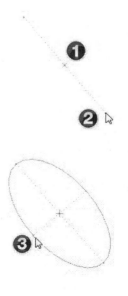

⸭ Points

This command creates points as you click in the graphics window.

1. On the ribbon, click **Sketch** tab > **Sketching** panel > **Points**.
2. Click in the graphics window to create points.

∿ Spline

This command creates a smooth B-spline curve passing through the points you select.

1. On the ribbon, click **Sketch** tab > **Sketching** panel **> Spline**.
2. Click to define points in the graphics window. A spline is created passing through the selected points.

If you want to create a closed spline, click the start point of the spline.

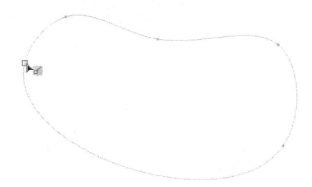

Dimensions

It is generally considered a good practice to ensure that every sketch you create is fully defined before moving on to creating features. The term, 'fully-defined' means that the sketch has a definite shape and size. You can fully-define a sketch by using

dimensions and constraints. As you create sketches in Creo Parametric, some dimensions are added to the sketch elements. These dimensions are called Weak dimensions and they do not have any control over the sketch geometry. If you want these dimensions to control the shape and size of the sketch geometry, you have to lock these dimensions.

You can lock a weak dimension by using the **Lock** option. Select the weak dimension and click the right mouse button. Select the **Lock** option from the menu and type-in a new value of the dimension. Press Enter to create the locked dimension. You can modify the dimension value by double-clicking on it and entering a new value.

↔ The Dimension command

You can add dimensions to a sketch by using the **Dimension** command. You can use this command to add all types of dimensions such as length, angle, and diameter and so on. This command creates a dimension based on the geometry that you select. For instance, to dimension a circle, activate the **Normal** command (On the ribbon, click **Sketch** > **Dimension** > **Dimension**), and then click on the circle. Next, move the pointer and click the Middle mouse button to position the dimension. Notice that a box pops up. Type-in a value in this box, and then press Enter to update the dimension.

If you click a line, this command creates a linear dimension. Move the pointer and middle-click to position the dimension.

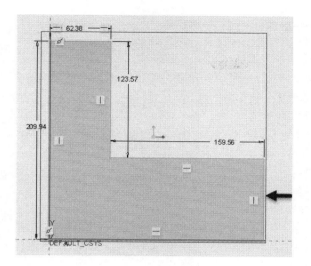

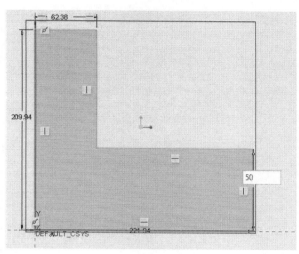

If you click on an inclined line, this command creates a dimension parallel to the line.

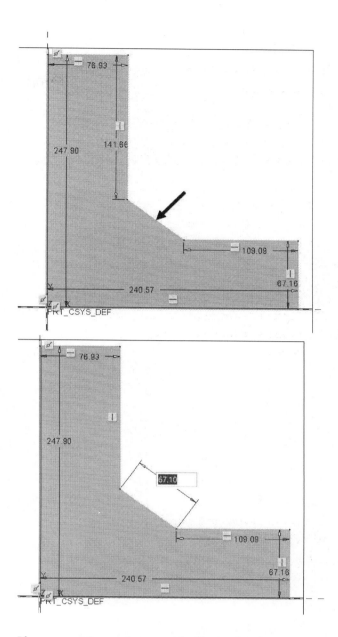

If you want to create an angle dimension between two elements, then activate the **Normal** command and select the elements. Next, move the pointer and click the middle mouse button to position the dimension. Type-in the angle value and press Enter.

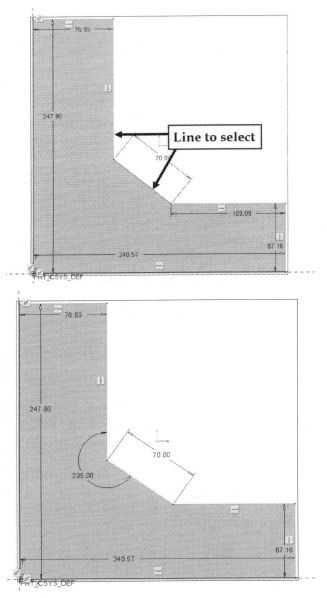

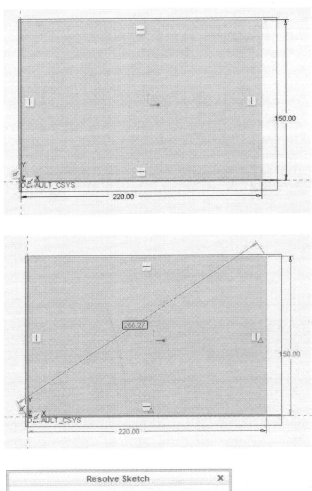

Resolve Sketch

When creating sketches for a part, Creo Parametric will not allow you to over-constrain the geometry. The term 'over-constrain' means adding more dimensions than required. The following figure shows a fully constrained sketch. If you add another dimension to this sketch (e.g. diagonal dimension), the **Resolve sketch** dialog appears.

Now, you have to delete one of the dimensions (or) convert the new dimension into reference. Click the **Dim > Ref** button to convert the dimension into reference. The reference dimension will be in blue color and **REF** will be added to it.

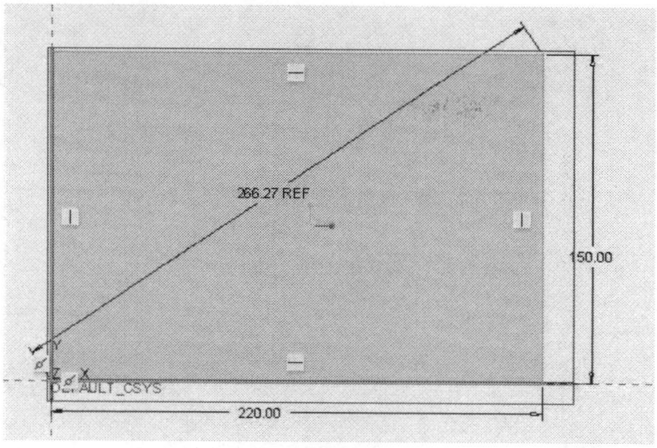

Now, if you change the value of the width, the reference dimension along the diagonal updates, automatically. Also, note that the dimensions, which are initially created, will be driving dimensions, whereas the dimensions created after fully defining the sketch are over constraining dimensions.

Modify

This command modifies all the dimensions in a sketch using the **Modify Dimensions** dialog.

1. On the ribbon, click the **Sketch > Editing > Modify**.
2. Select the dimension as shown.

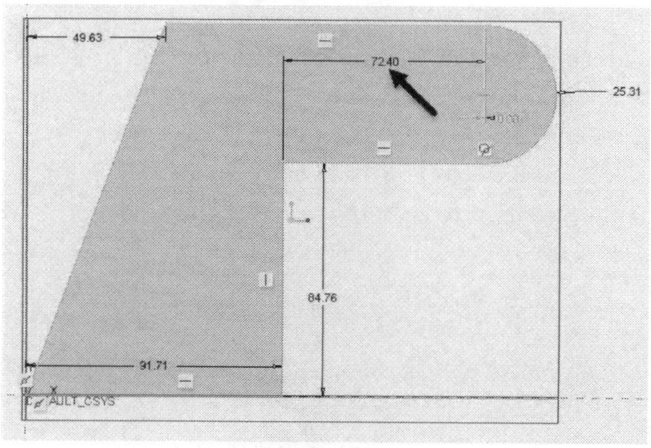

3. On the **Modify Dimensions** dialog, type-in a value in the box.

You can also use the dimension dragger located next to the dimension box to modify the value. The dimension value changes as you drag the dimension dragger. You can set the sensitivity of the dimension dragger by using the **Sensitivity** scroll bar.

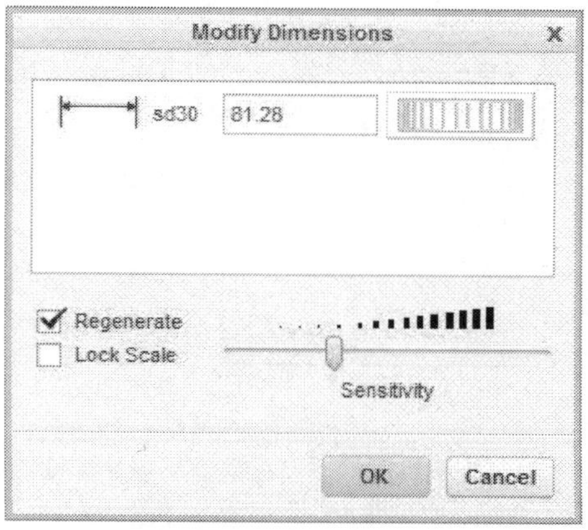

4. Check the **Regenerate** option to regenerate the sketch after clicking **OK**.
5. Click **OK** on the dialog.
6. Drag a box around the sketch to select all its dimensions.
7. Activate the **Modify** command.
8. On the **Modify Dimension** dialog, click in the dimension boxes one-by-one and enter new values.

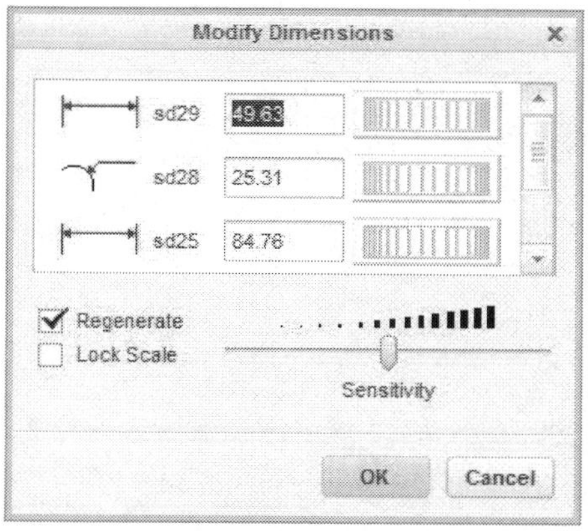

9. Click **OK** to update the dimension.

Constraints

Constraints are used to control the shape of a sketch by establishing relationships between the sketch elements. These constraints are available on the **Constrain** panel of the **Sketch** tab and are explained next.

Coincident

This constraint connects a point to another point.

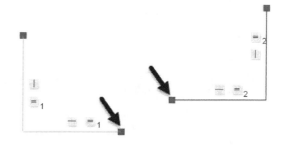

1. On the **Constrain** panel of the ribbon, click
    Coincident ⁻ᵒ⁻ .
2. Select two points. The selected points will be
    connected.

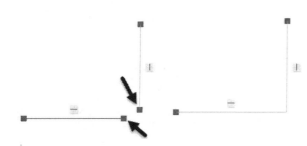

⊢ Horizontal

To apply the **Horizontal** constraint, click the
Horizontal icon on the **Constrain** panel and select a
line.

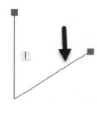

You can also align two points or vertices
horizontally.

⊢ Vertical

Use the **Vertical** command to make a line vertical.
You can also align two vertices vertically by using
this command.

⟋ Tangent

This command makes an arc, circle, or line tangent
to another arc or circle. On the **Constrain** panel, click
the **Tangent** icon and select a circle, arc, or line.
Select another circle, arc, or line. The two elements
will be tangent to each other.

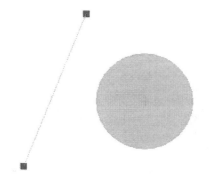

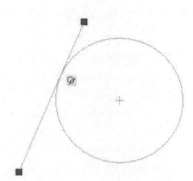

∥ Parallel

Use the **Parallel** command to make two lines parallel to each other.

Midpoint

Use the **Midpoint** command to make a point coincide with the midpoint of a line or arc.

1. On the **Constrain** panel, click the **Midpoint** icon.
2. Select and line/arc and a point.

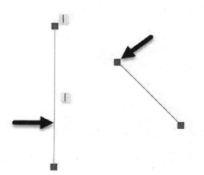

⊥ Perpendicular

Use the **Perpendicular** command to make two entities perpendicular to each other.

⁺⁺⁺ Symmetric

Use the **Symmetric** command to make two points or vertices symmetric about a centerline.

1. On the **Constrain** panel, click the **Symmetric** icon.
2. Click on the symmetric line.
3. Click on two points to be made symmetric.

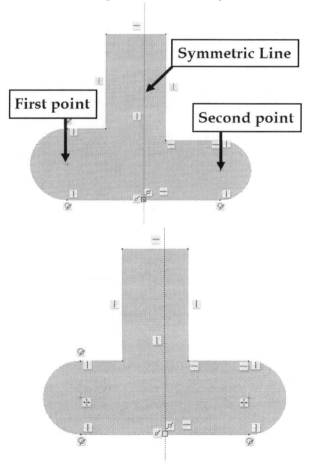

Symmetric Line

First point

Second point

Turning ON/OFF Dimensions and Constraints

As dimensions and constraints are created, they can be shown or hidden using the **Sketcher Display Filter** drop-down on the **Graphics** toolbar. When dealing with complicated sketches involving numerous constraints, you can deactivate the options on this drop-down to turn off the display of all dimensions, constraints, grid, and vertices.

⌾ Construction Mode

This command allows you to create construction elements. They support you to create a sketch of desired shape and size.

1. On the ribbon, click **Sketch** tab > **Sketching** panel > **Construction** Mode.
2. Activate any sketching command and create construction elements.

You can also convert a sketch element into construction element. To do this, select the sketch element, and then click the right mouse button. Select **Construction** from the shortcut menu that appears.

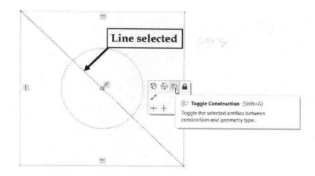

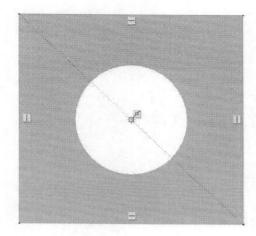

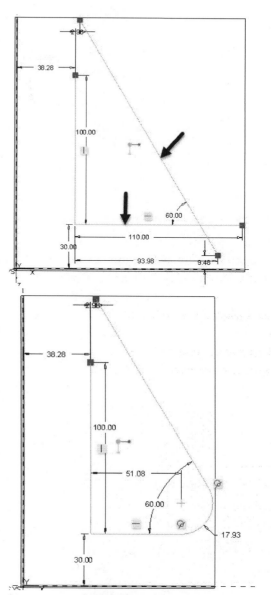

You can also convert the construction element back to a standard sketch element. To do this, click the right mouse button and select **Geometry** from the shortcut menu.

The Circular Trim command

This command fillets a sharp corner created by intersection of two lines, arcs, circles, and rectangle or polygon vertices.

1. On the ribbon, click **Sketch > Sketching > Fillet > Circular Trim**.
2. Select the intersecting elements to add a fillet.

You can modify the fillet size by changing its dimension value.

The elements to be cornered are not required to touch each other.

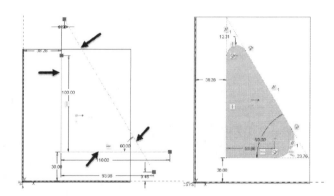

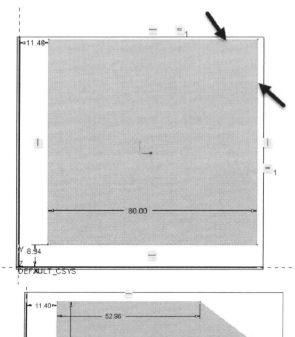

⌐ The Circular command

The **Circular Trim** command creates a fillet by trimming/extending the intersecting elements, automatically. Whereas, the **Circular** command (On the ribbon, click **Sketch > Sketching > Fillet > Circular**) creates a fillet and converts the intersecting elements in the construction elements.

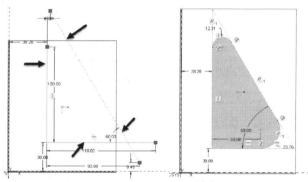

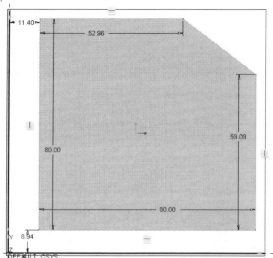

⌐ The Chamfer Trim command

This command replaces a sharp corner with an angled line.

1. On the ribbon, click **Sketch > Sketching > Chamfer > Chamfer Trim**.
2. Select the select the elements' ends to be chamfered.

⌐ The Delete Segment command

This command trims the end of an element back to the intersection of another element.

1. On the ribbon, click **Sketch** tab > **Editing** panel > **Delete Segment**.
2. Click on the element to trim.

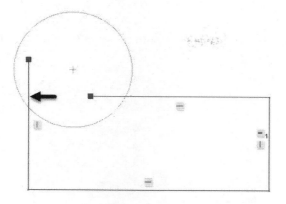

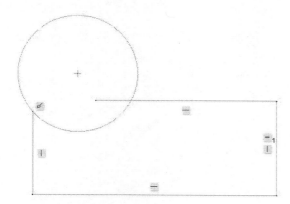

You can also trim the elements by pressing the left mouse button and dragging the pointer.

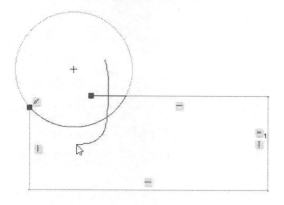

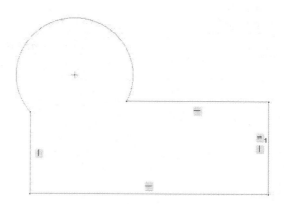

The Divide command

This command breaks a sketch element at a selected point.

1. On the ribbon, click **Sketch** tab > **Editing** panel > **Divide**.
2. Click on the sketch element to define the break point.

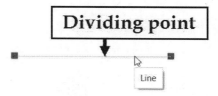

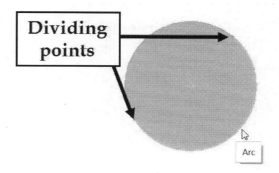

The Corner command

This command trims and extends elements to form a corner.

1. On the ribbon, click **Sketch** tab > **Editing** panel > **Corner**.

2. Select two intersecting elements. The elements will be trimmed and extended to form a closed corner.

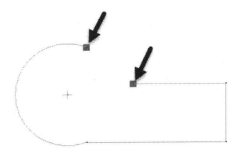

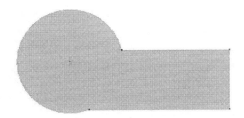

🗗 **The Mirror command**

This command creates a mirror copy of selected sketch elements.

1. Drag a selection box and select the elements to mirror.

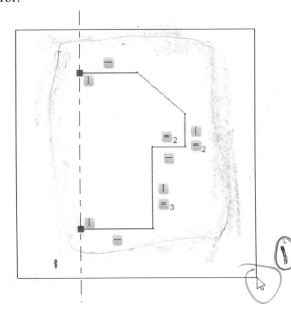

2. On the ribbon, click **Sketch** tab > **Editing** panel > **Mirror**.

3. Click on a line or centerline to define the mirror line.

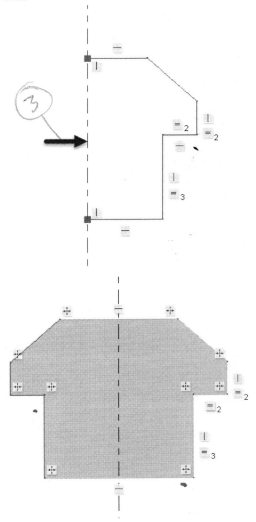

⟲ **The Rotate Resize command**

This command can be used to rotate or resize the selected elements.

1. Select the elements to rotate.

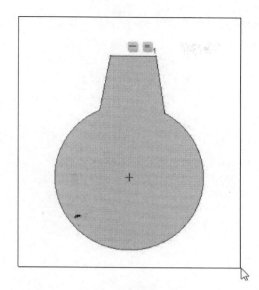

2. On the ribbon, click **Sketch** tab > **Editing** panel > **Rotate Resize**.

You will notice that the rotate and resize handles appear on the selected elements. Click and drag the rotate handle to rotate the selected elements.

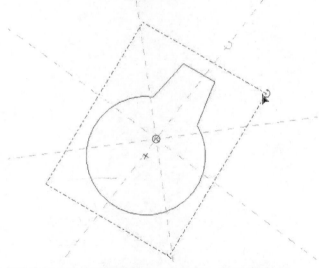

While rotating the element, you can define the center of rotation by clicking in the **Enter reference to rotate entity** box on the ribbon and selecting a point.

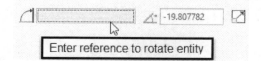

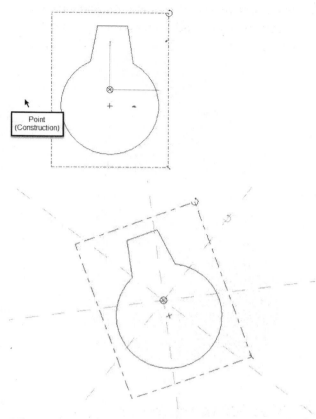

Likewise, use the resize handle to change the size of the elements.

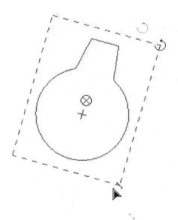

After rotating/resizing the elements, click the green check on the ribbon.

The Offset command

This command creates a parallel copy of a selected element or chain or closed loop of elements.

1. On the ribbon, click **Sketch** tab > **Sketching** panel > **Offset**.
2. Select an option from the **Type** dialog.

Use the **Single** option on the **Type** dialog to select a single element.

Use the **Chain** option to select connected elements. Select this option and click on two or more connected elements. The **Menu Manager** dialog pops up. You can click **Next** to view different sets of connected elements. Click **Accept** to select the desired chain of elements.

Use the **Loop** option to select a closed loop.

3. Type-in the offset distance value and click the green check.

4. Click **Close** on the **Type** dialog.

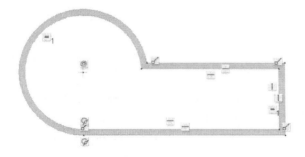

⬚ The Thicken command

This command offsets the sketch elements on both sides.

1. On the ribbon, click **Sketch** tab > **Sketching** panel > **Thicken**.
2. On the **Type** dialog, select an option from the **Select Thicken Edge** section.
3. Select an option from the **End caps** section.

The **Open** option creates an offset with open ends.

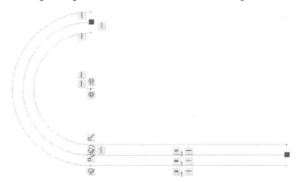

The **Flat** option closes the ends with a line.

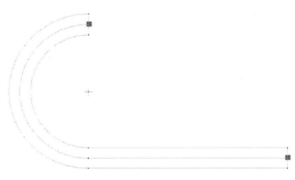

The **Circular** option closes the ends with an arc.

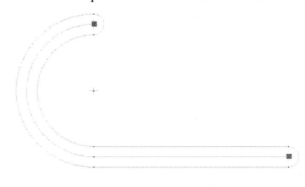

4. Select the elements to offset.
5. Type-in the total offset distance (both sides combined). Click the green check.
6. Type-in the offset distance on the outside. Click the green check.

7. Click **Close** on the **Type** dialog.

Palette

This command displays a palette showing various predefined polygons, shapes, profiles, and stars.

1. On the ribbon, click **Sketch > Sketching > Palette**.
2. On the **Palette** dialog, click the **Polygons** tab.
3. Under the **Polygons** tab, select **6-Sided Hexagon**.
4. Drag it into the graphics window.
5. Use the handles available on the polygon to move, rotate, and scale it.

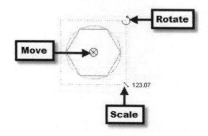

6. Click the green check on the Dashboard.
7. You can modify the dimensions to change the size and location of the polygon.

Likewise, you can insert other predefined shapes using the tabs available on the **Palette** dialog.

Examples

Example 1

In this example, you will draw the sketch shown below.

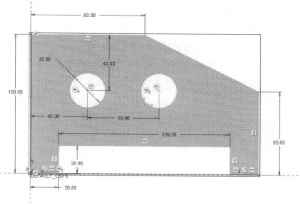

1. Start **Creo Parametric 4.0** by clicking the **PTC Creo Parametric 4.0** icon on your desktop.
2. Create a new folder with the name *Creo Parametric 4.0 Basics* on your drive.
3. On the ribbon, click **Home** tab > **Data** panel > **Select Working Directory**.
4. Go to the *Creo Parametric 4.0 Basics* folder and click **Organize > New Folder**.

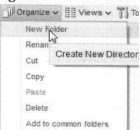

5. Type-in **Sketching** in the **New Folder** dialog and click **OK**.

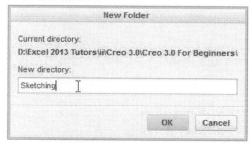

6. Again, click **OK** to set the *Sketching* folder as the working directory.
7. On the ribbon, click **Home** tab > **Data** panel > **New**.
8. On the **New** dialog, select **Type > Part** and **Sub-type > Solid**.
9. Type-in **Example1** in the **Name** box.

10. Uncheck the **Use default template** option and click **OK**.
11. On the **New File Options** dialog, select **solid_part_mmks**, and click **OK**.
12. On the ribbon, click **Model** tab > **Datum** panel > **Sketch** .
13. Click on the Front plane.

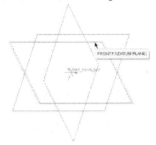

14. Accept the default values on the **Sketch** dialog and click **Sketch**.
15. On the **Graphics** toolbar, click the **Sketch View** icon to orient the sketch plane parallel to the screen.

16. On the ribbon, click **Sketch** tab > **Sketching** panel > **Line** .
17. Click on the origin point to define the first point of the line.
18. Move the pointer rightwards and click when the horizontal symbol appear on the line.

19. Move the pointer upwards and click when the vertical symbol appears. This creates a vertical line.

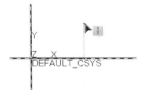

20. Move the pointer rightwards and click to create a horizontal line.

21. Create a closed loop by selecting points, as shown below. On the ribbon, click **Sketch** tab > **Operations** panel > **Select** icon to deactivate the **Line Chain** command.

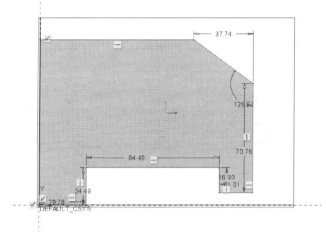

22. On the ribbon, click **Sketch** tab > **Constrain** panel > **Coincident** .
23. Click on the two horizontal lines at the bottom; they become coincident.

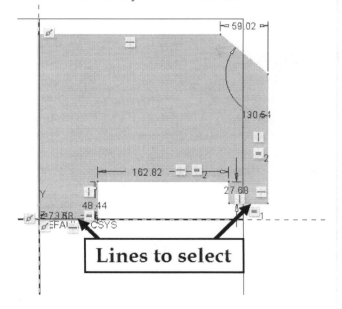

Lines to select

24. On the ribbon, click **Sketch** tab > **Constrain** panel > **Equal** ═.

25. Click on the two horizontal lines at the bottom. They become equal in length.

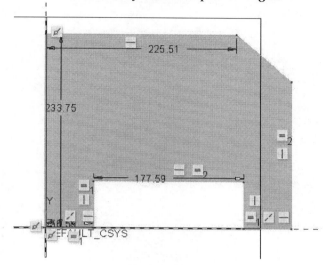

26. On the ribbon, click **Sketch** tab > **Operations** panel > **Select** drop-down > **One by One**.

27. On the ribbon, click **Sketch** tab > **Editing** panel > **Modify** .

28. Click on the horizontal dimension, as shown in figure.

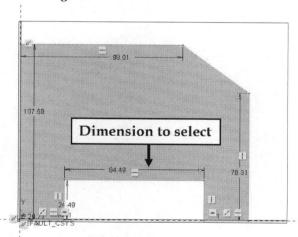

29. Type-in **120** on the **Modify Dimensions** dialog. Click **OK**.

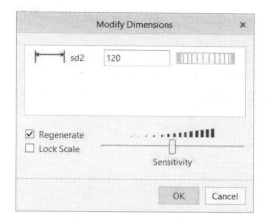

30. Likewise, activate the **Modify** command and change the other dimensional values. You can also select all the dimensions at a time by dragging a crossing window.

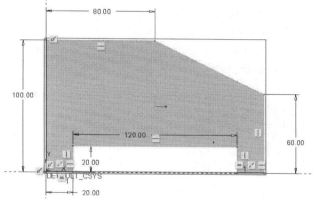

31. Click **OK** on the **Modify** dialog.

32. On the ribbon, click **Sketch** tab > **Sketching** panel > **Circle** drop-down > **Center and Point** .

33. Click inside the sketch region to define the center point of the circle. Move the pointer and click to define the diameter.

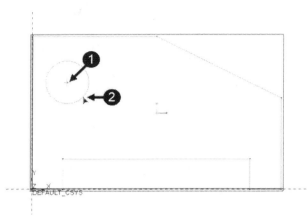

34. Likewise, create another circle.

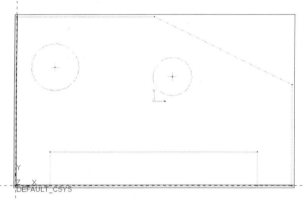

35. On the ribbon, click **Sketch** tab > **Constraint** panel > **Horizontal** ⊥.

36. Select the centerpoints of the circles.

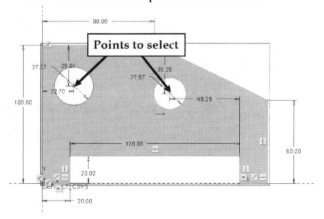

37. Apply the **Equal** = constraint between the two circles, if there is not equal.

38. Activate the **Modify** command and modify the dimension values of the circles and their positioning dimensions. Click **OK** on the dialog.

39. Press and hold the Ctrl key and select center points of the circles.

40. Click the right mouse button.

41. On the shortcut menu, click **Horizontal**.

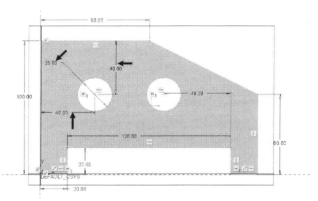

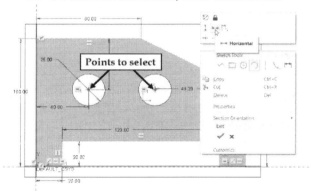

42. Type-in **50** in the value box and press Enter.

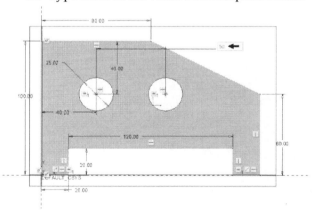

43. On the ribbon, click **Sketch** tab > **Close** panel > **OK** ✓.

44. On the **Quick Access Toolbar**, click the **Save** 🖫 icon (or) click **File > Save** on the Menu.

45. Click **OK** to save the part file.

46. Click **File > Close**.

Example 2

In this example, you will draw the sketch shown below.

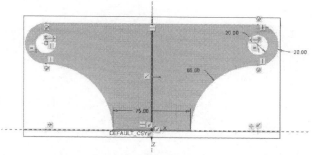

1. Start **Creo Parametric 4.0** by clicking the **PTC Creo Parametric 4.0** icon on your desktop.
2. On the **Quick Access Toolbar**, click the **New** icon.
3. On the **New** dialog, click **Type > Part**.
4. Type-in **Exampl2** in the **Name** box.
5. Uncheck the **Use default template** option and click **OK**.
6. On the **New File Options** dialog, select **solid_part_mmks**, and click **OK**.
7. To start a new sketch, click the **Sketch** icon on the **Datum** panel.
8. Click on the Top Plane, and then click **Sketch** to start the sketch.

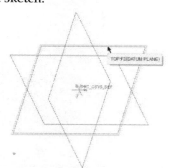

9. On the **Graphics** toolbar, click the **Sketch View** icon.
10. On the ribbon, click **Sketch** tab > **Sketching** panel > **Line Chain** .
11. Click in the second quadrant of the coordinate system to define the start point of the profile. Drag the pointer horizontally and click to define the endpoint.

12. On the ribbon, click **Sketch** tab > **Sketching** panel > **Arc** drop-down > **3-Point/Tangent End**.
13. Select the right endpoint of the line.
14. Move the pointer upwards right and click to define the second point of the arc.

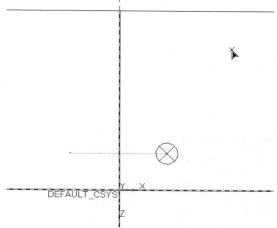

15. Move the pointer and click to define the third point of the arc.

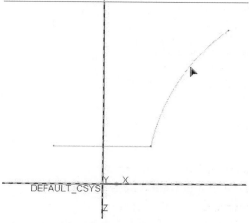

16. Select the endpoint of the arc.
17. Move the pointer rightwards and upwards, and then click to create an arc tangent to the previous arc.

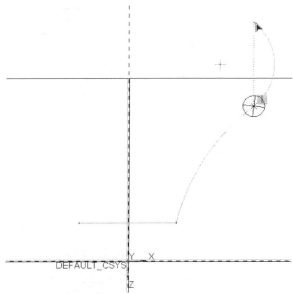

18. On the ribbon, click **Sketch** tab > **Sketching** panel > **Line Chain** .
19. Select the endpoint of the arc.
20. Move the pointer toward left and click to create a horizontal line.
21. Click the **3-Point/Tangent End** icon the **Sketching** panel.
22. Select the endpoint of the horizontal line.
23. Move the pointer leftwards and downwards, and then click when a vertical dotted line appears, as shown below.

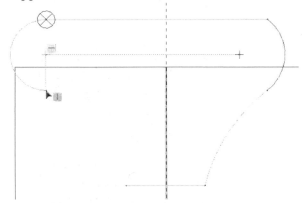

24. Select the endpoint of the arc. Move the pointer toward down and right, and then click on the start point to close the sketch.

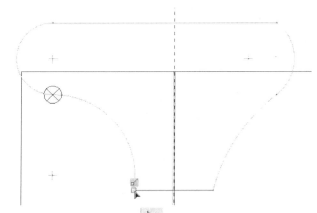

25. Click the **Select** icon on the ribbon to deactivate the command.
26. On the ribbon, click **Sketch** tab > **Sketching** panel > **Circle** drop-down > **Concentric** .
27. Select the top right arc to define the center of the circle.

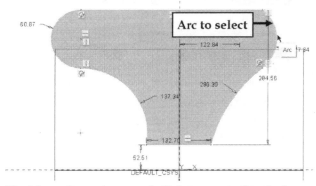

28. Move the pointer and click to create the circle.

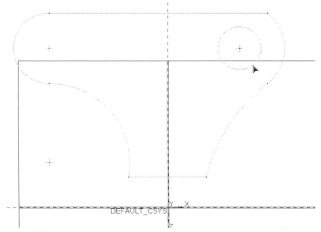

29. Click the **Select** icon on the ribbon to deactivate the command.

30. Again, activate the **Concentric** command and create another circle, as shown below.

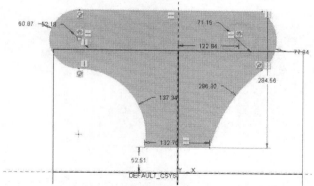

31. On the ribbon, click **Sketch** tab > **Sketching** panel **> Centerline**   .

32. Select the origin of the sketch.

33. Move the pointer vertically upward and click to create a vertical centerline.

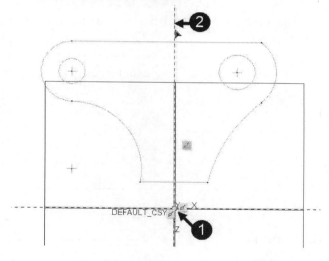

34. On the ribbon, click **Sketch** tab > **Constrain** panel > **Symmetric**   .

35. Select the centerline to define the symmetry line.

36. Select the centerpoints of the circles to make them symmetric.

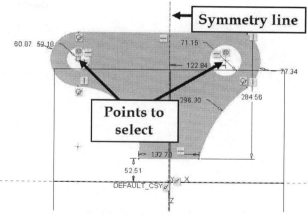

37. Select the centerline, and then the center points of the arcs.

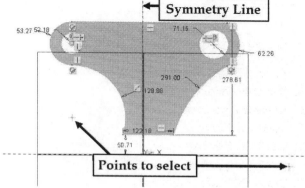

38. Activate the **Coincident** command, and then click on the bottom horizontal line and the centerpoint of the arc. They will be made coincident.

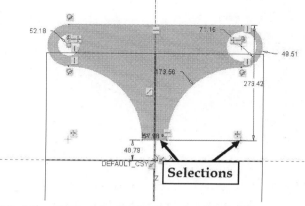

39. Likewise, make the bottom horizontal line coincident with the origin.

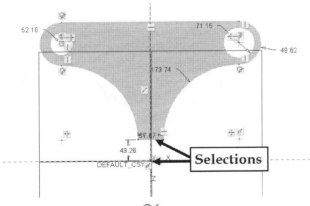

40. Click the **Tangent** icon on the **Constrain** panel.

41. Select the top horizontal line and the right arc. A tangent constrain is created between them.

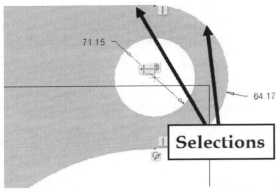

42. Apply the **Equal** constraint between the two circles.

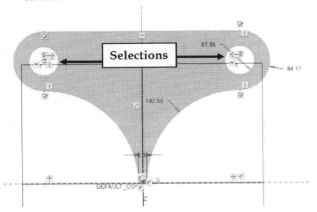

43. On the ribbon, click **Sketch** tab > **Editing** panel > **Modify** .

44. Click on the diameter value of the circle.

45. On the **Modify Dimension** dialog, uncheck the **Regenerate** option and type-in 20 in the value box.

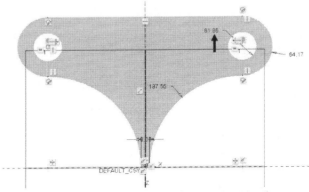

46. Likewise, select the other dimensions and change their values. Click **OK** to regenerate the dimensions.

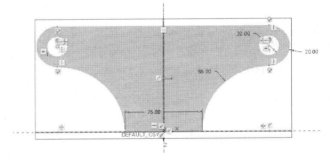

47. Click **OK** on the ribbon to complete the sketch.

48. To save the file, click **File > Save**. Next, click **OK**.

49. To close the file, click **File > Close**.

Questions

1. What is the procedure to create sketches in Creo Parametric?
2. List any two sketch constraints in Creo Parametric.
3. How to create constraints, automatically?
4. Describe the methods to create an ellipse.

5. How do you define the shape and size of a sketch?
6. How do you create a tangent arc?
7. Which command is used to apply different types of dimensions to a sketch?
8. List any two methods to create circles.
9. How do you create fillet?

Exercises
Exercise 1

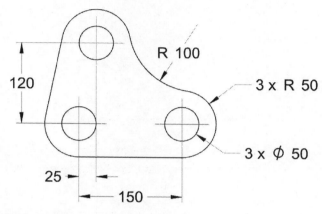

Exercise 2

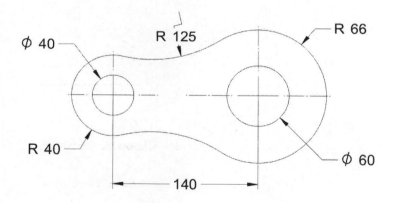

Exercise 3

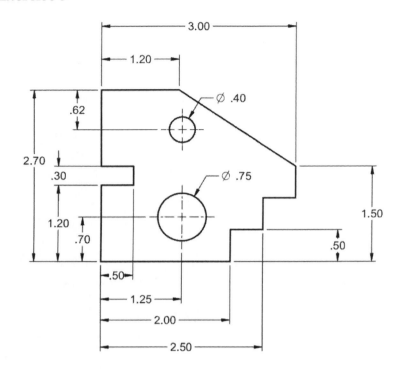

Chapter 3: Basic Features

Basic features are used to create basic and simple parts. Most of the times, they form the base for complex parts as well. These features are easy to create and require a single sketch. Now, you will learn the commands to create these features.

The topics covered in this chapter are:

- *Extrude Features*
- *Revolve Features*
- *Datum planes*
- *More Options in the Extrude and Revolve commands*
- *View commands*

Extrude

Extrusion is the process of taking a two-dimensional profile and converting it into 3D by giving it some thickness. A simple example of this would be taking a circle and converting it into a cylinder.

1. Once you have created a sketch profile or profiles you want to *Extrude*, activate the **Extrude** command (On the ribbon, click **Model** tab > **Shapes** panel > **Extrude**).
2. Click on the sketch profile to add thickness to it.

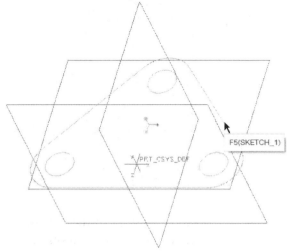

3. On the **Extrude** dashboard, type-in a value in the **Depth** box.

You can also click and drag the Extrude handle that appears on the preview. This changes the extrude thickness

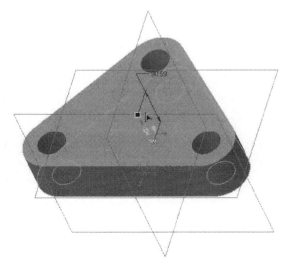

(or) Double-click in the value box that appears on the preview and type-in the Extrude depth.

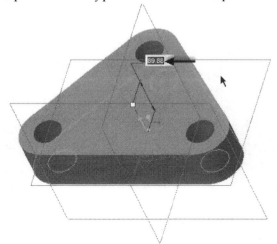

4. Click the **Reverse direction** button next to the **Depth** box, if you want to reverse the extrusion direction.
5. If you want to add equal thickness on both sides of the sketch, then select the **Both Sides** option from the drop-down next to the **Depth** box.

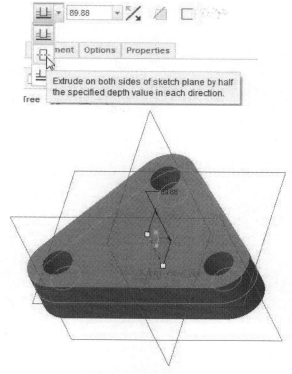

6. Click the green check on the dashboard to complete the *Extrude* feature.

⚛ Revolve

Revolving is the process of taking a two-dimensional profile and revolving it about a centerline to create a 3D geometry (shapes that are axially symmetric). While creating a sketch for the *Revolved* feature, it is important to think about the cross-sectional shape that will define the 3D geometry once it is revolved about an axis. For instance, the following geometry has a hole in the center.

This could be created with a separate *Cut* or *Hole* feature. But in order to make that hole part of the *Revolved* feature, you need to sketch the centerline of revolution so that it leaves a space between the profile and the centerline.

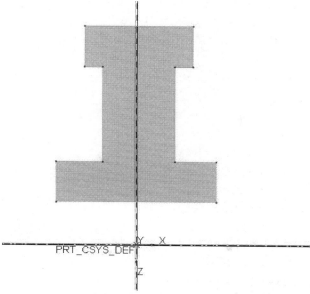

1. After completing the sketch, activate the **Revolve** command (On the ribbon, click **Model** tab > **Shapes** panel > **Revolve**).
2. Select the sketch, if not already selected. The sketch will be revolved by full 360 degrees.

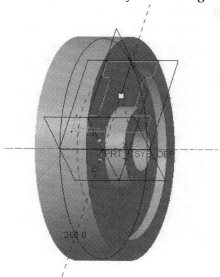

3. If you want to enter an angle of revolution, type-in a value in the **Angle** box on the dashboard.

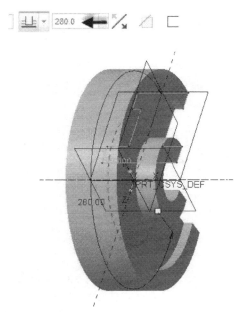

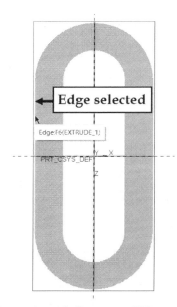

4. On the dashboard, click the green check to complete the *Revolved* feature.

☐ Project

This command projects the edges of a 3D geometry onto a sketch plane.

1. Activate the **Sketch** mode by selecting a plane or model face.
2. On the ribbon, click **Sketch** tab > **Sketching** panel > **Project**.
3. On the **Type** dialog, select the **Single, Chain,** or **Loop** option.
4. Click on the edges of the model geometry to project them on to the sketch plane.
5. Click **Close** on the **Type** dialog.

The projected element will be orange in color and fully constrained.

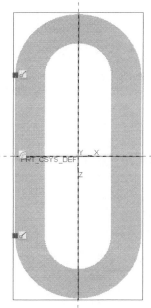

6. Complete the sketch and exit the Sketch mode.

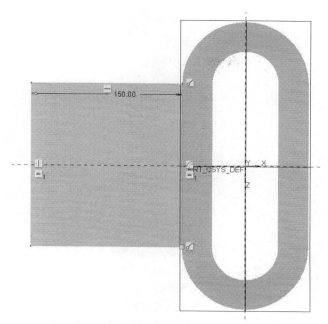

Creating Extruded Cuts

Creating Extruded cuts is similar to extruded features.

1. Draw a sketch on a plane or a model face.
2. Activate the **Extrude** command.
3. Select the sketch.

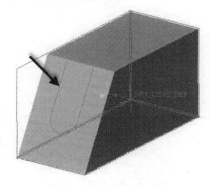

4. On the **Extrude** dashboard, click the **Remove Material** button.

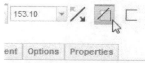

5. Type-in a value in the **Depth** box and click the **Reverse direction** button next to it.
6. Click the green check to complete the cut feature.

Creating Revolved Cuts

Revolved cuts are created by revolving a sketch about an axis.

1. Draw a sketch on a plane or a model face. Also, draw a centerline using the **Centerline** command.

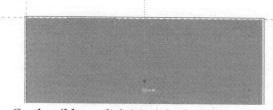

2. On the ribbon, click **Model** tab > **Shapes** panel > **Revolve**.
3. Select the sketch. If you have created the centerline, revolved cut will be created automatically.

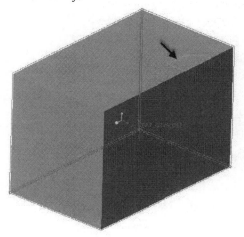

4. On the **Revolve** dashboard, click the **Remove Material** button.

5. Click the green check to complete the revolve cut feature.

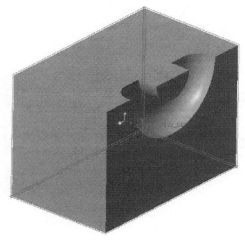

The Plane command

Each time you start a new part file, Creo Parametric automatically creates default datum planes. Planes are a specific type of elements in Creo Parametric, known as Datum features. These features act as supports to your 3D geometry. In addition to the default datum features, you can create your own additional planes. Until now, you have known to create sketches on any of the default datum planes (XY, YZ, and XZ planes). If you want to create sketches and geometry at locations other than default datum planes, you can create new datum planes manually. You can do this by using the **Plane** command.

Offset from plane

This method creates a datum plane, which will be parallel to a face or another plane.

1. Activate the **Plane** command (On the ribbon, click **Model > Datum > Plane**).
2. Select a flat face/plane.

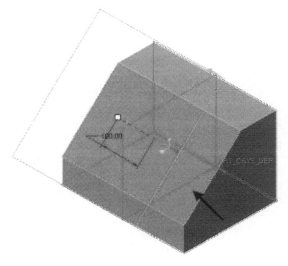

3. On the **Datum Plane** dialog, select **Offset** from the drop-down in the **References** section.
4. Drag the Offset handle that appears on the plane (or) type-in a value in the **Translation** box to define the offset distance.

On the dialog, you can type a negative value in the **Translation** box to create the plane on the other side of the model face/plane.

5. Click **OK** to create the offset plane.

Plane and Point

This method creates a plane parallel/normal to a flat face at a selected point.

1. Activate the **Plane** command.

2. Press the Ctrl key and select a flat face and point.

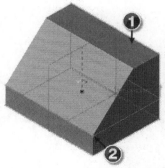

3. On the **Datum Plane** dialog, select the **Normal** option from the drop-down next to the plane reference. The datum plane is created normal to reference flat face and passing through the selected point.

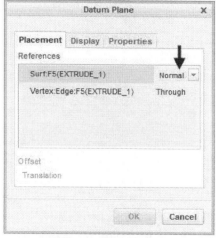

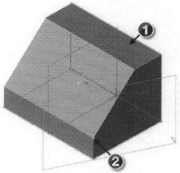

Plane and Edge

This method creates a plane, which is positioned at an angle or parallel or normal to a face or plane.

1. Activate the **Plane** command.

2. Select a flat face or plane to define the reference.
3. Press the Ctrl key and click on an edge of the part geometry to define the rotation axis.
4. Type-in a value in the **Rotation** box.

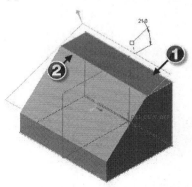

4. On the **Datum Plane** dialog, select the **Normal** option from the drop-down next to the plane reference. The datum plane is created normal to reference flat face and passing through the selected edge.

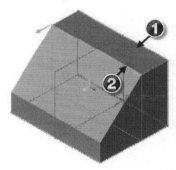

5. On the **Datum Plane** dialog, select the **Parallel** option from the drop-down next to the plane reference. The datum plane is created parallel to reference flat face and passing through the selected edge.

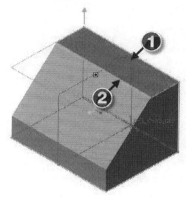

Through three points

This method creates a plane by selecting three points.

1. Activate the **Plane** command.
2. Press the Ctrl key and select three points from the model geometry.
3. Click **OK** to create a plane passing through the points.

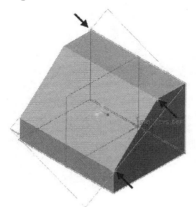

Through two Edges/lines

This method creates a plane by selecting two edges/lines.

1. Activate the **Plane** command.
2. Press the Ctrl key select two parallel edges/lines from the model geometry.
3. Click **OK**. A plane is created passing through the selected lines/edges.

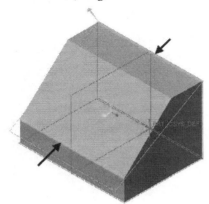

Point and Line/Curve/Edge

This method creates a datum plane, which will be normal (perpendicular) to a line, curve, or edge.

1. Activate the **Plane** command.
2. Press the Ctrl key and select an edge, line, curve, arc, or circle.
3. Click on a point of the selected element to define the location of the plane.
4. On the **Datum Plane** dialog, select the **Normal** option from the drop-down next to the curve reference. The datum plane is created normal to reference curve and passing through the selected point.

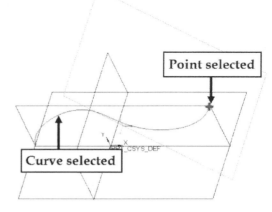

Tangent to surface

This method creates a plane tangent to a curved face.

1. Activate the **Plane** command.
2. Select a curved face.
3. Press the Ctrl key and select an edge.
4. On the **Datum Plane** dialog, select the **Tangent** option from the drop-down next to the surface reference. The datum plane is created tangent to reference surface and passing through the selected edge.

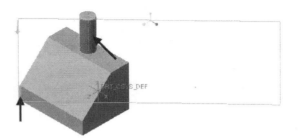

Mid Plane

This method creates a plane, which lies at the midpoint between two selected faces. Activate the **Plane** command. Press hold the Ctrl key, and then select two faces of the model geometry which are parallel to each other. Click **OK** to create the mid plane.

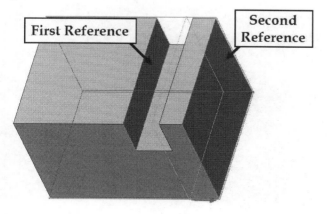

First Reference

Second Reference

You can also create a plane passing through the intersection point of the two selected planes or faces. Activate the **Plane** command. Press hold the Ctrl key, and then select two intersecting surfaces. On the **Datum Plane** dialog, select **Bisector1** or **Bisector 2** option from the drop-down located next to the second surface. Click **OK** to create the passing through the intersection of selected surfaces.

Bisector 1

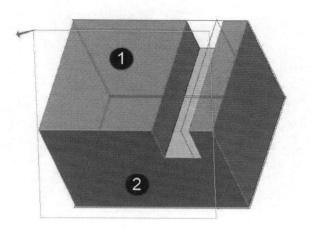

Bisector 2

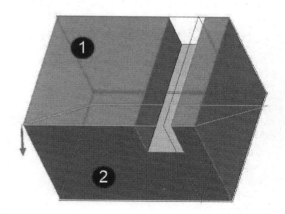

Axis

The **Axis** command (On the ribbon, click **Model > Datum > Axis**) creates an axis in the 3D space. The methods to create axis using this command are explained next.

Point-Point

Press the Ctrl Key and select two points.

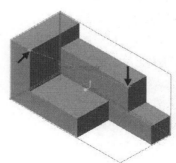

Point and Edge/line

Press the Ctrl Key and select a point and edge.

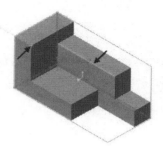

On the **Datum Plane** dialog, select the **Normal** option from the drop-down next to the edge reference. The datum axis is created normal to reference edge and passing through the selected point.

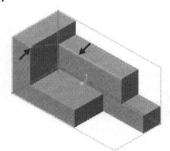

On a planar face

1. Click on a planar face. An axis appears with two reference handles.
2. Click the right mouse button and select the Offset Reference.
3. Press the Ctrl key and select two faces that are perpendicular to the placement face.
4. On the **Datum Plane** dialog, type the values in the Offset references section.

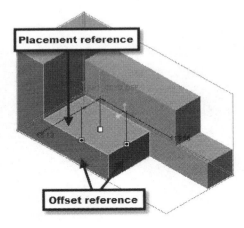

Additional options of the Extrude command

The **Extrude** command has some additional options to create a 3D geometry, complex features, and so on. These options are also available on the **Revolve** dashboard.

Depth

On the **Extrude** dashboard, the **Options** tab has options to define the start and end depths of the *Extrude* feature. These options are **Blind, Symmetric, To Next, Through All, Through Until,** and **To Selected**.

The **To Next** option extrudes the sketch through the face next to the sketch plane.

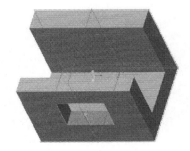

The **Through Until** option extrudes the sketch up to a selected surface. Activate the Extrude command and select the sketch to be extruded. On the **Extrude** dashboard, select **Through Until** from the drop-down, and then click on a surface. The sketch will be extruded up to the selected surface.

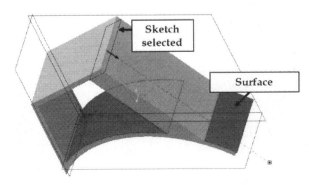

The **To Selected** option extrudes the sketch from the sketch plane up to a selected planar face, point, curve, and surface.

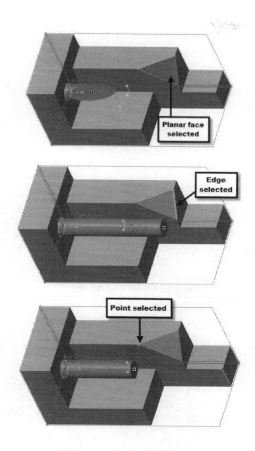

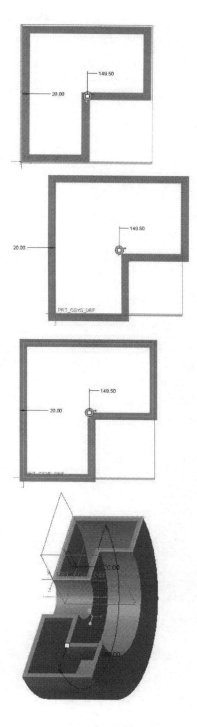

The **Through All** option extrudes the sketch throughout the 3D geometry.

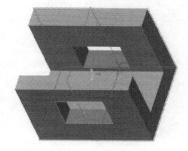

⌐ Thicken Sketch

The **Thicken Sketch** icon will help you to add thickness to the selected sketch. Click this icon on the **Extrude** or **Revolve** dashboard to add thickness to the sketch. Type-in thickness value in the box located next to this icon. Click the **Flip** icon next to the box to change the thickness side. You can add thickness to inside, outside, or both sides of the sketch using this icon.

Extruding Open Profile

The **Extrude** command can also create a feature using an open profile. It uses the adjacent edges of the open profile to form a closed loop. Activate the **Extrude** command and select the open sketch.

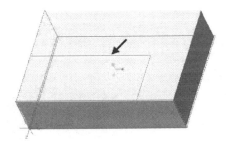

A preview of the *Extrude* feature appears. Click on the horizontal arrow to change the material side. On the dashboard, type-in a value in the **Depth** box located on the **Extrude** ribbon, and then press Enter.

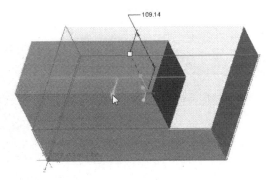

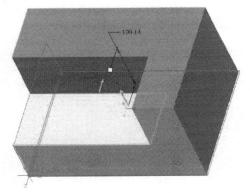

Use the **Remove Material** ⬜ icon to create cutouts.

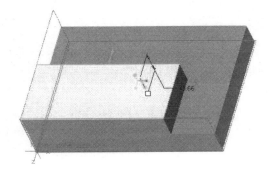

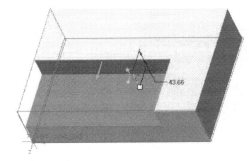

Add taper

The **Add taper** option will help you to apply draft to the extrusion. It applies a draft to the extrusion from the sketch plane.

1. Activate the **Extrude** command and select the sketch.
2. Click the **Options** tab on the Dashboard and check the **Add taper** option.
3. Type the taper angle in the angle box.

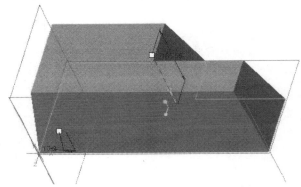

4. Set the depth type to **Symmetric**. Notice that the taper angle is applied with reference to the sketch plane.

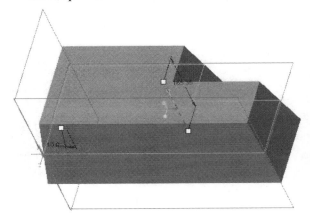

Editing Model Properties

Creo Parametric allows you to edit the model
properties such as material, units, and so on.

1. Click **File > Prepare > Model Properties**. The
    Model Properties dialog displays the physical
    properties, parameters, features properties, and
    so on.
2. On the **Model Properties** dialog, click the
    change link located next to the **Material**
    property.
3. On the Materials dialog, double-click on anyone
    of the folders available in the list box.

4. On the **Materials** dialog, select the material from
    the list and click the arrow [→] icon pointing
    toward right. The selected material appears in
    the **Materials in Model** section.

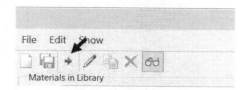

5. Click **OK** to assign the material to the geometry.
6. Click the 'i' icon located next to **Mass
    Properties**. The **Mass Properties Report** appears
    showing physical properties such as density,
    mass, volume, and so on. If you want to change
    the mass properties, click the **Change** button
    located at the bottom right corner. The **Mass
    Properties** dialog appears. On this dialog,
    change the density value and click **OK** to change
    all the properties.

7. Close the **Mass Properties Report**.

Likewise, you can change other model properties.

8. Click **Close** on the **Model Properties** dialog.

View commands

The model display in the graphics window can be determined using various view commands. Most of these
commands are located on **Graphics** toolbar or on the **View** ribbon tab. The following are some of the main view
commands:

🔍	**Refit**	The model will be fitted in the current size of the graphics window so that it will be completely visible.
✋	**Pan**	Activate this command and press the left mouse button. Drag the pointer to move the model view on the plane parallel to screen.

Basic Features

56

	Orient mode	Activate this command and press the middle mouse button. Drag the pointer to rotate the model view.
	Zoom In	Activate this command and create a box by specifying its corners. The area inside the box is magnified.
	Zoom Out	Click this icon to zoom out of the geometry.
	Sketch View	Click this icon to orient the sketch plane parallel to the screen.
	Shading with Reflections	This option represents the geometry with shades and reflections
	Shading with Edges	This option represents the model with shades along with visible edges.
	Shading	This option represents the model with shades without visible edges.

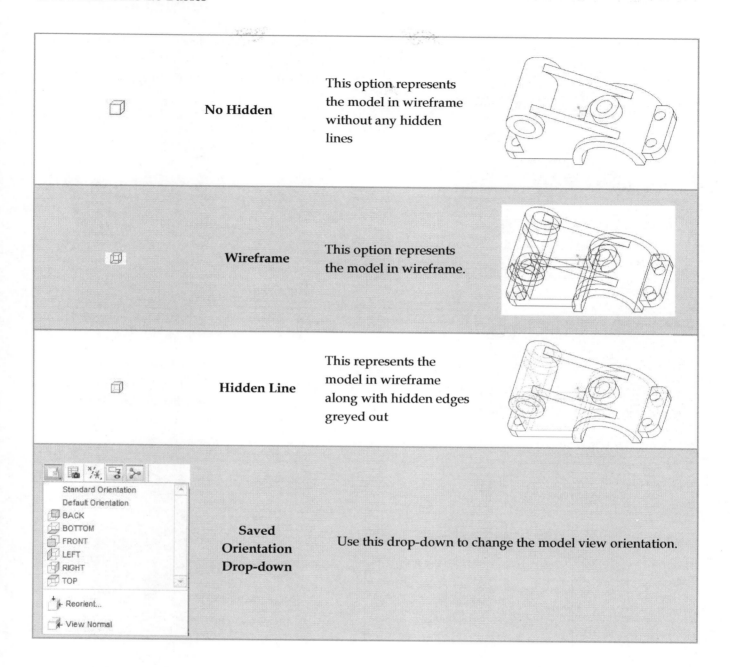

	No Hidden	This option represents the model in wireframe without any hidden lines	
	Wireframe	This option represents the model in wireframe.	
	Hidden Line	This represents the model in wireframe along with hidden edges greyed out	
	Saved Orientation Drop-down	Use this drop-down to change the model view orientation.	

Measure Commands

The measure commands help you to measure the physical properties of geometry. These commands are explained next.

 Summary

This command displays the measurements of the selected element based on the element type. For

example, if you select a face, it displays the area and perimeter.

1. On the ribbon, click the **Analysis** tab > **Measure** > **Summary**.
2. Click on an element to display its measurements.

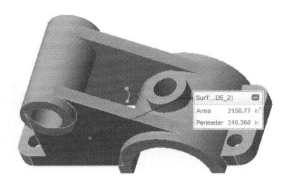

3. Press the Ctrl Key and select another element. A summary appears showing the measurements of both the elements.

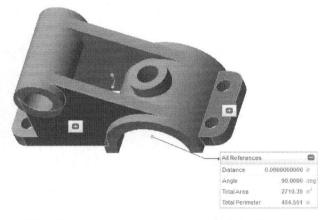

4. Click the right mouse button and click **Clear**.

∿ Length

This command measures the length of the selected edge or curve.

1. On the ribbon, click the **Analysis > Measure > Length**.

Examples

Example 1

In this example, you will create the part shown below.

2. Click on the edge. The curve length of the edge will appear.
3. Click the right mouse button and select **Clear**.

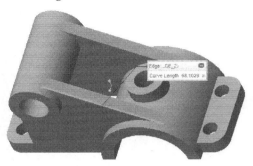

⊢⋅ Distance

This command measures the distance between two elements.

1. On the ribbon, click the **Analysis > Measure > Distance**.
2. Press the Ctrl key and click on two elements. The distance between the two elements will appear.
3. Click the right mouse button and select **Clear**.

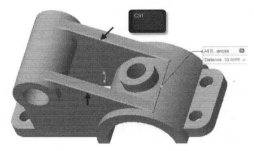

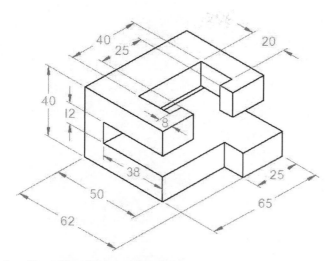

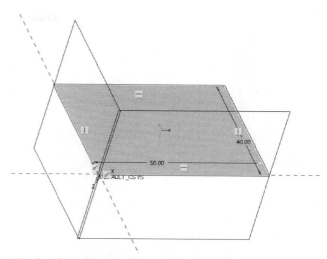

1. Start **Creo Parametric 4.0**.
2. Create the *Basic Features* folder and set it as current working folder.
3. On the Quick Access Toolbar, click the **New** button.
4. On the **New** dialog, select **Types > Part**, and then type-in **C03-Example1**.
5. Uncheck the **Use default template** option and click **OK**.
6. On the **New File Options** dialog, select **solid_part_mmks**, and click **OK**.
7. On the ribbon, click **Model** tab > **Datum** panel > **Sketch**.
8. Select the Front plane and click the **Sketch** button.
9. On the ribbon, click **Sketch** tab > **Sketching** panel > **Rectangle** drop-down > **Corner Rectangle**.
10. Click the origin point to define the first corner of the rectangle.
11. Move the pointer toward top right and click to define the second corner.
12. On the ribbon, click **Sketch** tab > **Operations** panel > **Select** drop-down > **One by One**.
13. On the ribbon, click **Sketch** tab > **Editing** panel > **Modify**.
14. Modify the dimensions of the rectangle (refer to the **Modify** section of Chapter 2 to learn how to modify dimensions).

15. On the ribbon, click **Sketch** tab > **Close** panel > **OK**.
16. On the ribbon, click **Model** tab > **Shapes** panel > **Extrude**.
17. On the **Extrude** dashboard, type-in **65** in the **Depth** box.
18. Select the **Both sides** option from the drop-down next to the **Depth** box.
19. Click the green check on the dashboard.

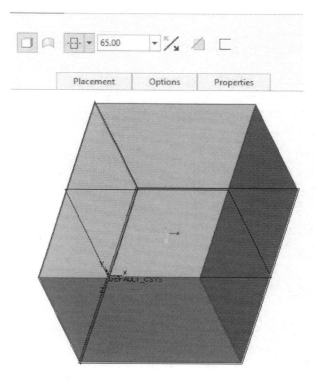

20. On the ribbon, click **Model** tab > **Datum** panel > **Sketch**.

21. Click on the front face of the model geometry.
22. On the **Sketch** dialog, click in the **Reference** box and select the right face of the model.

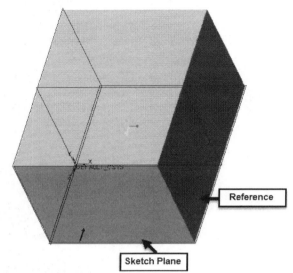

Reference

Sketch Plane

23. Click the **Sketch** button.
24. On the **Graphics** toolbar, click the **Sketch View** icon. This orients the sketch parallel to the screen.
25. On the ribbon, click **Sketch** tab > **Sketching** panel > **Rectangle** drop-down > **Corner Rectangle**.
26. Modify the dimensions, as shown below (refer to the **Modify** section of Chapter 2 to learn how to modify dimensions).

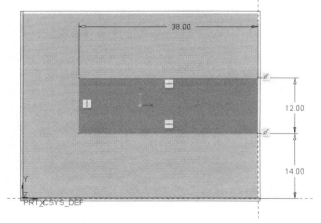

27. On the ribbon, click **Sketch** tab > **Close** panel > **OK**.
28. On the **Graphics** toolbar, click **Saved Orientations** drop-down > **Standard Orientation**.

29. On the ribbon, click **Model** tab > **Shapes** panel > **Extrude**.
30. Select the sketch.
31. On the ribbon, click the **Remove Material** button.
32. Click the **Reverse Direction** button next to the **Depth** box.
33. Select the **Through All** option from the drop-down next to the **Depth** box.
34. Click the green check on the dashboard.

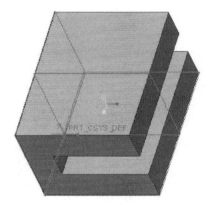

35. On the ribbon, click **Model** tab > **Datum** panel > **Sketch**.
36. Click on the top face of the model geometry.
37. On the **Sketch** dialog, click in the **Reference** box and select the right face of the model.

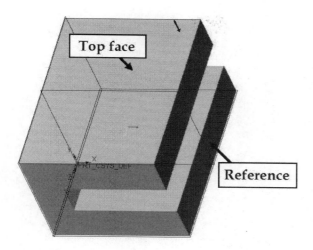

38. Click the **Sketch** button.
39. On the **Graphics** toolbar, click the **Sketch View** icon. This orients the sketch parallel to the screen.
40. On the ribbon, click **Sketch** tab > **Sketching** panel > **Line Chain** ⌄.
41. Draw the sketch, as shown below.

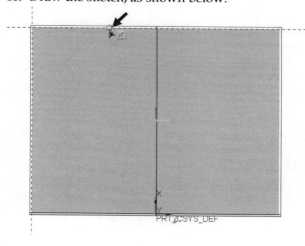

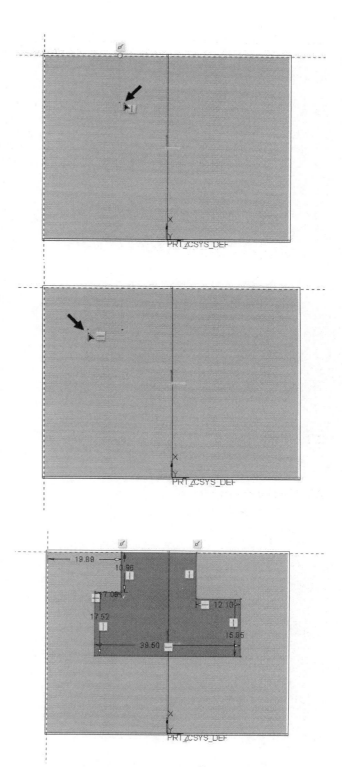

42. On the ribbon, click **Sketch** tab > **Constrain** panel > **Equal** ═.
43. Select the two vertical lines, as shown below.

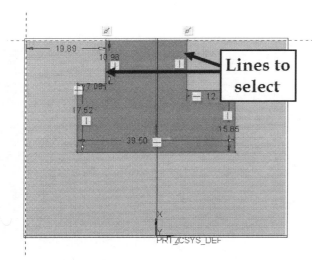

44. Likewise, apply the **Equal** constraint to the horizontal lines.

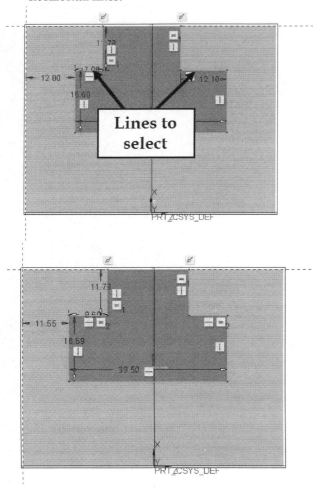

45. Modify the dimensions of the sketch, as shown below (refer to the **Modify** section of Chapter 2 to learn how to modify dimensions).

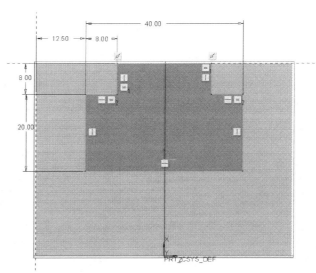

46. Click **OK** on the ribbon.
47. Change the view to **Standard Orientation**.
48. On the ribbon, click **Model** tab > **Shapes** panel > **Extrude**.
49. Select the sketch and click the **Remove Material** button on the dashboard.
50. Click the **Reverse Direction** button next to the **Depth** box.
51. Select **Extrude up to next surface** option from the drop-down next to the **Depth** box.

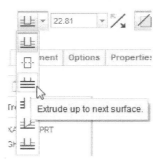

52. Click the green check on the dashboard to create the cut.

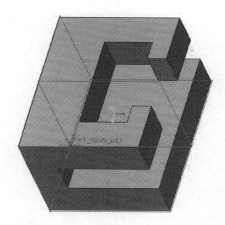

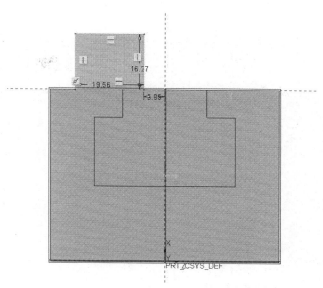

53. On the ribbon, click **Model** tab > **Datum** panel > **Sketch**.
54. Click on the top plane to define the sketching plane.
55. On the **Sketch** dialog, click in the **Reference** box and select the right face of the model geometry.

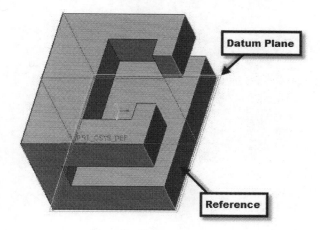

56. Click the **Sketch** button.
57. On the **Graphics** toolbar, click the **Sketch View** icon. This orients the sketch parallel to the screen.
58. Create a sketch, as shown below.

59. On the ribbon, click **Sketch** tab > **Constrain** panel > **Coincident** ━━ .
60. Select the edge and the line, as shown below. This will make them coincident.

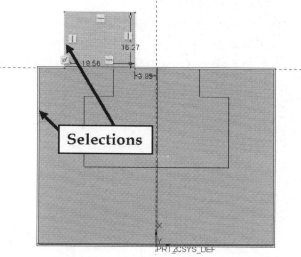

61. Modify the dimensions, as shown below (refer to the **Modify** section of Chapter 2 to learn how to modify dimensions).

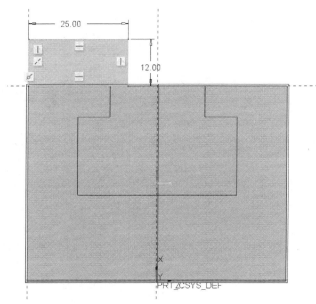

62. Click **OK** on the ribbon.
63. Change the view to **Standard Orientation.**
64. Activate the **Extrude** command and select the sketch.
65. On the **Extrude** dashboard, select the **Extrude to selected point, curve, plane or surface** option from the drop-down next to the **Depth** box.

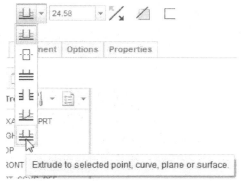

66. Select the horizontal face of the part geometry, as shown in figure.

67. Click the green check to complete the part.

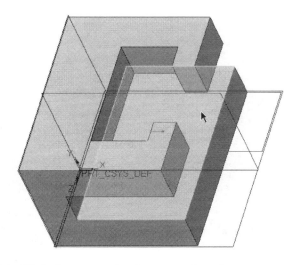

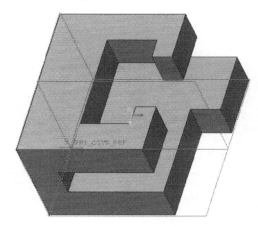

68. Save and close the file.

Example 2

In this example, you will create the part shown below.

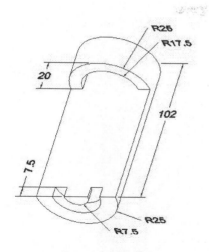

1. Start **Creo Parametric 4.0**.
2. On the Quick Access Toolbar, click the **New** button.
3. On the **New** dialog, select **Types > Part**, and then type-in **C03-Example2** in the **Name** box.
4. Uncheck the **Use default template** option and click **OK**.
5. On the **New File Options** dialog, select **solid_part_mmks**, and click **OK**.
6. Draw a sketch on the top plane, as shown below.

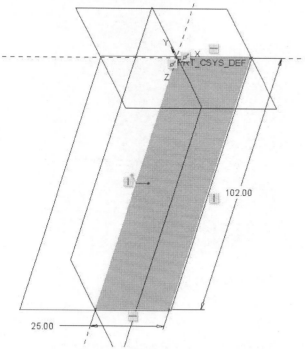

7. On the ribbon, click **OK** to exit the **Sketch** mode.
8. On the ribbon, click **Model** tab > **Shapes** panel > **Revolve** .

9. Select the sketch.
10. Click on the line passing through the origin.

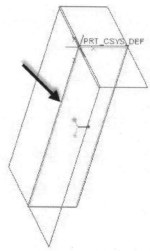

11. On the **Revolve** dashboard, type-in 180 in the **Angle** box and click the **Reverse Direction** button.

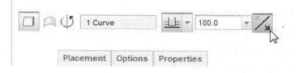

12. Click the green check to create the *Revolved* feature.

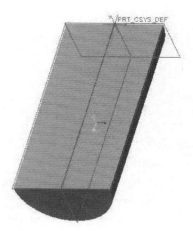

13. On the ribbon, click **Model** tab > **Datum** panel > **Sketch**.
14. Click on the top face of the model geometry.
15. On the **Sketch** dialog, click in the **Reference** box and select the front face of the model.

16. Click the **Sketch** button to start the sketch.
17. Draw the sketch and create a centerline, as shown below.

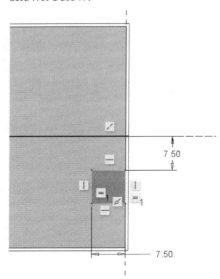

18. Click **OK** on the ribbon.
19. Activate the **Revolve** command and select the sketch, if not already selected.
20. On the **Revolve** dashboard, click the **Remove material** button.
21. Click the green check to complete the revolved cut.

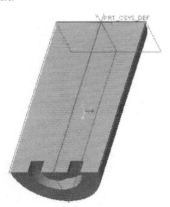

22. Activate the **Sketch** command and click on the top face of the model.
23. On the **Sketch** dialog, click in the **Reference** box and select the back face of the model.
24. Click the **Sketch** button to start the sketch.
25. On the ribbon, click **Sketch > Setup > References**.
26. Click the side edges of the geometry, and click **Close**.

27. Create the sketch and centerline, as shown below.

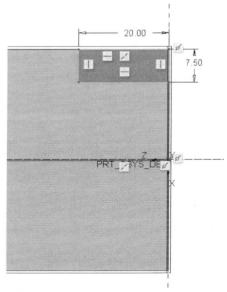

28. Click **OK** on the ribbon.
29. Activate the **Revolve** command and select the sketch, if not already selected.
30. Type-in 180 in the **Angle** box on the dashboard.
31. Click the green check on the dashboard.

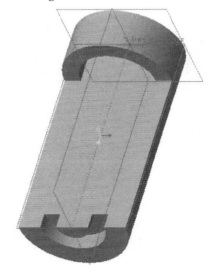

32. Save and close the file.

Questions

1. How do you create parallel planes in Creo Parametric?
2. List any two depth types available on the **Extrude** dashboard.

3. List the commands to create basic features.
4. How do you create angled planes in Creo Parametric?

Exercises
Exercise 1

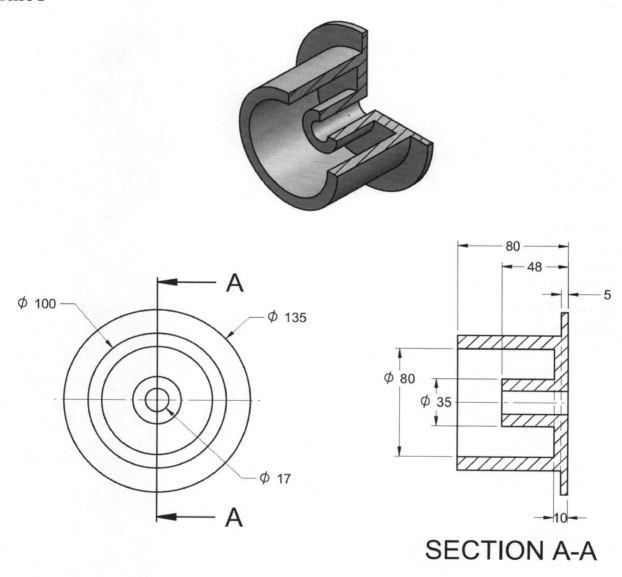

SECTION A-A

Exercise 2

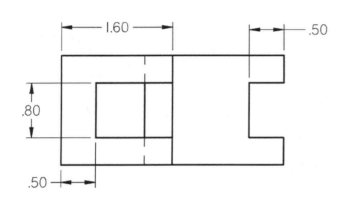

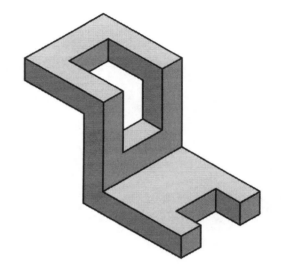

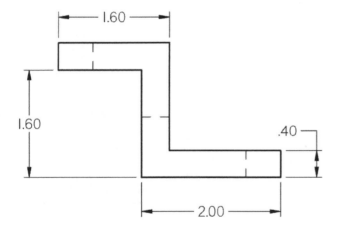

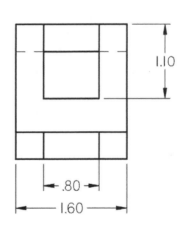

Exercise 3

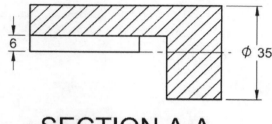

SECTION A-A

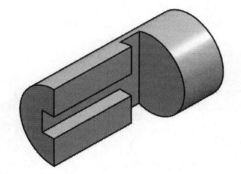

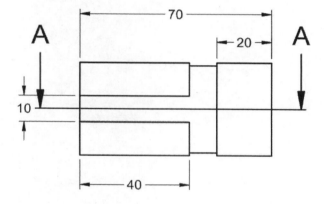

Chapter 4: Holes and Placed Features

So for, all of the features that were covered in previous chapter were based on two-dimensional sketches. However, there are certain features in Creo Parametric that do not require a sketch at all. Features that do not require a sketch are called placed features. You can simply place them on your models. However, you must have some existing geometry to add these features. Unlike a sketch-based feature, you cannot use a placed feature for a first feature of a model. For example, to create a *Round* feature, you must have an already existing edge. In this chapter, you will learn how to add Holes and placed features to your design.

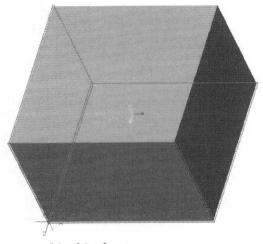 

The topics covered in this chapter are:

- *Holes*
- *Threads*
- *Rounds*
- *Chamfers*
- *Drafts*
- *Shells*

Hole

As you know, it is possible to use the *Extrude* command to create cuts and remove material. But, if you want to drill holes that are of standard sizes, the **Hole** command is a better way to do this. The reason for this is it has many hole types already predefined for you. All you have to do is choose the correct hole type and size. The other benefit is when you are going to create a 2D drawing, Creo Parametric can automatically place the correct hole annotation. Activate this command (On the ribbon, click **Model > Engineering > Hole**) and click on a face to add hole.

You can select a flat or cylindrical face. You will notice that **Hole** dashboard appears. There are options on this dashboard that make it easy to create different types of holes. The procedures to create various types of holes are explained next.

Simple Hole

1. To create a simple hole feature, click the **Create simple hole** icon on the **Hole** dashboard.
2. On the **Hole** dashboard, type-in a value in the **Diameter** ⌀ box.

3. If you want a through hole, click **Drill Depth** drop-down > **Drill to intersect with all surfaces**. If you want a blind hole, then select **Depth value** from the **Drill Depth** drop-down. Next, type-in a value in the **Depth** box.

4. If you want a V-bottom hole, then click **Use standard hole profile** icon on the dashboard.

5. Click the **Shape** tab and type-in a value in the **Angle** box. You can define the drill depth up to the shoulder or tip of the hole using the **Shoulder** or **Tip** options, respectively.

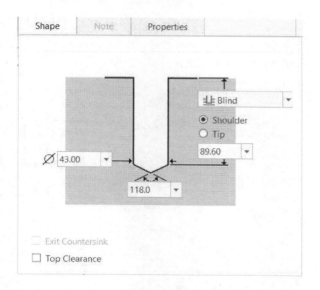

You can also create Counterbored or Countersunk holes using the **Adds Counterbore** or **Adds Countersunk** icons.

A counterbore hole is a large diameter hole added at the opening of another hole. It is used to accommodate a fastener below the level of the work piece surface. Click the **Adds Counterbore** icon on the dashboard and edit the dimensions on the **Shape** tab.

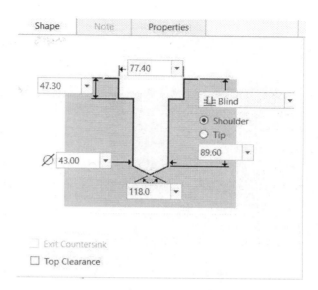

A countersunk hole has an enlarged V-shaped opening to accommodate a fastener below the level of work piece surface. Click the **Adds Countersink** icon on the dashboard and edit the dimensions on the **Shape** tab.

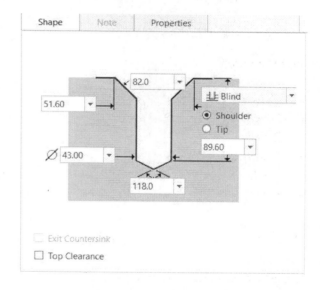

6. Click and drag anyone of the green handles attached to the holes onto the side face of the model.

7. Likewise, drag another handle onto the side face perpendicular to the previous face.

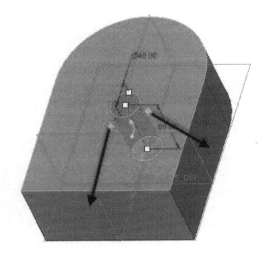

8. Modify the offset dimensions to define the hole position.

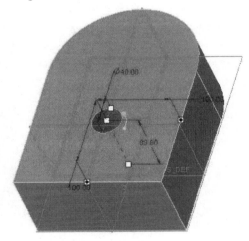

9. Click the green check on the dashboard to create the hole.

Coaxial Hole

You can create holes coaxial to a cylindrical face.

1. Create a datum axis by activating the **Axis** command and selecting the edge of a cylindrical face.

2. Activate the **Hole** command.
3. Press the Ctrl key and click on the datum axis and the face on which the hole is to be placed.

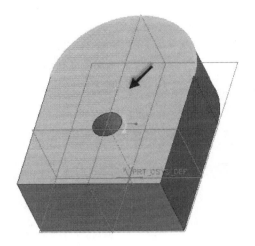

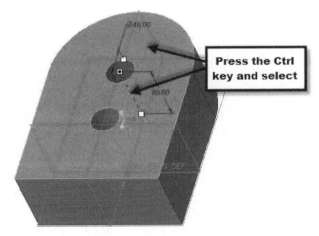

Press the Ctrl key and select

4. Set the other options on the dashboard and click the green check.

Radial and Diameter Holes

You can create a hole at a radial distance from an axis.

1. Activate the **Hole** command and click on the placement face.
2. On the **Hole** dashboard, click the **Placement** tab and select **Type > Radial**.
3. Click in the **Offset References** section on the **Placement** tab.
4. Press the Ctrl key and select an axis and plane. The axis is used as the reference to define the

radial distance and the plane is used to define the angle.

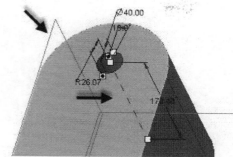

5. Modify the radial and angle values to define the location of the hole.
6. Click the green check.

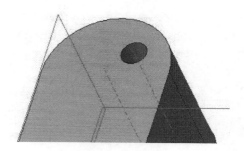

Likewise, you can create a hole by specifying the diameter distance from an axis.

Standard Hole

Creo Parametric allows you to create holes based on UNF, ISO, and UNC standards. You can create a thread, clearance or tapered hole using the standard charts.

1. Activate the **Hole** command and click the **Create standard hole** icon on the **Hole** dashboard.
2. Select the standard from the **Thread type** drop-down.
3. Select the screw size from the **Screw size** drop-down.
4. Define the hole depth on the dashboard. You can also use the **Adds countersink** and **Adds counterbore** options to create countersink or counterbored holes.

5. Click on the placement face and position the hole.

Likewise, you can add a clearance hole to the model.

1. Activate **Hole** command and click **Create standard hole** icon on the **Hole** dashboard.
2. Deactivate the **Adds tapped hole** icon.
3. Click the **Create clearance hole** icon on the Dashboard.
4. Set the standard and screw size on the Dashboard.
5. Click the **Shape** tab on the Dashboard.
6. Select the type of **Fit** from the drop-down.

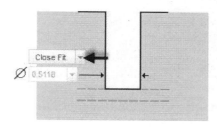

7. Define the hole depth.
8. Click on the placement face and position the hole.

Tapered Hole

Tapering is the process of decreasing the hole diameter toward one end. A tapered hole has a smaller diameter at the bottom.

1. Activate **Hole** command and click the **Create standard hole** icon on the **Hole** dashboard.

2. Activate the **Adds tapped hole** icon.
3. Click the **Create tapered hole** icon on the Dashboard.
4. Set the standard and screw size on the Dashboard.
5. Define the hole depth.
6. Click on the placement face and position the hole.

The Cosmetic Thread command

This command adds a cosmetic thread/tap feature to a cylindrical face. A thread is added to the outer cylindrical face, whereas a tap is added to the inner cylindrical face (holes). You add thread/tap features to a 3D geometry so that when you create a 2D drawing, Creo Parametric can automatically place the correct thread annotation.

1. On the ribbon, click **Model > Engineering > Cosmetic Thread**.

2. To create a thread, click on the outer cylindrical face of the part geometry.
3. Click on the end face of the cylindrical feature to define the limiting face.
4. On the **Cosmetic Thread** Dashboard, type-in the thread diameter, thread depth, and pitch values.
5. Use the arrow that is displayed on the preview to change the thread direction.

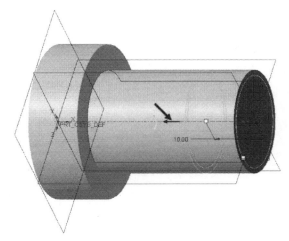

6. On the **Cosmetic Thread** Dashboard, click the **Properties** tab to view the thread properties. You can use the **Open** button to import the thread properties (or) use the **Save** button to save the properties for future use.

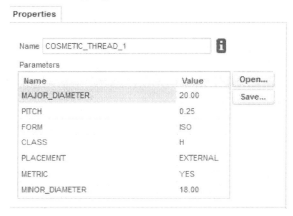

You can also create a standard thread.

1. On the **Cosmetic Thread** Dashboard, click the **Define standard thread** icon.
2. Set the standard and thread size.
3. Click the **Properties** tab to view and modify the thread properties.

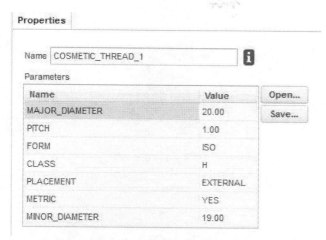

4. Click the green check on the dashboard.

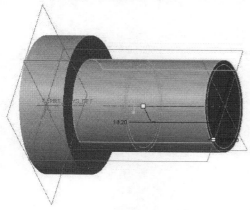

The Round command

This command breaks the sharp edges of a model and rounds them. It does not need a sketch to create a round. All you need to have is model edges.

1. On the ribbon, click **Model > Engineering > Round**.
2. Select the edge to round. If you want to create multiple rounds with same radius, then press Ctrl and select multiple edges. By mistake, if you have selected a wrong edge you can deselect it by pressing Ctrl and selecting the edge again.

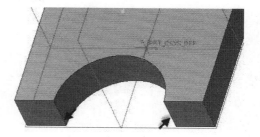

3. You can change the radius by typing a value in the **Radius** box available on the **Round** Dashboard. As you change the radius, all the selected edges will be updated. This is because they are all part of one instance. If you want the edges to have different radii, you must select edges without pressing Ctrl key.
4. Click **OK** to finish this feature. The *Round* feature will be listed in the Model Tree.

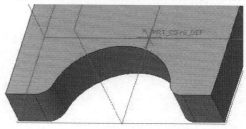

If you want to select all the edges that are tangentially connected, then simply click on anyone of the tangentially connected edges.

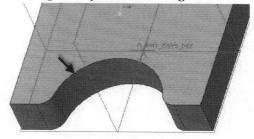

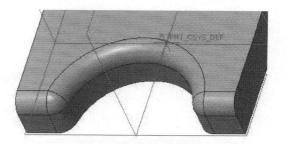

Conic Rounds

By default, the rounds have a circular arc profile. However, if you want to create a round with conical arc profile, then click the **Sets** tab on the Dashboard and select **Conic** from the **Cross-section** drop-down. Next, type-in a value in the **Conic parameter** box.

The rounds with different conic parameters are shown below.

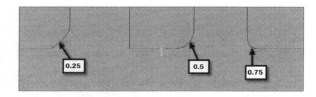

Corner Transition

If you create a round on three edges that come together at a corner, you have the option to control how these three rounds are blend together.

1. Activate the **Round** command and select the three edges that meet together at a corner.
2. On the **Round** dashboard, click the **Switch to transition mode** icon.
3. Click on the corner segment.

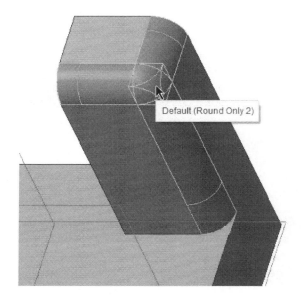

4. On the Dashboard, select **Intersect** from the drop-down.
5. Click the **Preview** icon.

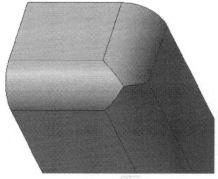

6. Click the **Resume** icon.
7. On the **Round** dashboard, click the **Switch to transition mode** icon.
8. Click on the corner segment.
9. On the Dashboard, select **Corner Sphere** from the drop-down.
10. Type-in 0.4 in the **R** box and press Enter. Notice the L1, L2, and L3 boxes on the Dashboard. You can type-in the setback distances in these boxes.

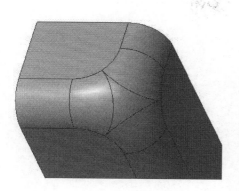

Likewise, you can create other transitions at the corners.

Variable Radius Rounds

Creo Parametric allows you to create a round with a varying radius along the selected edge.

1. Activate the **Round** command.
2. Click on the edge to round.
3. Click the right mouse button and select **Make variable**. Two separate radii are added at the ends.

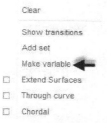

4. On the dashboard, click the **Sets** tab.
5. Click the right mouse button on the table available at the bottom of the **Sets** tab and select **Add radius**. A new radius is added to the round.

6. Click and drag the radius handle to move it to the center.

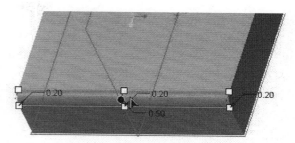

7. Type-in the radii values in the table available at the bottom on the **Sets** tab. You can also modify the radii by dragging the radii handles.

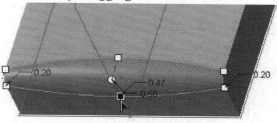

You can also convert the variable radius round to constant radius one by clicking the right mouse button and selecting **Make constant**.

8. Click the green check to complete the feature.

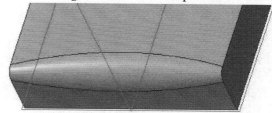

Chordal Round

You can create a round by specifying the chord length of the round instead of a radius. The chord length is the distance between the endpoints of the round profile.

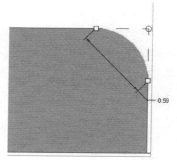

1. Activate the **Round** command and click on the
   edge to round.
2. Click the right mouse button and select **Chordal**.
3. Type-in a value in the **Chordal Length** box on
   the dashboard.

Face-Face Round

The **Round** command also allows you to create a
round between two faces.

1. Activate the **Round** command.
2. Press the Ctrl key and click on two faces
   connected to each other.

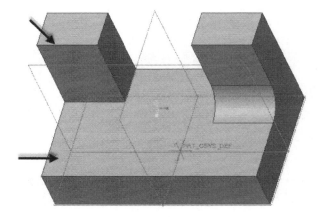

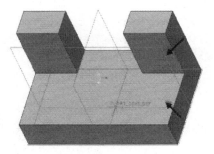

3. Type-in a value in the **Radius** box.
4. Click the green check on the Dashboard.

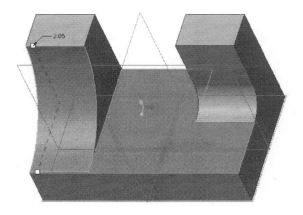

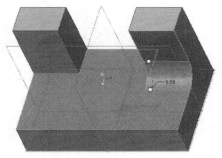

3. Click the green check on the Dashboard.

Full round

This option creates a full round between two
selected edges.

1. Activate the **Round** command.
2. Press the Ctrl key and click on two edges having
   a common face.
3. Click the right mouse button and select **Full
   round**.

Face-Edge round

The **Round** command also allows you to create a
round by selecting a face and a limiting edge.

1. Activate the **Round** command.
2. Press the Ctrl key and click on a face and edge.
   A round is created between the face and edge.

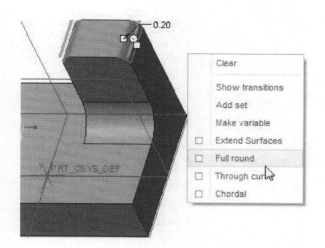

A round appears replacing the common face.

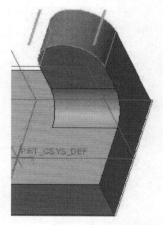

4. Click the green check on the Dashboard.

The Edge Chamfer command

The **Edge Chamfer** and **Round** commands are commonly used to break sharp edges. The difference is that the **Edge Chamfer** command adds a bevel face to the model. A chamfer is also a placed feature.

1. On the ribbon, click **Model > Engineering > Chamfer**.
2. On the **Edge Chamfer** dashboard, select the chamfer mode from the drop-down. You can select **D x D, D1 x D2, Angle x D, 45 x D, O x O,** or **O1 x O2**.

The **D x D** option defines the chamfer size by using a single distance value.

The **D1 x D2** option defines the chamfer size by using the vertical and horizontal distances.

The **Angle x D** option defines the chamfer size by using angle and distance values

The **45 x D** option defines the chamfer size by using the distance specified at a 45-degree angle. You can use this type only for perpendicular faces.

3. If you select **Angle x D**, then type-in the angle and distance values of the chamfer.
4. Click on the edge(s) to chamfer.
5. Click the green check.

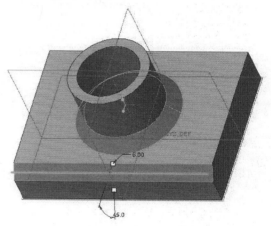

Draft

When creating cast or plastic parts, you are often required to add draft on them so that they can be moulded. A draft is an angle or taper applied to the faces of parts to make it easier to remove them from a mold.

1. On the ribbon, click **Model > Engineering > Draft**.
2. Press the Ctrl key and click on the faces to draft. You can select all the tangentially connected faces by clicking on any single face.
3. On the Dashboard, click in the **Draft Hinge** box and select a flat face or plane. This defines the

draft hinge. The draft angle will be measured with reference to this face.

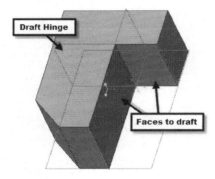

4. Type-in a value in the **Angle** box located on the Dashboard. This defines the draft angle. You can click the **Flip** icon to reverse the draft angle.

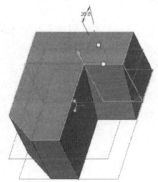

5. Click in the **Draft Hinge** box and select the plane located at an offset from the bottom face.

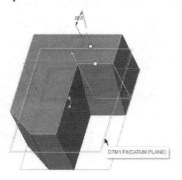

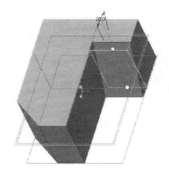

Split Drafts

If you want to add a draft only up to a certain height, then create a plane at that height. Activate the **Draft** command and select the faces to draft.

Click in the **Draft Hinge** box and select the plane. On the Dashboard, click the **Split** tab and select **Split options > Split by draft hinge**. Select the plane perpendicular to the draft faces.

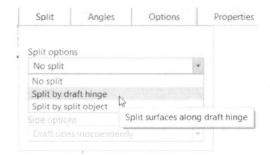

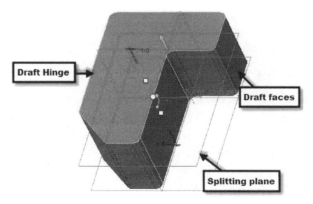

On the **Split** tab, select **Side options > Draft sides independently**. Enter different draft angles for each side.

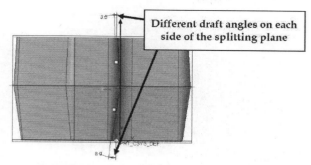

On the **Split** tab, select **Side options > Draft sides dependently**. Enter a single draft angle for both sides about a splitting plane.

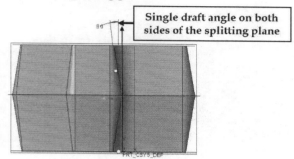

On the **Split** tab, select **Side options > Draft first side only**. Draft the first side only.

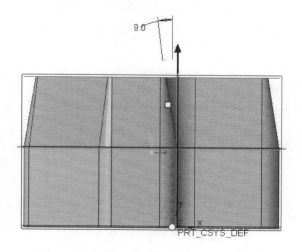

On the **Split** tab, select **Side options > Draft second side only**. Draft the second side only.

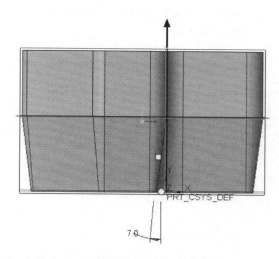

Variable Pull Direction Draft

This command creates a variable pull direction draft.

1. On the ribbon, click **Model > Engineering > Draft > Variable Pull Direction Draft** .
2. Click on the top face to define the draft reference.
3. On the Dashboard, click in the **Draft Hinges** box and select the edge, as shown below.
4. Type-in a value in the **Angle** box on the Dashboard.

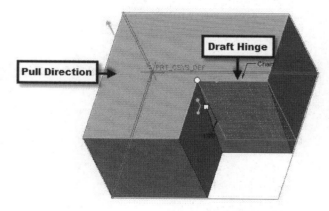

5. On the Dashboard, click the **References** tab and click the **New set** option.
6. Select a new draft hinge and type-in a new angle value.

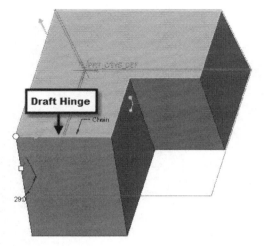

7.   Click the green check to complete the feature.

Shell

The **Shell** is another useful feature that can be
applied directly to a solid model. It allows you to
take a solid geometry and make it hollow. This can
be a powerful and timesaving technique, when
designing parts that call for thin walls such as
bottles, tanks, and containers. This command is easy
to use.

1.   You should have a solid part, and then activate
     this command by clicking **Model > Engineering
     > Shell** on the Ribbon.
2.   Select the faces to remove.
3.   Type-in the wall thickness in the **Thickness** box.
4.   If you want to add different thickness to some
     faces, then click the **Reference** tab on the
     Dashboard. Next, click in the **Non-default
     thickness** box, and then select the faces to add
     different thickness. You will notice that a
     thickness value appears in the Non-default
     thickness box. Double-click on the value and
     change it.

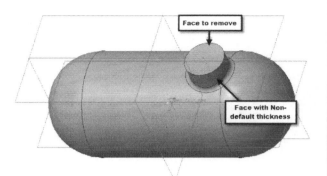

5.   Click **OK** to finish the feature.

If you want to shell the solid body without
removing any faces, then simply type-in a value in
the **Thickness** box and click the green check. This
creates the shell without removing any faces.
Change the **Display style** to **Wireframe** or **Hidden
Lines** to view the shell.

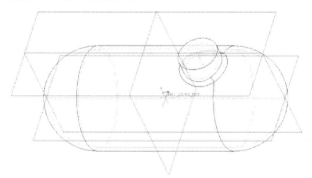

Profile Rib

This command creates stiffening ribs to add
structural stability, strength and support to your
designs. Just like any other sketch-based feature, a
rib feature requires a two dimensional sketch.

1.   On the ribbon, click **Model > Engineering > Rib
     drop-down > Profile Rib**.

2. Click on a datum plane to define the sketch location.

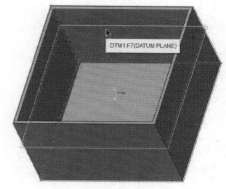

3. Create a sketch, as shown in figure.

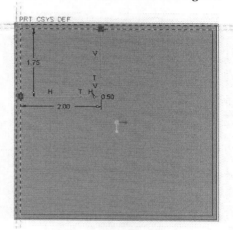

4. Click **OK** on the ribbon. The preview of the geometry appears.

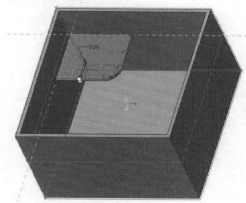

You can add material to either side of the sketch line or evenly to both sides using the **Flip** icon located on the Dashboard.

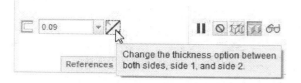

5. Click the **Flip** icon and see that the preview changes.
6. Type-in the thickness value of the rib feature in the **Thickness** box (or) drag the thickness handle.
7. On the Dashboard, click the **References** tab and click **Flip** to reverse the material side.

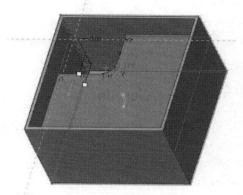

8. Again, click the **Flip** button on the **References** tab.
9. Click the green check to complete the feature.

Trajectory Rib

This command is similar to the **Profile Rib** command, but creates ribs in the direction perpendicular to the sketch.

1. On the ribbon, click **Model > Engineering > Rib drop-down > Trajectory Rib**.
2. Click on the face to define sketch plane.

10. Create a sketch, as shown in figure.

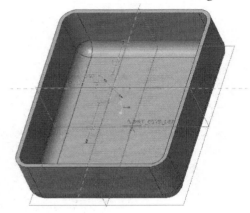

3. Click **OK** on the ribbon. The preview of the geometry appears.

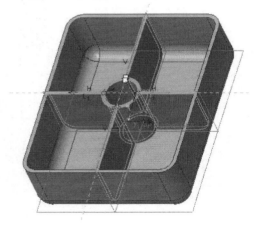

4. Type-in the thickness value of the rib feature in the **Thickness** box (or) drag the thickness handle.

5. On the Dashboard, click the **Adds draft** icon.

6. Click the **Add rounds on internal edges** icon.

7. Click the **Add rounds on exposed edges** icon.

8. On the Dashboard, click the **Shape** tab and modify the shape dimensions (thickness, draft angle, and round radius).

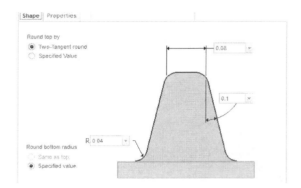

9. Click the green check to complete the feature.

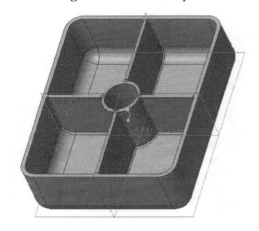

Examples

Example 1

In this example, you will create the part shown below.

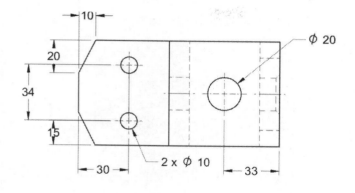

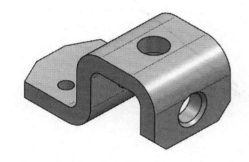

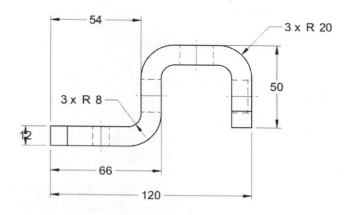

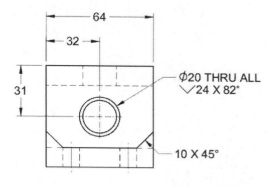

1. Start **Creo Parametric 4.0**.
2. Create the *Placed Features* folder and set it as current working folder.
3. On the Quick Access Toolbar, click the **New** button.
4. On the **New** dialog, select **Types > Part**, and then type-in **C04-Example1**.
5. Uncheck the **Use default template** option and click **OK**.
6. On the **New File Options** dialog, select **solid_part_mmks**, and click **OK**.
7. On the ribbon, click **Model** tab > **Shapes** panel > **Extrude**.
8. Click on the Front plane.
9. Draw the sketch and modify dimensions, as shown in figure (refer to the **Modify** section of Chapter 2 to learn how to modify dimensions).

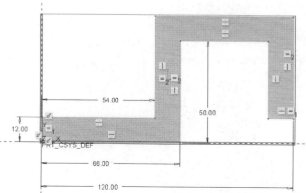

10. Extrude the sketch up to 64 mm depth.

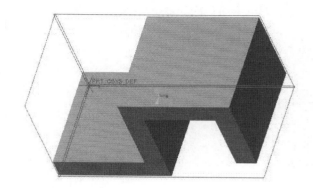

11. On the ribbon, click **Model** tab > **Engineering** panel > **Hole** .

12. Select the right-side face of the model geometry.

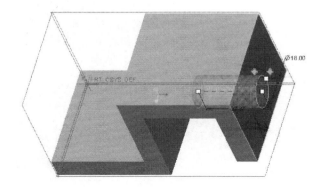

You will notice that there are two green handles attached to the hole. These handles are used to define the location of the hole.

13. Click on the horizontal green handle and align it with the vertical edge of the model.

14. Likewise, align the vertical green handle to the top horizontal edge.

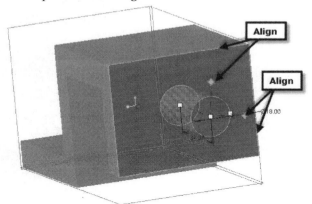

15. On the **Hole** dashboard, click the **Placement** tab.

16. On the **Placement** tab, type-in 31 and 32 in the vertical and horizontal offset boxes, respectively.

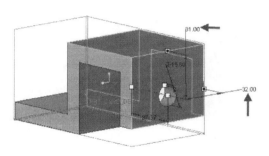

17. On the dashboard, click the **Create standard hole** icon.

18. Click the **Adds countersink** icon.

19. On the dashboard, set the hole standard to ISO.

20. Set the screw size to M20x1.5.

21. Select the **Drill to intersect with all surfaces** option from the drop-down.

22. Click on the **Shape** tab, and set the angle and countersink diameter to 82 and 24, respectively.

23. Select the **Thru Thread** option. This creates the thread throughout the hole.

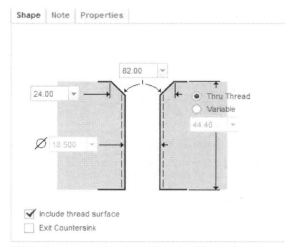

24. Click the green check on the dashboard to create the hole.

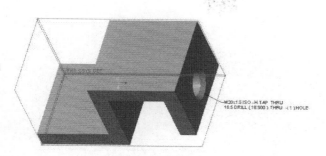

25. Activate the **Hole** command and click on the top face of the part geometry.

26. Align the green handles of the hole to the horizontal and vertical edges of the face.

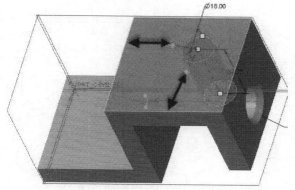

27. Change the horizontal and vertical offset distances of the hole to 33 and 32, respectively.

28. Type-in **20** in the **Diameter** box.

29. Select the **Drill up to next surface** option from the drop-down.

30. Click the green check on the dashboard to create the hole.

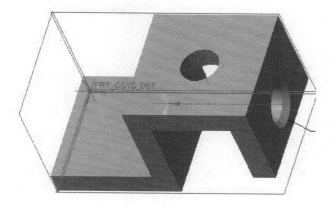

31. Likewise, create two more holes of 10 mm diameter each. Refer to the dimensions given at the starting of the example.

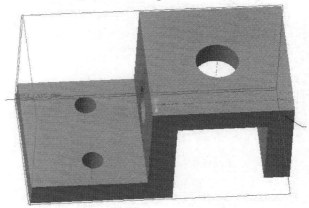

Chamfer Edges

1. On the ribbon, click **Model** tab > **Engineering** panel > **Chamfer** .

2. On the **Edge Chamfer** dashboard, select **D1 x D2** from the drop-down.

3. Set the **D1** and **D2** values to **10** and **20**, respectively.

4. Press the Ctrl key and click on the side vertical edges as shown.

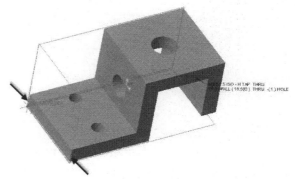

5. Click the green check to apply chamfers.

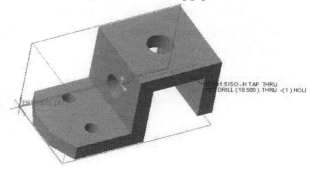

Round Edges

1. On the **Graphics** toolbar, click **Display Style** drop-down > **Wireframe**.

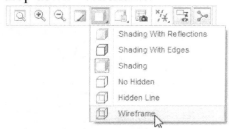

2. On the ribbon, click **Model** tab > **Engineering** panel > **Round** .
3. On the ribbon, type-in 8 in the **Radius** box. Press Enter.

4. Click on the horizontal edges of the geometry, as shown below.

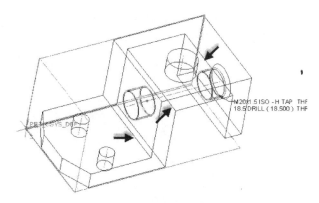

5. Click the green check to add rounds.
6. Activate the **Round** command and type-in 20 in the **Radius** box. Press Enter.
7. Click on the outer edges of the model, as shown below. Click the green check to complete the round feature.

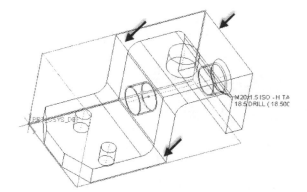

8. On the **Graphics** toolbar, click **Display Style** drop-down > **Shading**.

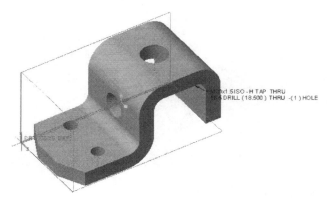

9. On the ribbon, click **Model** tab > **Engineering** panel > **Chamfer** .
10. On the **Edge Chamfer** dashboard, select **D x D** from the drop-down.
11. Set the **D** value to **10**.
12. Click on the lower corners of the part geometry.

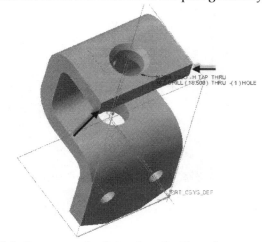

13. Click the green check to chamfer the edges.

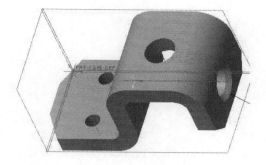

14. On the **Graphics** toolbar, click **Saved Orientations Drop-down > Standard Orientation**.
15. Save and close the file.

Example 2

In this example, you will create the part shown next.

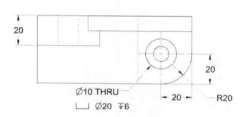

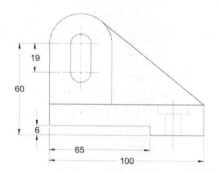

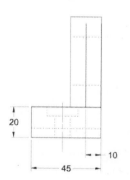

1. Start **Creo Parametric 4.0**.
2. Create the *Placed Features* folder and set it as current working folder.
3. On the Quick Access Toolbar, click the **New** button.
4. On the **New** dialog, select **Types > Part**, and then type-in **C04-Example2**.
5. Click **OK**.

6. On the **New File Options** dialog, select the **solid_part_mmks** template. Click **OK** to start the file.
7. Activate the **Extrude** command and click on the top plane.
8. On the ribbon, click **Sketch** tab > **Sketching** panel > **Rectangle** drop-down > **Corner Rectangle**.
9. Select the origin point to define the first corner of the rectangle.

10. Move the pointer toward bottom right corner, and then click to the create the rectangle.

11. Modify the dimensions of the rectangle, as shown (refer to the **Modify** section of Chapter 2 to learn how to modify dimensions).

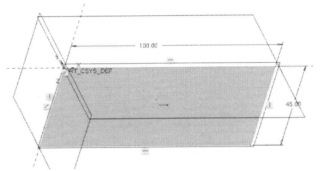

12. Extrude the rectangle up to a depth of 20 mm.

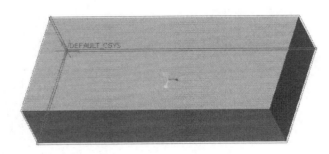

13. Activate the **Extrude** command, and then click on the Front Datum plane.

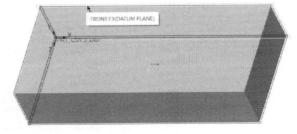

14. Click **Sketch View** on the Graphics toolbar.

15. Create the sketch, as shown.

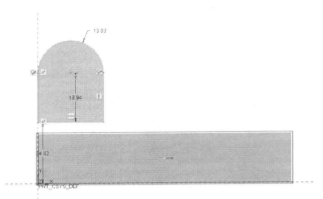

16. Make the horizontal line coincident with the top horizontal edge.

17. Modify the dimensions of the sketch (refer to the **Modify** section of Chapter 2 to learn how to modify dimensions).

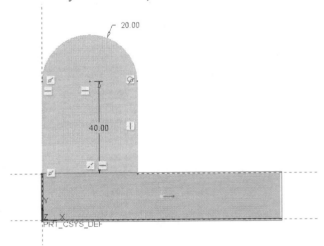

18. Click **OK** on the **Sketch** tab of the ribbon.

19. Type 20 in the **Depth** box of the **Extrude** Dashboard, and then click the green check.

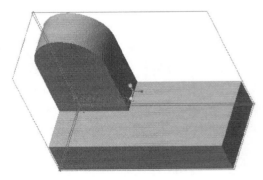

20. Activate the **Sketch** command and select the Front datum plane.

21. Click in the **Reference** box and select the right face of the model.

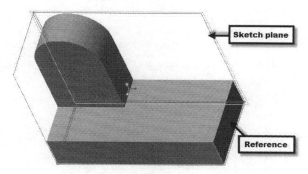

22. Click the **Sketch** button to start the sketch.
23. On the ribbon, click **Sketch** tab > **Setup** panel > **References** .
24. Select the top face of the first feature, right and curved faces of the second feature.

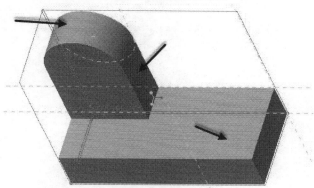

25. Close the **References** dialog.
26. Activate the **Line** command and click on the curved edge.

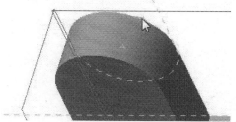

27. Move the pointer and click to create a line.

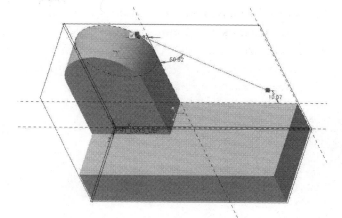

28. On the ribbon, click **Sketch** tab > **Constrain** panel > **Coincident** .
29. Select the bottom end point of the line.
30. Select the horizontal reference line; the end point of the line is made coincident with the horizontal reference line.

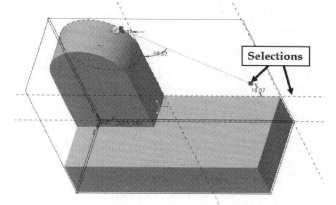

31. Likewise, make the end point of the line coincident with the vertical reference line.

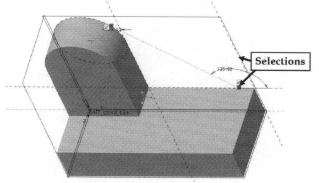

32. On the ribbon, click **Sketch** tab > **Constrain** panel > **Tangent** .

33. Select the line and the curved face of the second feature; the line is made tangent to the curve face.

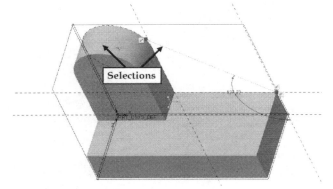

34. Click **OK** ✔ on the ribbon.
35. On the ribbon, click **Model** tab > **Engineering** panel > **Rib** drop-down > **Profile Rib** .
36. Select the sketch line, if not selected.
37. On the **Profile Rib** dashboard, click the **References** tab, and then click the **Flip** button. You can also click the arrow that appears on the sketch line. This changes the rib direction.

38. On the dashboard, type-in 10 in the thickness box.
39. Click the **Change thickness option** button until the thickness side is changed, as shown.

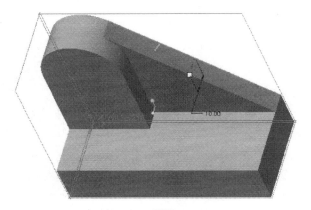

40. Click the green check ✔ to complete the rib feature.

41. Activate the **Extrude** command and click on the front face of the second feature.
42. Draw the sketch for the slot feature. You can use the **Palette** command to do this (refer to the **Palette** section of Chapter 2 to learn how create predefined shapes).

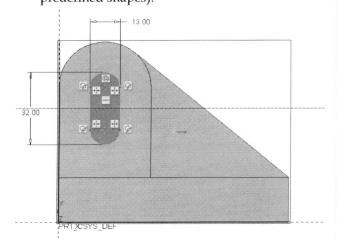

43. Exit the sketch and create the *Extrude cut* feature.

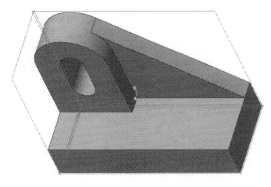

44. Create a sketch on the front face of the base.

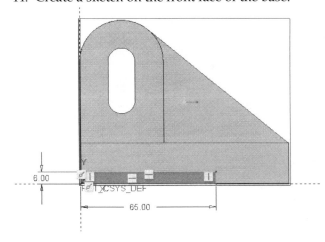

45. Create another *Extrude cut* feature throughout the model.

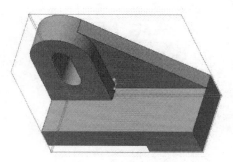

46. On the ribbon, click **Model** tab > **Engineering** panel > **Round** .

47. Select the lower right corner edge of the first feature.

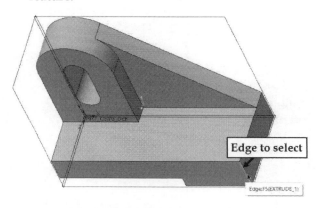

Edge to select

Edge:F5(EXTRUDE_1)

48. Type 20 in the **Radius** box on the **Round** dashboard.

49. Click the green check.

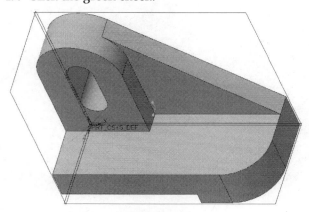

50. On the ribbon, click **Model** tab > **Datum** panel > **Axis** .

51. Select the round face of the model, as shown.

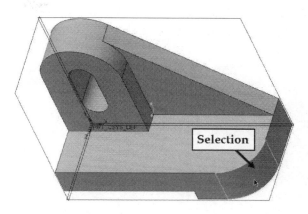

Selection

52. Click **OK** on the **Datum Axis** dialog to create the axis at the center point of the selected round face.

53. On the ribbon, click **Model** tab > **Engineering** panel > **Hole** .

54. Press hold the Ctrl key, and then click on the top face of the first feature and the axis.

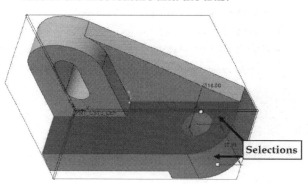

Selections

55. On the **Hole** dashboard, click the **Create Standard hole** icon.

56. Click the **Adds Counterbored** icon on the **Hole** dashboard.

57. Set the **Standard** to **ISO**.

58. Select **M10X1.25** from the **Screw Size** drop-down.

59. Select the **Through All** from the **Specify drill depth type** drop-down.

60. Click the **Shape** tab on the **Hole** dashboard, and then specify the settings, as shown.

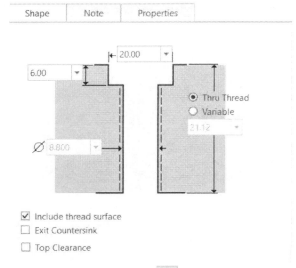

Shape	Note	Properties

20.00

6.00

Thru Thread
○ Variable
21.12

Ø 8.800

☑ Include thread surface
☐ Exit Countersink
☐ Top Clearance

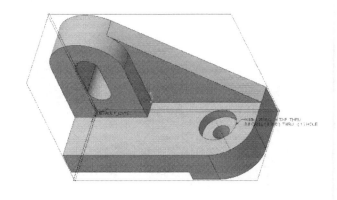

62. Save and close the file.

61. Click the green check ✓.

Questions

1. What are Placed features?
2. Which option allows you to create a chamfer with unequal setbacks?
3. Which command allows you create a variable radius blend?
4. When you create a thread on a cylindrical face, the thread diameter will be calculated automatically or not.

Exercises

Exercise 1

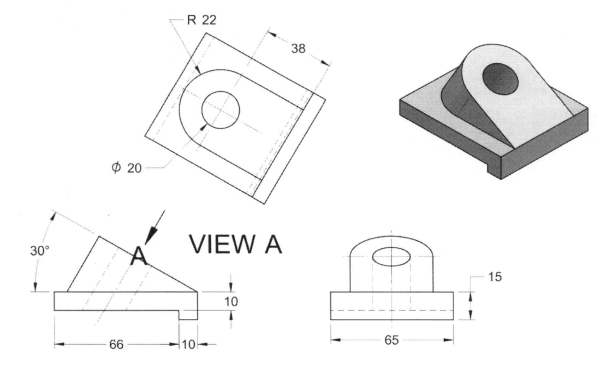

R 22

38

Ø 20

30°

VIEW A

10

66

10

15

65

Exercise 2

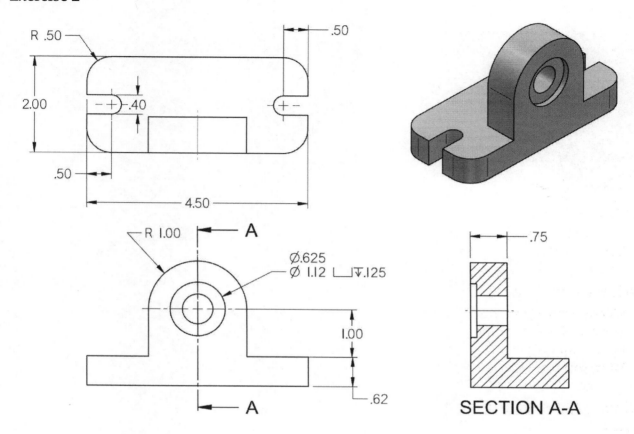

SECTION A-A

Exercise 3

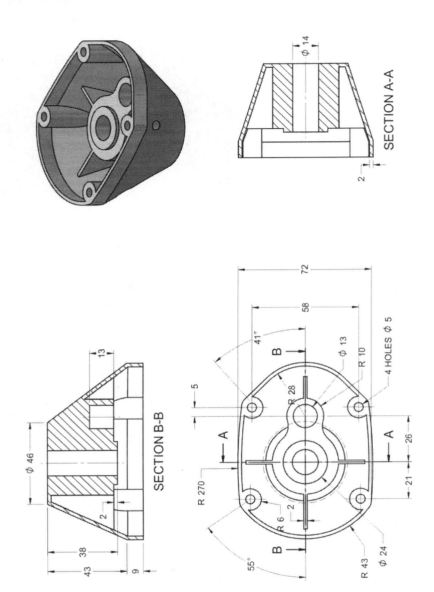

SECTION A-A

φ 14

2

SECTION B-B

13

φ 46

2

38

43

9

72

58

41°

5

B

R 28

A

A

R 270

R 6

2

B

55°

R 43

φ 24

φ 13

R 10

4 HOLES φ 5

26

21

Exercise 4

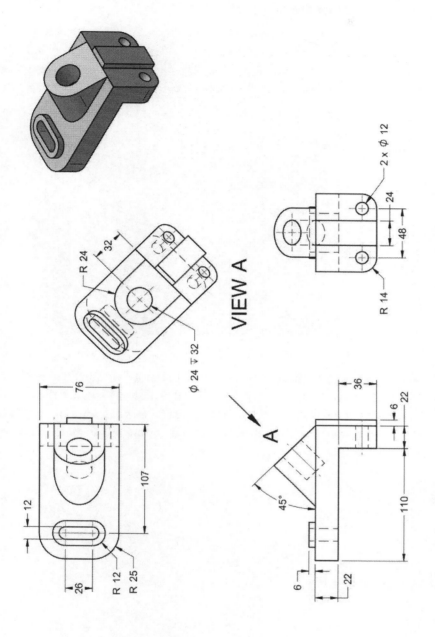

VIEW A

R 24

32

Ø 24 ⊽ 32

2 x Ø 12

24

48

R 14

76

107

12

26

R 12

R 25

36

6

22

110

45°

6

22

Chapter 5: Patterned Geometry

When designing a part geometry, oftentimes there are elements of symmetry in each part or there are at least a few features that are repeated multiple times. In these situations, Creo Parametric offers you some commands that save your time. For example, you can use mirror features to design symmetric parts, which makes designing the part quicker. This is because you only have to design a portion of the part and use the mirror feature to create the remaining geometry.

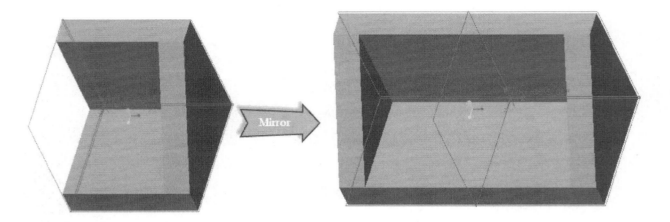

In addition, there are some transformation commands to replicate a feature throughout a part quickly. They save you time from creating additional features individually and help you modify the design easily. If the design changes, you only need to change the first feature and the rest of the pattern features will update, automatically. In this chapter, you will learn to create mirrored and pattern geometries using the commands available in Creo Parametric.

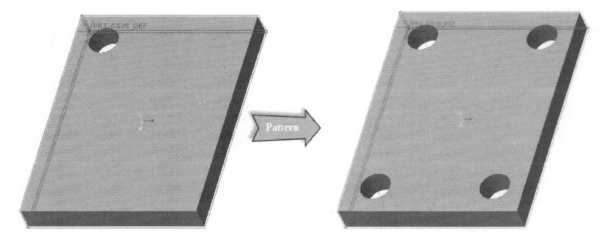

The topics covered in this chapter are:

- *Mirror* features
- *Mirror the entire body*
- *Save a mirrored copy of the part*
- *Direction Patterns*
- *Axis Patterns*
- *Reference Patterns*
- *Curve Patterns*
- *Point Patterns*

The Mirror command

If you are designing a part that is symmetric, you can save time by using the **Mirror** command. Using this command, you can replicate individual features or the entire body. To mirror features (3D geometry), you need to have a face or plane to use as a mirroring element. You can use a model face, default plane, or create a new plane, if it does not exist where it is needed.

1. Press and hold the Ctrl key and select the features to mirror from the Model Tree.

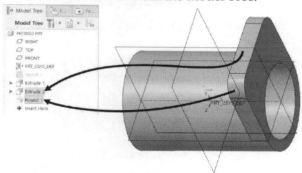

2. On the ribbon, click **Model > Editing > Mirror**.

3. Select the plane/face about which the features are to be mirrored.

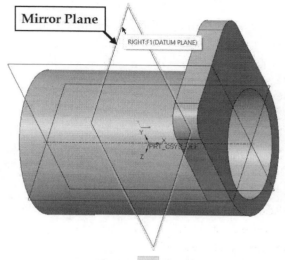

4. Click the green check ✓ on the **Mirror** dashboard.

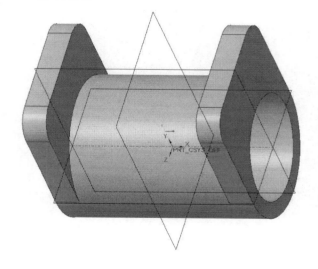

Now, if you make changes to original feature, the mirror feature will be updated, automatically.

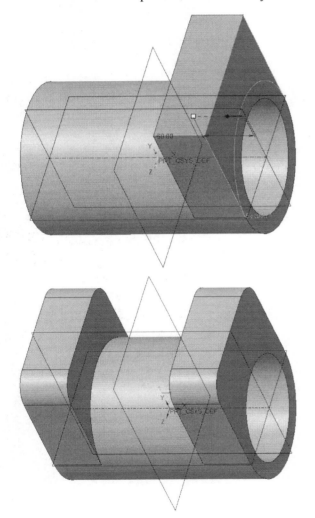

Mirror the Entire body

If the part you are creating is completely symmetric, you can save more time by creating half of it and mirroring the entire geometry rather than individual

features.

1. In the Model Tree, click the part name.

2. Activate the **Mirror** command and click on the mirror plane.

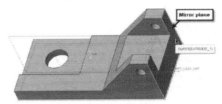

3. Click the green check on the **Mirror** dashboard to mirror the complete body.

Save a Mirrored copy of the Part

Creo allows you to save a mirror copy of the part.

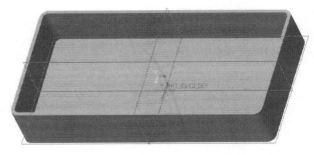

1. On the **File** menu, click **Save As > Mirror Part**.

2. On the **Mirror Part** dialog, select **Geometry only** to mirror only the part geometry. You cannot edit the individual features of the geometry. The **Geometry with features** option allows you to edit the features of the mirrored part.

3. Examine the other options and check the **Preview** option. The preview of the mirrored part appears. Note that you cannot define the mirror plane as the program defines it, automatically.

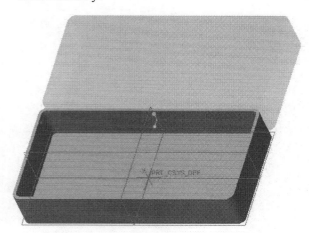

4. Type the name of the mirrored copy and click **OK**.

The Pattern command

This command replicates a feature using different references such as direction, axis, surface boundary, dimension, an existing pattern, table, curve, and randomly arranged points. On the ribbon, click **Model > Editing > Pattern** to activate this command. The different types of patterns that can be created using this command are explained next.

Direction

This option replicates a feature using a directional reference such as plane, face, edge, or axis.

1. Select the feature to pattern.

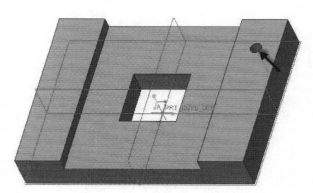

2. On the ribbon, click **Model > Editing > Pattern**.
3. On the **Pattern** dashboard, select **Direction** from the drop-down available on the left side.
4. Select the edge along the Z-axis to define the first direction of the pattern.

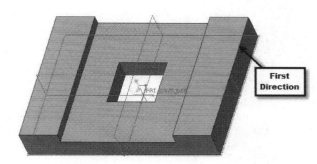

5. Specify number of instances as **4** and spacing between them as **30**.

6. Use the **Flip** icon to correct the pattern direction, if required.
7. Click the green check on the dashboard to create the direction pattern.

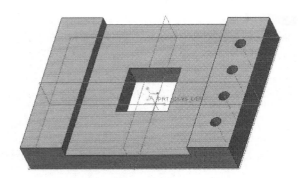

8. In the Model tree, click on **Pattern 1 of Hole 1** and select **Edit Definition**.

9. On the **Pattern** dashboard, click the **Dimensions** tab.

10. Under the **Direction 1** section, click in the **Dimension** field and select the diameter of the hole.

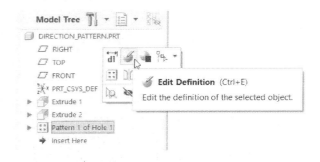

11. Type-in 2 in the **Increment** box in the **Direction 1** section. The diameter of the hole is increased by 2 for each increment.

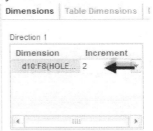

12. Click the green check 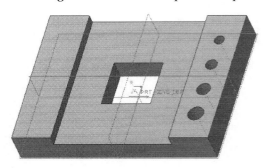 to update the pattern.

13. In the Model tree, click on **Pattern 1 of Hole 1** and select **Edit Definition**.

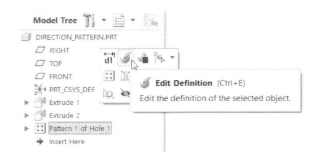

14. Click in the **Second Direction** box on the **Pattern** dashboard.

15. Select the edge along the X-axis to define the second direction.

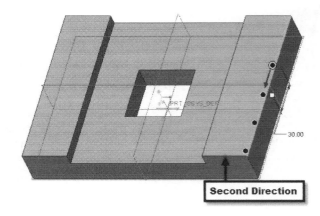

16. Specify number of instances as **5** and spacing between them as **40**.

17. Use the **Flip** icon to correct the pattern direction, if required.

18. Click the green check to update the pattern.

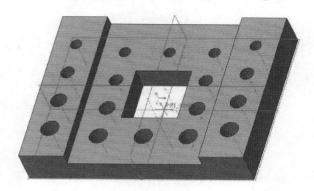

19. In the Model tree, click the right mouse button on **Pattern 1 of Hole 1** and select **Edit Definition**.

20. On the **Pattern** dashboard, click the **Dimensions** tab.

21. Under the **Direction 2** section, click in the **Dimension** field and select the diameter of the hole.

22. Type-in -1 in the **Increment** box under the **Direction 2** section. The diameter of the hole is decreased by **1** for each increment along the second direction.

23. Click the green check to update the pattern.

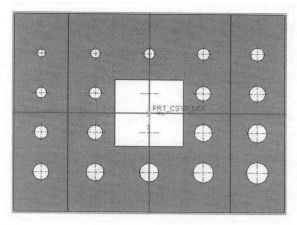

24. In the Model tree, click the right mouse button on **Pattern 1 of Hole 1** and select **Edit Definition**.

25. On the pattern preview, click the black dots at the center to suppress them.

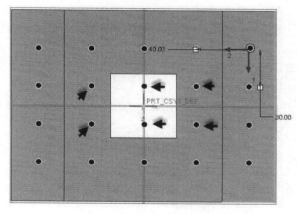

26. Click the green check to update the pattern.

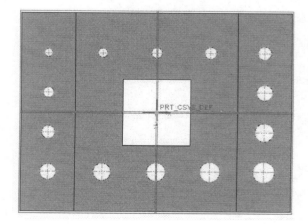

Axis

This option patterns the selected features in a circular fashion.

1. On the **Graphics** toolbar, make sure that the **Axis Display** is turned ON.

2. Select the feature to pattern and activate the **Pattern** command.

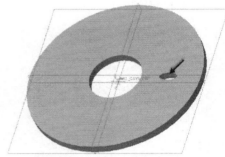

3. On the **Pattern** dashboard, select **Axis** from the drop-down available on the left side.
4. Select a Datum axis or Csys axis to define the center of the pattern.

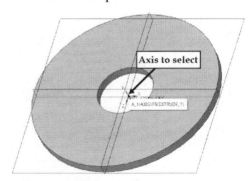

5. Type-in the number of instances value on the Dashboard.

Deactivate the **Set Angular extent** icon, if you want to type-in the instance count and the angle between individual instances.

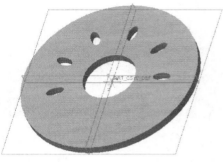

Activate the **Set Angular extent** icon, if you want to type-in the instance count and extent angle. The angle between the instances will be calculated, automatically. For example, enter 5 in the **Instance(s)** box and 360 in the **Angular Extent** box. This creates five instances including the original one. The angle between the instances will be 72 (360/5).

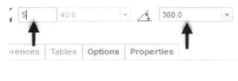

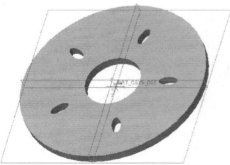

On the **Options** tab, uncheck **Follow axis rotation** to pattern the feature with the original orientation.

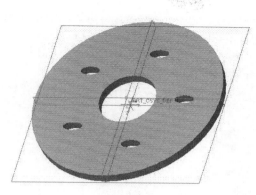

You can check the **Use alternate origin** option and select a datum point, coordinate system, curve end, or vertex to define the origin of the pattern.

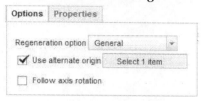

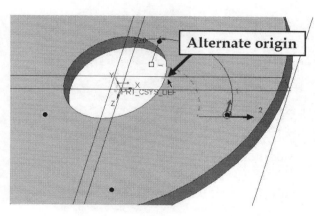

Check the **Follow axis rotation** option to change the orientation of the instances, as they are patterned in the circular fashion.

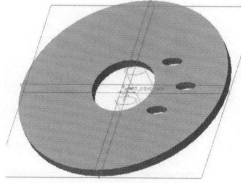

You can also create pattern instances in second direction. Specify the number of instances and spacing value on the Dashboard.

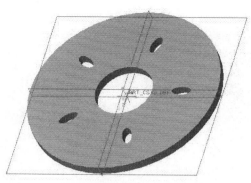

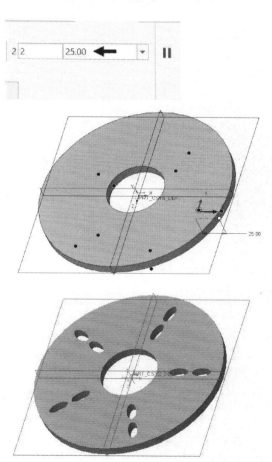

Reference

This option patterns a feature using an existing pattern. The feature should be associated with the feature of the existing pattern.

1. Select the feature associated with an existing

pattern.

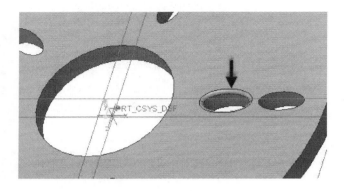

2. Activate the **Pattern** command. The **Reference** option is active on the **Pattern** dashboard.
3. Click the green check to create the reference pattern.

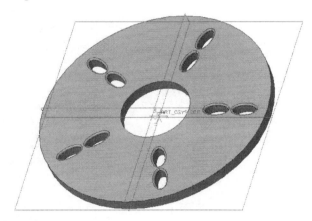

Curve

The **Curve** option creates a pattern along a selected curve.

1. Select the feature to pattern and activate the **Pattern** command.

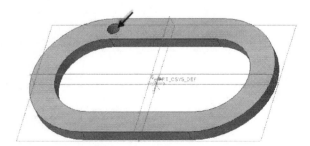

2. On the **Pattern** dashboard, select **Curve** from the drop-down available on the left side.

3. On the **Pattern** dashboard, click the **References** tab, and then click the **Define** button.
4. Click on the top face of the model, and click the **Sketch** button.
5. On the **Sketch** ribbon, click **Sketching > Offset**.
6. On the **Type** dialog, select **Chain.**

7. Click on the two inner edges, as shown.

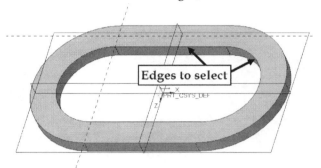

8. On the **Menu Manager**, click **Next** until all the inner edges are highlighted.

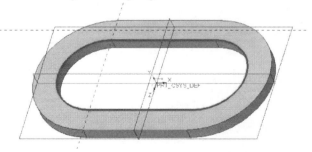

9. Click **Accept** on the **Menu Manager** to accept the selection.
10. Click **Yes** on the **Convert to Loop** dialog.

11. Type -25 in the offset box, and then click the green check.

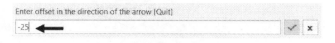

12. Click **Close** on the **Type** dialog.

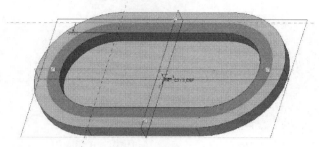

13. Click **OK** on the **Sketch** ribbon. The pattern preview appears and the sketch origin is used as pattern origin. However, you can change the origin of the pattern by clicking the **Options** tab and checking the **Use alternate origin** option.

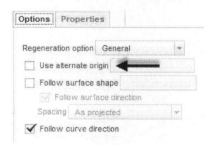

14. On the **Pattern** dashboard, click the **Use Member Quantity** icon and type 12 in **Quantity** box.

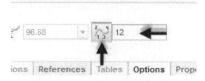

15. Click the green check to complete the pattern.

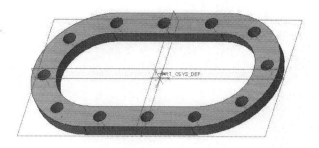

Point

This option patterns the selected features by using user-defined points.

1. Start a sketch and place datum points, as shown below. You need to divide the sketch entities by using the **Divide** command, and then place the datum points (refer to **The Divide command** section in Chapter 2 to learn how to divide sketch entities).

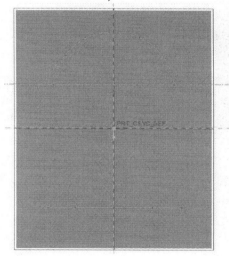

2. Exit the sketch.
3. On the ribbon, click **Model > Datum > Point**, and place points, as shown below.

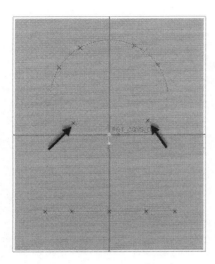

4. Create a hole or any other feature to pattern.

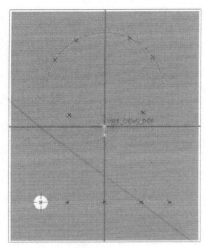

5. Select the feature to pattern and activate the **Pattern** command.
6. On the **Pattern** dashboard, select **Point** from the drop-down available on the left side.
7. Activate the **Sketch** icon on the dashboard and select the sketch.

Examples

Example 1

In this example, you will create the part shown below.

8. Click the green check.

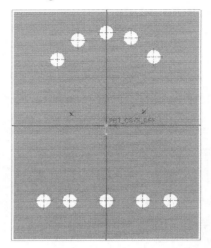

9. In the model tree, click the right mouse button on the Pattern and select **Edit Definition**.
10. On the **Pattern** dashboard, click the **Datum Points** icon, and select the datum points.
11. Click the green check.

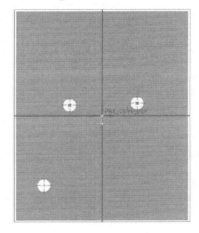

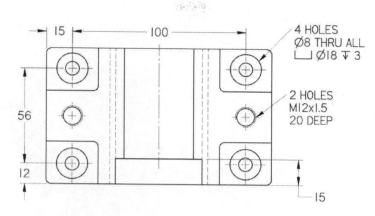

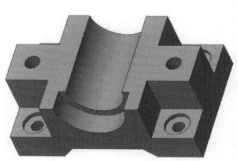

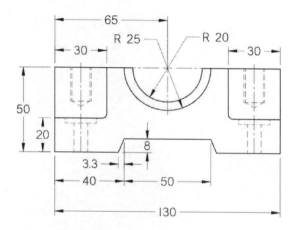

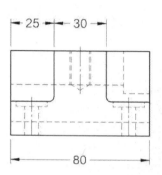

1. Start **Creo Parametric 4.0**.
2. Create the *Patterned Geometry* folder.
3. On the ribbon, click **File > Manager Session > Select Working Directory**.

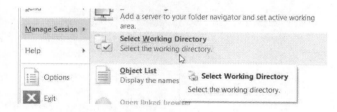

4. Browse to the location of the *Patterned Geometry* folder, and then click **OK**.
5. On the Quick Access Toolbar, click the **New** button.
6. On the **New** dialog, select **Types > Part**, and then type-in **C05-Example1**.
7. Uncheck the **Use default template** option and click **OK**.

8. On the **New File Options** dialog, select the **solid_part_mmks** template. Click **OK** to start the file.
9. Activate the **Extrude** command and click on the Front plane
10. Create a rectangular sketch using the **Center Rectangle** command.
11. Modify the dimensions, and then click **OK** on the ribbon.

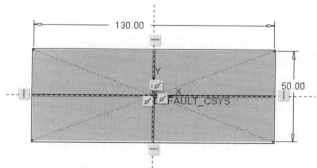

12. On the dashboard, type-in **80** in the **Depth** box.

13. Select the **Both sides** option from the drop-down next to **Depth** box.
14. Click the green check to complete the *Extrude* feature.

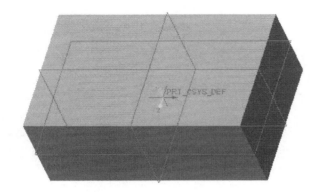

15. On the ribbon, click **Model** tab > **Datum** panel > **Sketch**.
16. Click on the top face of the part geometry.
17. On the **Sketch** dialog, click in the **Reference** box and select the right face of the model.
18. Click **Sketch** to start the sketch.
19. Create a rectangular sketch and click **OK**.

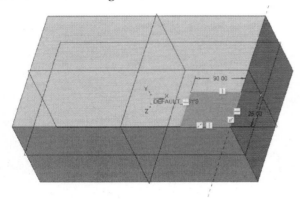

20. Activate the **Extrude** command.
21. Create the *Extruded cut* feature of **30 mm** depth.

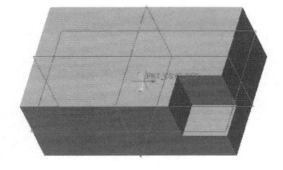

22. Activate the **Hole** command and click on the bottom face of the *Extruded cut* feature.

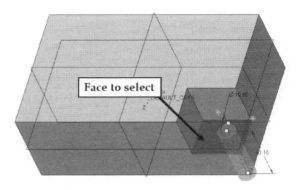

23. Align the green handles of the hole to the horizontal and vertical edges of the placement face.
24. Change the horizontal and vertical offset distances of the hole to 15 and 12, respectively.

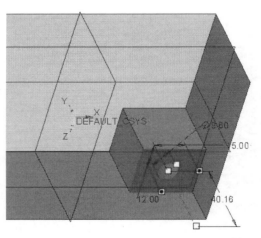

25. On the dashboard, click the **Creates standard hole** icon.
26. On the dashboard, click the **Adds counterbore** icon.
27. Set the thread standard to ISO.
28. Set the screw size to 10x1.5.
29. Select the **Drill to intersect with all surfaces** option from the drop-down.

31. Click the **Shape** tab on the Dashboard.
32. Type-in **18** and **3** in the **Diameter** and **Depth** boxes, respectively.

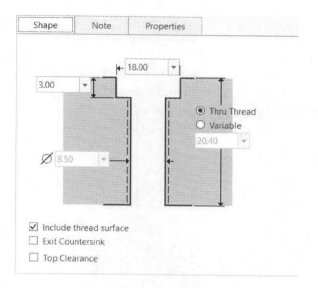

33. Click the green check to create the hole.

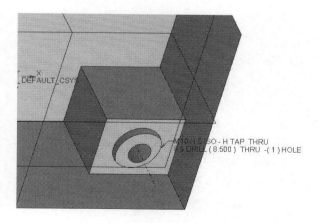

34. Activate the **Hole** command and click on the top face of the model.
35. Align the green handles of the hole to the horizontal and vertical edges of the face.
36. Change the horizontal and vertical offset distances of the hole to 15 and 40, respectively.

30. Click the **Shape** tab and select **Thru Thread** option.

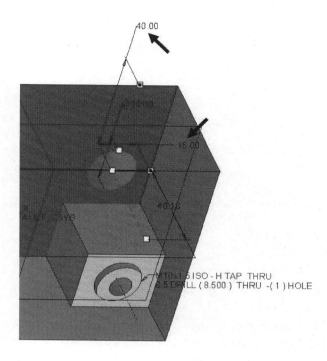

37. On the dashboard, select the **Creates standard hole** icon.
38. Set the thread standard to **ISO**.
39. Set the screw size to **12x1.5**.
40. Select the **Drill to intersect with all surfaces** option from the drop-down.
41. Click the **Shape** tab on the dashboard and select **Thru Thread** option.
42. Click the green check to create the hole.

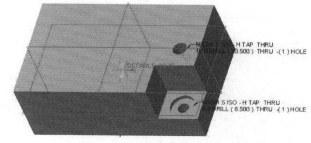

43. Select the *Extruded cut* feature from the Model Tree.

44. On the ribbon, click **Model** tab > **Editing** panel > **Pattern** drop-down > **Pattern**  .

45. On the dashboard, select the **Direction** option from the drop-down located at the left side.

46. Click on the top front edge of the part geometry to define the first direction of the pattern.

47. Click in the second direction reference box and select the top-right edge of the part geometry. This defines the second direction.

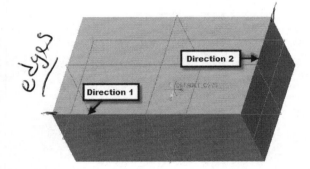

52. Select the counterbore hole and click the Pattern icon on the ribbon.

53. On the **Pattern** dashboard, select **Direction** from the drop-down located the left side.

54. Specify the same parameters used in the previously created pattern.

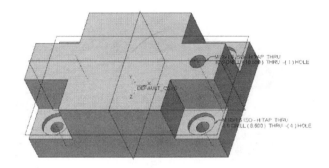

48. Enter members in first direction as **2** and spacing value as **100**.

49. Enter members in second direction as **2** and spacing value as **55**.

50. Click the **Flip the second direction** button on the dashboard.

55. Select the simple threaded hole from the Model Tree.

56. On the ribbon, click **Model** tab > **Editing** panel > **Mirror** .

57. Select the Right plane to define the mirroring plane.

58. Click the green check on the dashboard to mirror the hole.

51. Click the green check to complete the pattern.

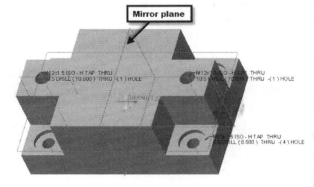

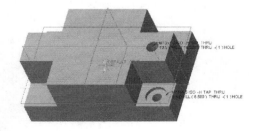

59. On the ribbon, click **Model** tab > **Engineering**

panel > **Hole**.

60. On the **Hole** dashboard, click **Datum** drop-down > **Axis**.

61. Press the Ctrl key and click on the top face of the model and the right plane.

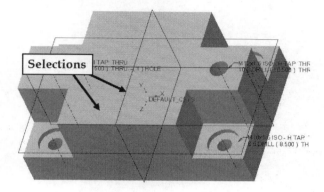

62. Click OK to create the axis at the intersection of the two selected planes.

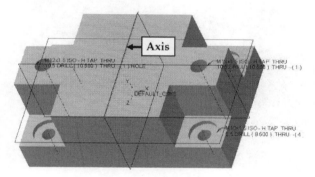

63. Click **Resume** on the Hole dashboard; the hole preview appears on the axis.

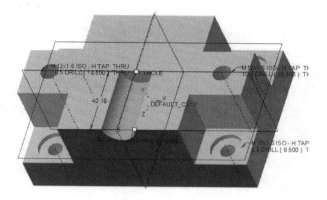

64. Click the Standard Hole icon on the Hole dashboard.

65. Click **Adds counterbore** icon on the Hole dashboard.

66. Click the **Shape** tab and specify the parameters, as shown.

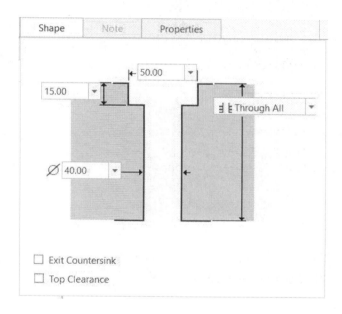

67. Click **OK** to create the counterbore hole.

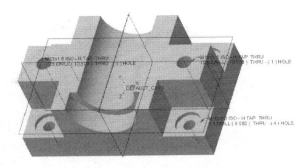

68. Activate the **Sketch** command and click on the front face of the model.

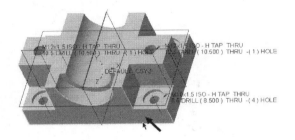

69. On the **Sketch** dialog, click in the **Reference** box and select the bottom face of the model.

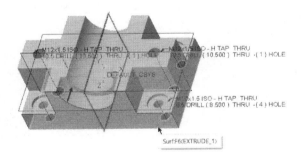

70. Click **Sketch** on the **Sketch** dialog.
71. Create the sketch, as shown below.

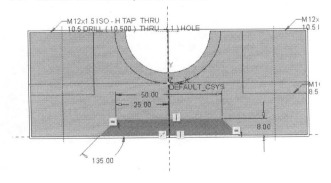

72. Create the *Extruded cut* throughout the model geometry.

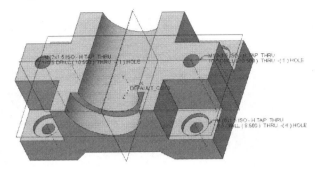

73. Round the sharp edges of the *Extrude cut* features. The round radius is 2 mm.

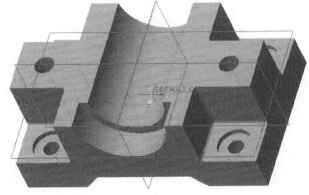

74. Save and close the part file.

Questions

1. Describe the procedure to create a mirror feature.
2. List any two types of patterns.
3. Describe the procedure to create a curve pattern.
4. List the methods to define spacing in a direction pattern.

Exercises
Exercise 1

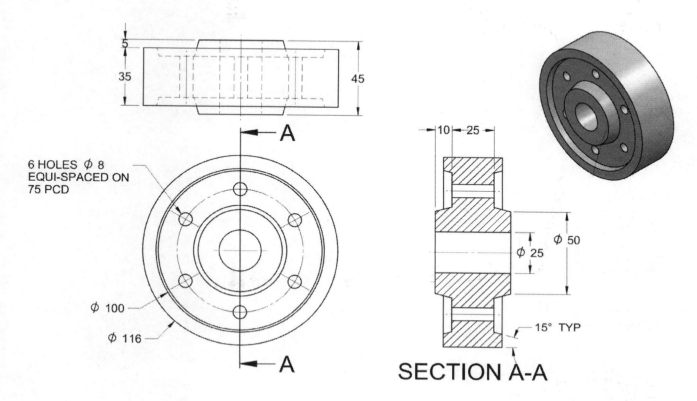

6 HOLES ⌀ 8
EQUI-SPACED ON
75 PCD

⌀ 100

⌀ 116

⌀ 50

⌀ 25

15° TYP

SECTION A-A

Exercise 2

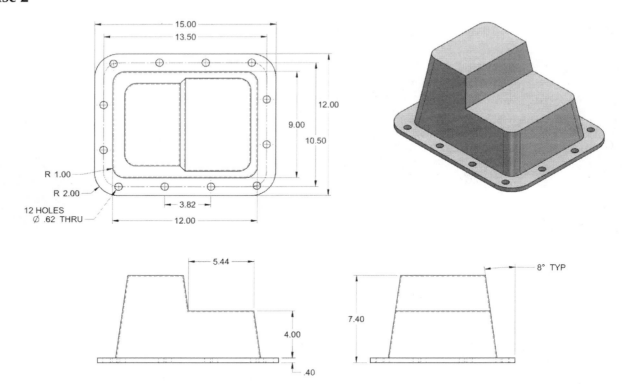

SHEET THICKNESS = 0.079 in

Exercise 3 (Inches)

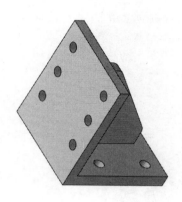

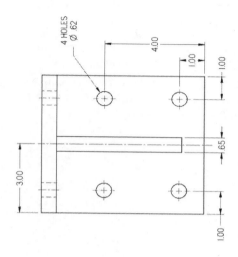

4 HOLES
Ø .62

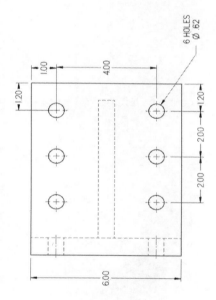

6 HOLES
Ø .62

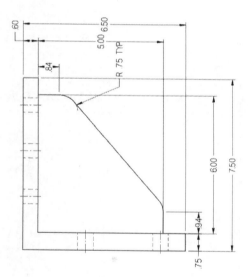

R .75 TYP

Chapter 6: Sweep Features

The Sweep feature is one of the basic features available in Creo Parametric that allow you to generate a solid geometry. It can be used to create simple geometry as well as complex shapes. A sweep is composed of two items: a cross-section and a trajectory. The cross-section controls the shape of sweep while the trajectory controls its direction. For example, look at the angled cylinder shown in figure. This is created using a simple sweep with the circle as the profile and an angled line as the trajectory.

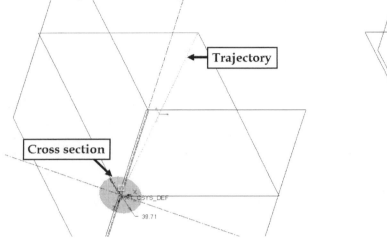
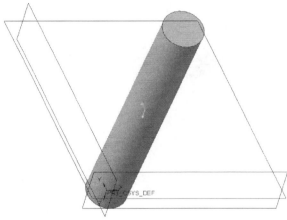

By the making the path a bit more complex, you can see that a sweep allows you to create the shape you would not be able to create using commands such as Extrude or Revolve.

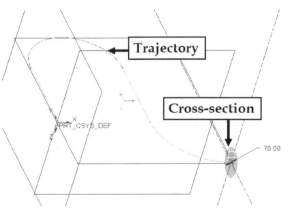
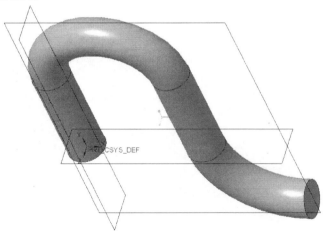

The topics covered in this chapter are:

- *Creating sweep features*
- *Avoiding errors and intersections*
- *Various types of trajectories that can be used to create sweep features*
- *Merging end faces of the sweep*
- *Swept cutouts*

The Sweep command

The sweep feature requires two elements: a trajectory and cross section. The cross section defines the shape of the sweep along the trajectory. A trajectory is used to control the direction of the cross section and it can be a sketch or an edge.

1. To create a sweep, you must first create a trajectory.
2. Create a trajectory by drawing a sketch. It can be an open or closed sketch.

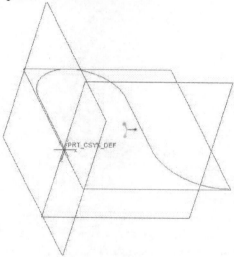

3. On the ribbon, click **Model > Shapes > Sweep**.
4. Select trajectory and click the **Create or edit sweep section** icon on the Dashboard.
5. Sketch the cross section on the plane normal to the trajectory.

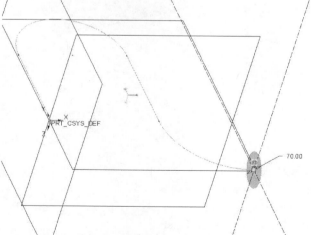

6. On the ribbon, click **OK** to exit the sketch mode. The preview of the sweep feature appears.

Sweep Features

7. Click the green check to complete the feature.

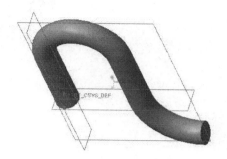

Creo Parametric will not allow the sweep to result in a self-intersecting geometry. As the cross section is swept along a trajectory, it cannot comeback and cross itself. For example, if the cross section of the sweep is larger than the trajectory, the resulting geometry will intersect and the sweep will fail.

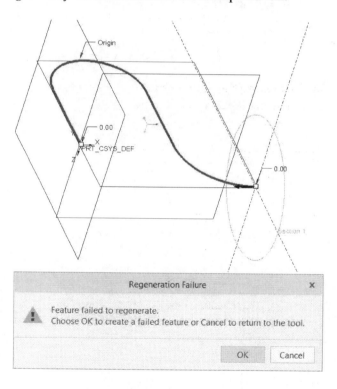

A sweep cross section must be created as a sketch. However, a trajectory can be a sketch, curve, or edge. The following illustrations show various types of center curves and resultant sweep features.

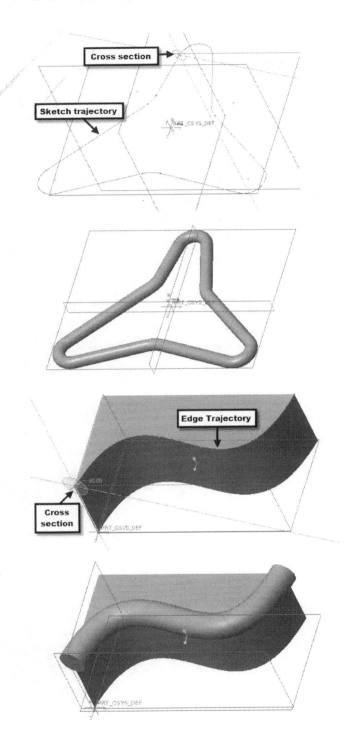

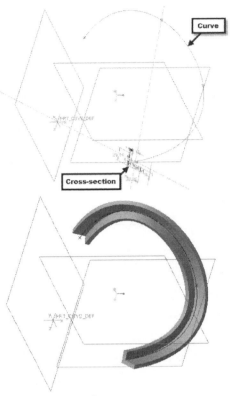

Thin Sweep feature

You can create a thin sweep feature by using the **Create a thin feature** icon. After defining the trajectory and cross section, click the **Create a thin feature** ⌐ icon on the Dashboard and type-in a thickness value.

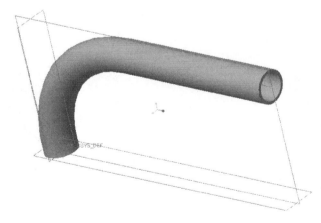

Remove Material

In addition to adding sweep features, Creo Parametric allows you to remove geometry using the **Remove material** option.

1. Activate the **Sweep** command and select the edge to define the trajectory.

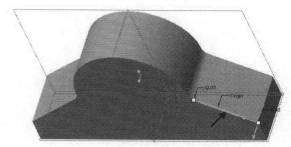

2. If you want to select tangentially connected edges, then click the **References** tab on the Dashboard and click the **Details** button.
3. On the **Chain** dialog, select the **Rule-based** option, and then select the **Tangent** rule.
4. Click **OK** to close the dialog. The tangentially connected edges are selected.

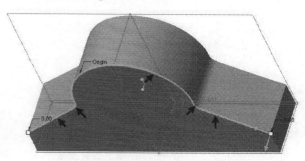

5. Click the **Create or edit sweep section** icon on the Dashboard.
6. Sketch the cross section and click **OK**.

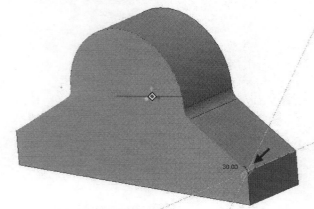

7. On the Dashboard, click the **Remove material** icon.

8. Click **Preview** on the Dashboard. You will notice that sweep is not created throughout the geometry.

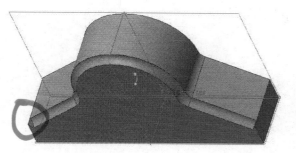

Notice that the swept cut not created up to the end of the model geometry.

9. Click the **Resume** icon.
10. On the Dashboard, click the **References** tab and select **Horizontal/Vertical Control > Automatic**.

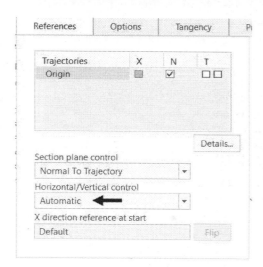

11. On the Dashboard, click the **Options** tab and check the **Merge ends** option. The resultant swept cutout will be throughout the geometry.

12. Click the green check to complete the feature.

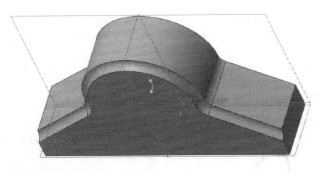

⚙ Helical Sweep

This command creates are spring shape feature.

1. On the ribbon, click **Model > Shapes > Sweep > Helical Sweep**.
2. On the **Helical Sweep** Dashboard, click the **References** tab.
3. Click the **Define** button next to the **Helical sweep profile** box.
4. Select the Front datum plane and click **Sketch**.
5. Click the **Sketch View** ⚙ icon on the **Graphics** toolbar.
6. On the **Sketch** ribbon, click **Sketching > Centerline**.
7. Create a vertical centerline passing through the sketch origin.
8. On the **Sketch** ribbon, click **Sketching > Line**.
9. Create a vertical line on the left side of the centerline.
10. Change the distance between the centerline and line to 2.
11. Change the length of the line to 5.

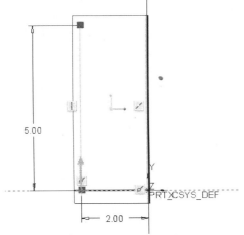

12. Click **OK** on the ribbon.

13. Click the **Create or edit sweep section** ✎ icon on the Dashboard.
14. Create a circle of 0.75 diameter at the intersection of construction lines.

15. Click **OK** on the ribbon.
16. Type-in 1 in the **Pitch** ⚙ box located on the Dashboard.
17. Use the **Left Hand Rule** ⚙ or **Right Hand Rule** ⚙ icon to define the helix direction.
18. Click the green check to complete the feature.

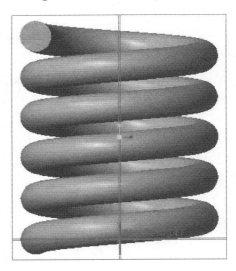

You can add hooks and other extensions to the ends using the **Sweep** command.

Helical Sweep cutout

The **Helical Sweep** command can also be used for creating cutouts.

1. Create a cylinder with diameter and length as 3 and 5, respectively.
2. Activate the **Helical Sweep** ⚙ command.

3. On the **Helical Sweep** Dashboard, click the **References** tab.
4. Click the **Define** button next to the **Helical sweep profile** box.
5. Select the Front datum plane and click **Sketch**.

   Click the **Sketch View** icon on the **Graphics** toolbar.
6. On the **Sketch** ribbon, click **Sketching > Centerline**.
7. Create a vertical centerline passing through the sketch origin.
8. On the **Sketch** ribbon, click **Sketching > Line**.
9. Create a vertical line on the right side of the centerline.
10. Modify the dimensions of the line, as shown below.

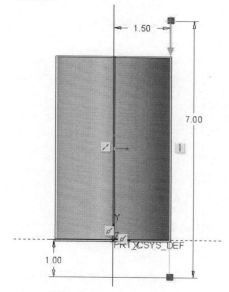

19. Click the **Create or edit sweep section** icon on the Dashboard.
20. Create the cross section and click **OK**.

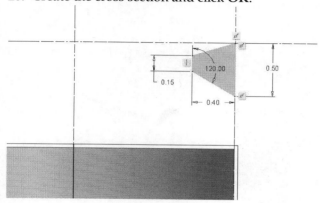

21. On the Dashboard, click the **Remove material** icon.
22. Type-in 0.7 in the **Pitch** box located on the Dashboard.
23. Define the helix direction, and click the green check.

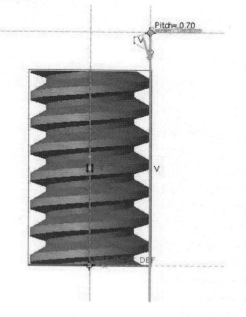

Examples

Example 1

In this example, you will create the part shown below.

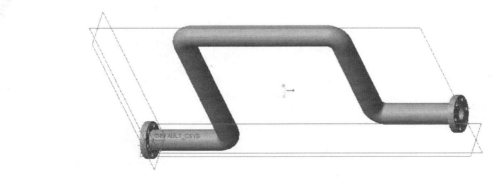

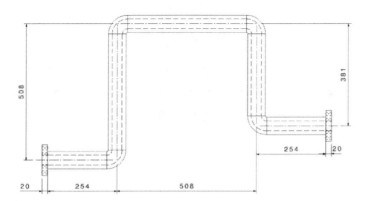

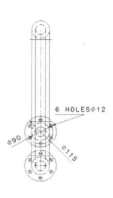

PIPE I.D. 51

PIPE O.D. 65

1. Start **Creo Parametric 4.0**.
2. Create the *Swept Features* folder and set it as current working folder.
3. On the Quick Access Toolbar, click the **New** button.
4. On the **New** dialog, select **Types > Part**, and then type-in **C06-Example1**.

5. Click **OK**.
6. On the **New File Options** dialog, select the **solid_part_mmks** template. Click **OK** to start the file.
7. On the Front plane, create the sketch shown below.

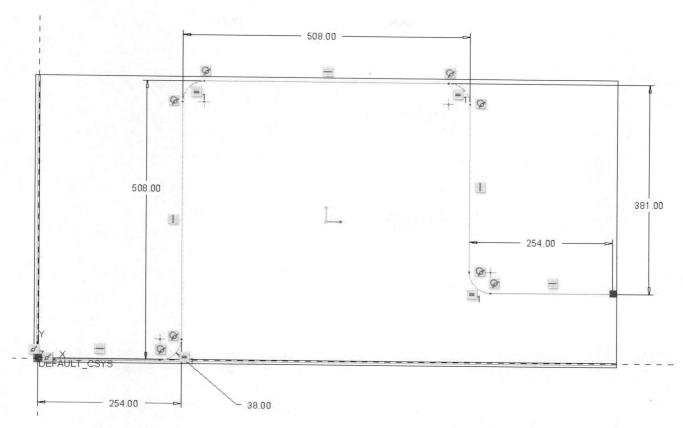

8. Exit the sketch mode and change the orientation to Standard.
9. On the ribbon, click **Model** tab > **Shapes** panel > **Sweep** drop-down > **Sweep** .
10. Select the sketch.

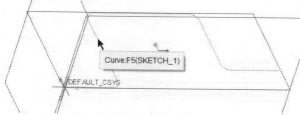

11. On the **Sweep** dashboard, click the **Create or edit sweep section** icon.
12. On the ribbon, click **Sketch** tab > **Sketching** panel > **Circle** drop-down > **Center and Point**.
13. Create a circle of 65 mm diameter at the origin.

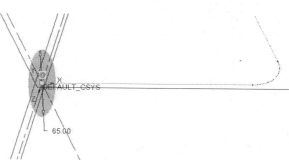

14. Click the **OK** button on the **Sketch** tab.
15. On the **Sweep** dashboard, click the **Create a thin feature** icon.
16. Type-in **14** in the thickness value box.
17. Click the green check to create the sweep feature.

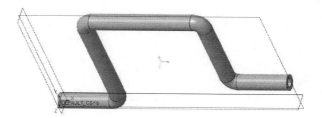

Sweep Features

18. Activate the **Extrude** command and click on the front-end face of the *Sweep* feature.

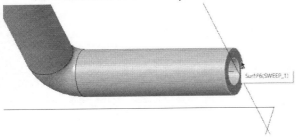

19. On the **Sketch** dashboard, click the **Project** icon.
20. On the **Type** dialog, select the **Single** option.
21. Click on the inner edges of the front-end face.

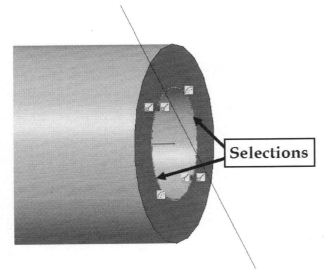

22. Close the **Type** dialog.
23. Draw a circle of 115 diameter.

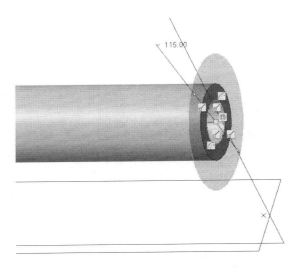

24. Click **OK** to complete the sketch.
25. Type-in **20** in the **Length** box and click the green check to complete the *Extrude* feature.

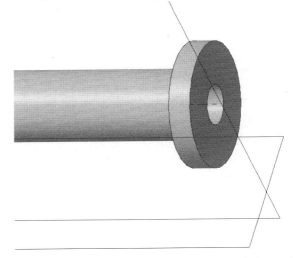

26. Activate the **Hole** command and click on the front face of the *Extrude* feature.
27. Set the hole diameter to 12.
28. On the Dashboard, click the **Placement** tab and select **Type > Radial**.
29. Click in the **Offset References** box and select the axis of the cylindrical face.
30. Press the Ctrl key and select the Front plane.

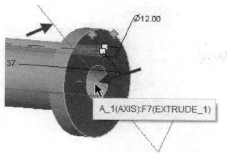

31. Specify the angle as 0 and radius dimension as 45.

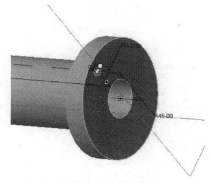

32. Select the **Drill up to next surface** ≣ option from the drop-down located next to the diameter box.

33. Click the green check to create the hole.

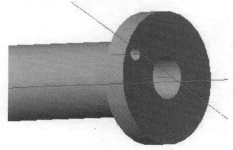

34. Select the small hole from the part geometry.

35. On the ribbon, click **Model** tab > **Editing** panel > **Pattern** drop-down > **Pattern** .

36. On the dashboard, select the **Axis** option from the drop-down located at the left side.

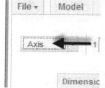

37. Select the axis of the *Extruded* feature, as shown below.

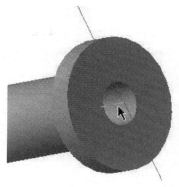

38. On the dashboard, click the total angle button and set the angular extent to 360.

39. Set the number of pattern instances to 6.

40. Click the green check to complete the pattern.

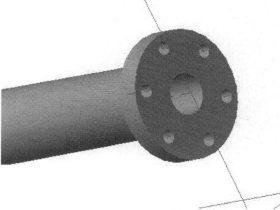

41. Select the *Extrude* feature and activate the **Pattern** command.

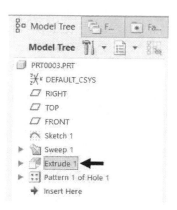

42. On the dashboard, select the **Point** option from the drop-down located at the left side.

43. Click the **Use points from datum point feature** icon.

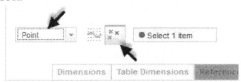

44. On the dashboard, at the right-side, click **Datum** drop-down > **Point** drop-down > **Offset Coordinate system**.

45. Select the Default Coordinate system.

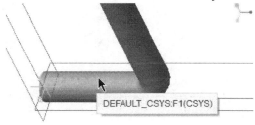

46. On the **Datum Point** dialog, type-in **-10** in the **X Axis** box.

47. Click **OK** to create a new datum point.

48. On the dashboard, click the **Resume** ▶ icon.

49. Click the green check to create the pattern.

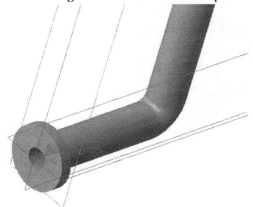

50. Select the circular pattern of the holes from the Model tree.

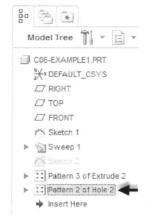

51. Activate the **Pattern** ⊞ command.

52. Make sure that the **Reference** option is selected in the pattern type drop-down.

53. Click the green check to create the reference pattern.

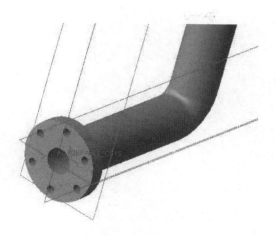

54. Save and close the part file.

Questions

1. List the types of trajectories that can be used to create *Sweep* features.
2. What is the use of **Merge ends** option?
3. List the options to define the helix direction.

Exercises
Exercise1

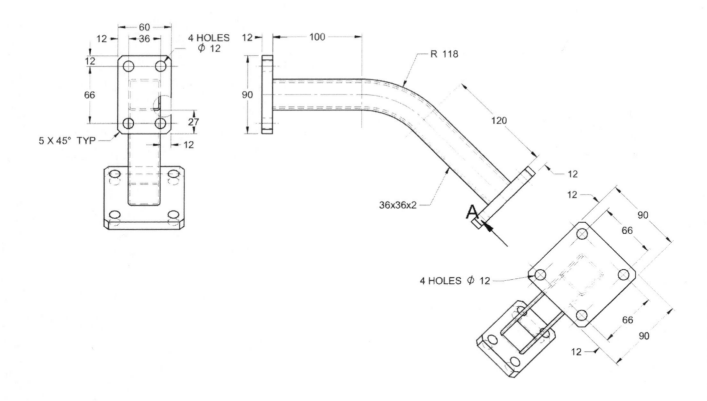

Chapter 7: Blend Features

A blend feature is one of the advanced features available in Creo Parametric that allows you to create simple as well as complex shapes. A basic blend feature is created by defining two cross-sections and joining them together. For example, if you create a blend feature between a circle and a square, you can easily change the cross-sectional shape of the solid. This ability is what separates the blend solid feature from the sweep feature.

The topics covered in this chapter are:

- *Blend features*
- *Blend Cut outs*
- *Types of Cross sections*
- *Rotational Blends*
- *Swept Blends*

The Blend command

This command creates a feature between different cross-sections.

1. To create this type of feature, first create two or more sections on different planes. The planes can be parallel or perpendicular to each other.
2. On the ribbon, click **Model > Shapes > Blend**.

3. On the **Blend** Dashboard, click the **Blend with selected sections** $\sim$ icon.
4. Select the first cross section.
5. On the **Sections** tab, click the **Insert** button and select the second cross section.

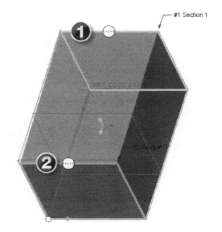

6. Again, click **Insert** and select the third cross section.

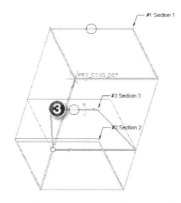

7. On the **Sections** tab, select the third section from the **Sections** list, and then click the **Move Up** button. The third section is moved to middle and the preview changes.

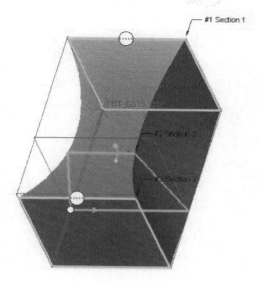

8. Click and drag the origin of the third section. Notice that the blend is twisted.

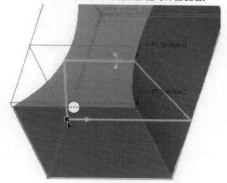

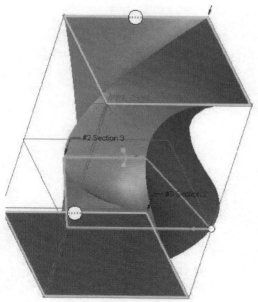

9. Drag the origin back to its initial position.

10. On the Dashboard, click the **Options** tab and set the **Blended surfaces** to **Straight**. Notice that the transition between the sections is changed to straight.

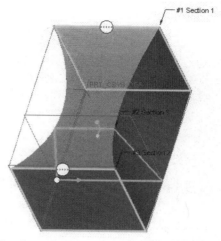

11. Again, set the **Blended surfaces** to **Smooth**. Click the green check to complete the feature.

Creating Blend Cut-outs

Like other standard features such as extrude, revolve and sweep, the blend feature can be used to add or remove material.

1. Activate the **Blend** command.
2. On the **Blend** Dashboard, click the **Sections** tab.
3. With the **Sketched sections** option selected, click the **Define** button next to the **Sketch** box.
4. Click on the front face of the model.

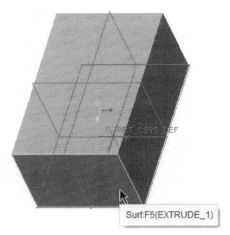

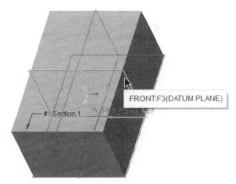

5. Click the **Sketch** button.
6. Create the first cross-section and click **OK** on the ribbon.

10. Create the second section and click **OK** on the ribbon.

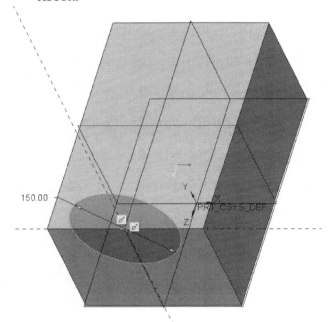

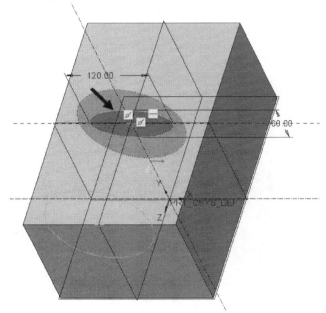

7. On the Dashboard, click the **Sections** tab. Notice that the **Section 2** definition is activated. In addition, the **Offset dimension** option is selected to define the sketch plane by an offset value. You can type-in the offset value in the **Offset from** box.
8. On the **Sections** tab, select the **Reference** option to define the sketch plane, manually.
9. Select the Front datum plane and click the **Sketch** button.

11. On the **Sections** tab, click the **Insert** button and select the **Reference** option.
12. Select the back face of the geometry and click **Sketch**.
13. Create the third section and click **OK** on the ribbon.

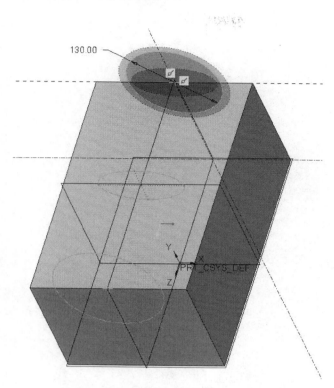

14. Click the **Remove material** ⬜ icon on the Dashboard.
15. Click the green check to complete the feature.

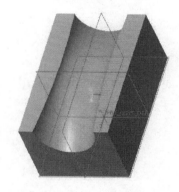

Types of the Cross-sections

In addition to 2D sketches, you can also use different element types to define cross-sections by using different element types. For instance, you can use existing model faces, surfaces, and curves.

Blends between existing model faces

The **Blend** command can be used to join to two solids.

1. Activate the **Blend** command.

2. On the **Blend** Dashboard, click the **Blend with selected sections** ∿ icon.
3. Click on an edge of the solid as shown.

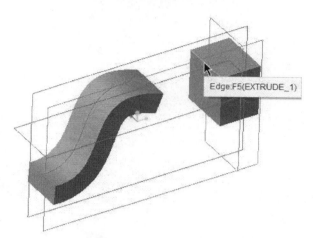

4. On the **Sections** tab, click the **Details** button.
5. On the **Chain** dialog, select the **Rule-based** option and set the **Rule** to **Complete Loop**.
6. Click on the end face of the solid. Click **OK** on the **Chain** dialog.

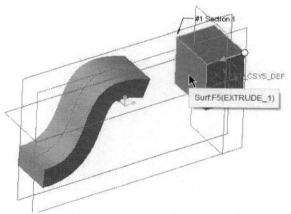

7. On the **Sections** tab, click the **Insert** button to define the second section.
8. Likewise, select the edge chain of the other solid as shown.
9. On the **Sections** tab, click the **Details** button.
10. On the **Chain** dialog, select the **Rule-based** option and set the **Rule** to **Complete Loop**.
11. Click on the end face of the solid. Click **OK** on the **Chain** dialog.

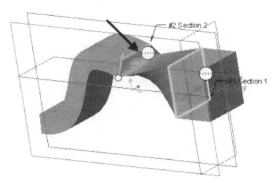

12. Click and drag the origin of the second cross section. The twist is removed.

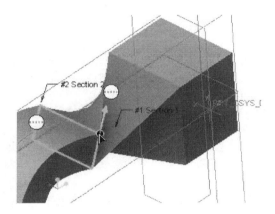

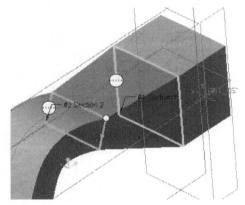

13. On the Dashboard, click the **Options** tab and make sure that the **Blend Surfaces** is set to **Smooth**.
14. On the Dashboard, click the **Tangency** tab.
15. Set the boundary condition of the **Start Section** to **Tangent**. An edge is highlighted.
16. Click on the face associated with the highlighted edge.

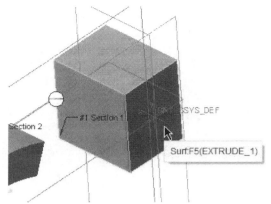

17. Likewise, select the faces associated with other highlighted edges. The blend faces at the start section become tangent to the side faces of the start section.

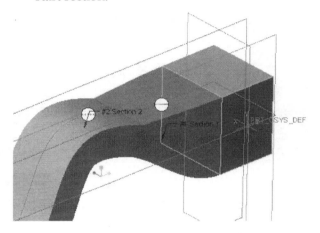

18. Change the boundary condition of the **End Section** to **Normal**. The blend faces become normal to the end section face.

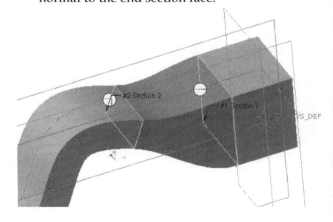

19. Click the green check to complete the model.

Cross Sections with different number of sides

Sections used for creating blend feature should have a matching number of segments. For example, a three-sided section will blend nicely to another three-sided section despite the differences in the shape of the individual segments. The **Blend** command does a good job of generating smooth faces to join them.

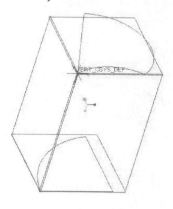

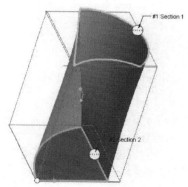

On the other hand, a four-sided section and two-sided section will result in an error.

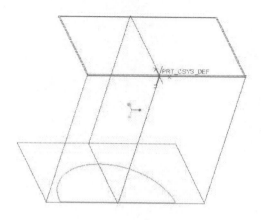

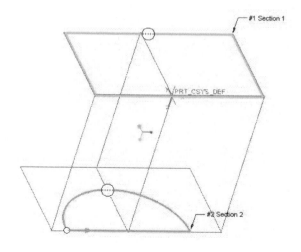

To get the desired result, you have to break one of the sections so that they have equal number of segments.

1. Click **Cancel** on the **Blend** dashboard.
2. Click the right mouse button on the arc sketch in the Model tree. Select **Edit Definition** to activate the sketch.
3. Activate the **Divide** command (click **Sketch > Editing > Divide** on the ribbon) and break the arc into three segments (refer to **The Divide command** section of Chapter 2 to learn how to divide segments). You can also use dimensions to define the exact location of the break points.

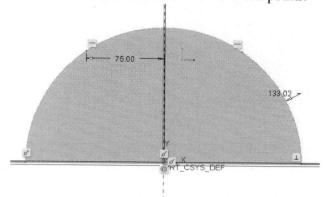

4. Now, exit the **Sketch** mode and activate the **Blend** command.
5. Create a blend by selecting sections.

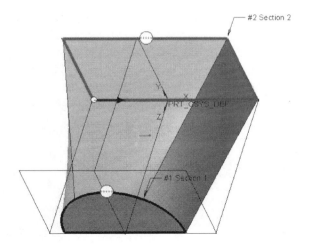

6. Click the green check to complete the feature.

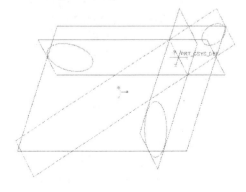 Rotational Blend

The **Rotational Blend** command creates blend feature through cross sections having a common axis. The difference between the **Rotational Blend** and **Blend** command is shown in figure. The **Blend** command simply blends the cross-sections whereas the **Rotational Blend** command blends the cross-sections by rotating them about a common axis.

Blend feature

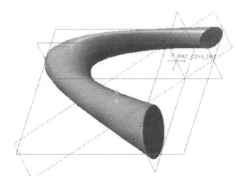

Rotational Blend feature

1. On the ribbon, click **Model > Shapes > Rotational Blend** .
2. On the **Rotational Blend** Dashboard, click the **Blend with selected sections** icon.
3. Select the first cross section.
4. Click the right mouse button and select **Insert**.
5. Select the second cross section.
6. Likewise, select the third cross section.

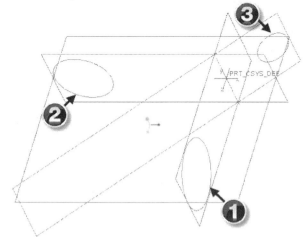

7. Click and drag the origin point of the third cross section. A smooth blend is created between the

sections.

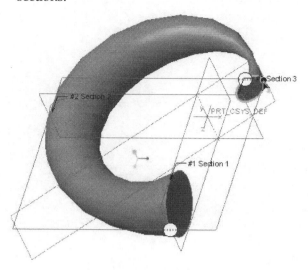

13. On the **Options** tab, check the **Connect end and start sections** option. Notice that the blend is closed.

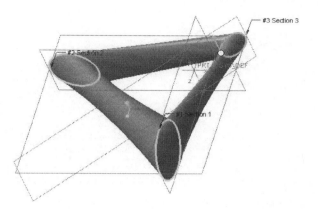

14. Set the **Blended surfaces** to **Smooth**.

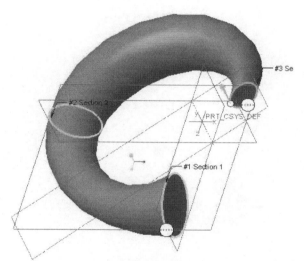

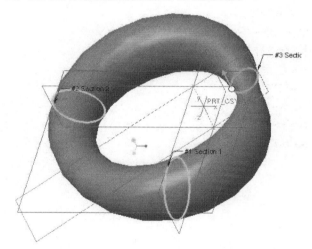

15. Click the green check to complete the feature.

🖉 Swept Blend

When you create a **Blend** feature, the material is added between the cross sections. The shapes of the cross sections control the blend feature. You do not have much control over the direction of the blend feature. The **Swept Blend** command allows you to control the direction by adding a trajectory. The trajectory controls the way the blend features is transformed between the sections. You can define the trajectory using a curve or sketch.

1. Create three sections and a trajectory as shown.

12. On the Dashboard, click the **Options** tab and set the **Blended surfaces** to **Straight**. Notice that the transition between the sections is changed to straight.

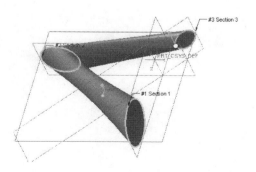

Likewise, you can change the boundary condition between sections using the **Tangency** options.

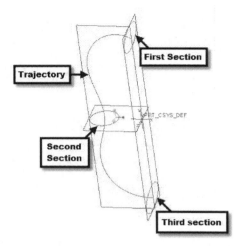

2. On the ribbon, click **Model > Shapes > Swept Blend** .
3. Select the trajectory passing through the sections.
4. On the dashboard, click the **Sections** tab.
5. Select the **Selected Sections** option
6. Select the first section.
7. Click the **Insert** button on the **Sections** tab.
8. Select the third section. The preview of the swept blend appears.

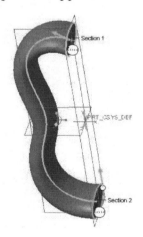

Examples

Example 1

In this example, you will create the part shown below.

9. On the **Sections** tab, select **Section 1**, and then click the **Insert** button.

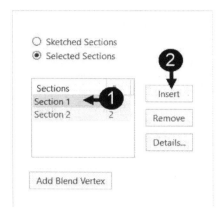

10. Select the second section. The preview of the swept blend changes as shown.

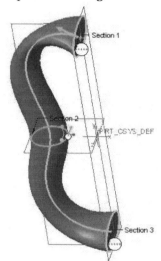

You can use the **Tangency** tab to control the continuity at the start and end sections.

11. Click the green check to complete the feature.

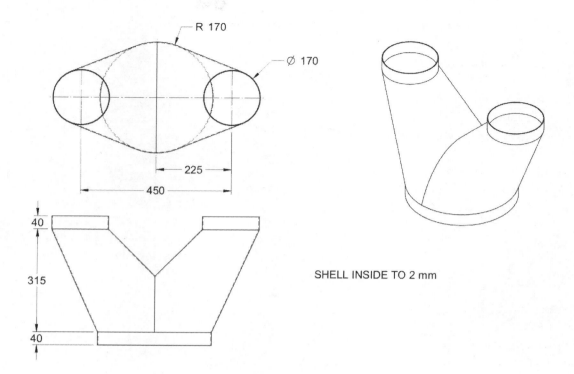

R 170

Ø 170

225

450

40

315

40

SHELL INSIDE TO 2 mm

1. Start **Creo Parametric 4.0**.
2. Create the *Blend Features* folder and set it as current working folder.
3. On the Quick Access Toolbar, click the **New** button.
4. On the **New** dialog, select **Types > Part**, and then type-in **C07-Example1**.
5. Click **OK**.
6. On the **New File Options** dialog, select the **solid_part_mmks** template. Click **OK** to start the file.
7. Start a new sketch on the Top plane and draw a circle of 340 mm diameter.

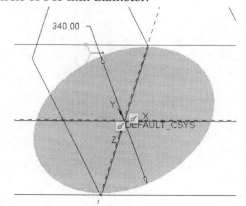

340.00

8. Exit the sketch.

9. Create the *Extrude* feature with 40 mm depth.

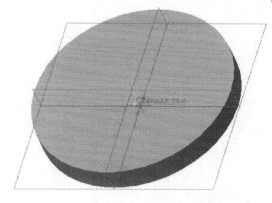

10. On the ribbon, expand the **Shapes** panel and click the **Blend** icon.
11. On the **Blend** dashboard, click the **Sections** tab.
12. Click the **Define** button and select the top face of the model.

13. On the **Sketch** dialog, click the **Sketch** button.

14. On the ribbon, click **Sketch** tab > **Sketching** panel > **Circle** drop-down > **Concentric**.
15. Create a circle of 340 diameter concentric to the *Extrude* feature.
16. Click **OK** on the ribbon. Now, you need to create the second section.
17. On the **Blend** dashboard, type-in 315 in the offset box and click the edit 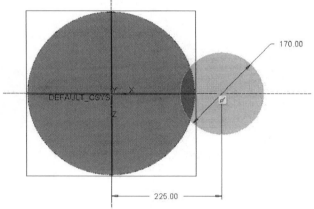 icon next to it.
18. Create a sketch, as shown below. Click **OK** on the ribbon to complete the sketch.

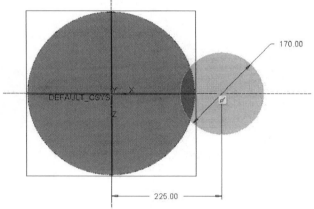

19. On the **Blend** dashboard, click the green check to create the blend feature.

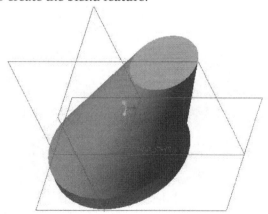

20. Activate the **Extrude** command and click on the top face of the blend feature.
21. Draw a circle of 170 mm diameter and add dimensions to it. Exit the sketch.
22. Create an *Extrude* feature of the 40 mm depth.

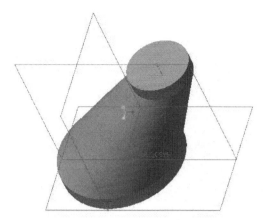

23. Press the Ctrl key and select the Blend feature and the Extrude feature on top of it.

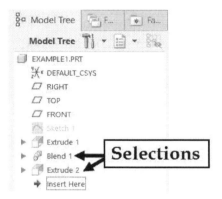

24. Activate the **Mirror** command.
25. Select the right plane to define the mirroring plane.
26. Click the green check to mirror the selected feature.

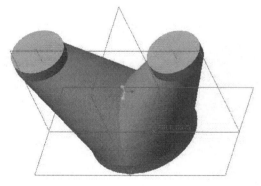

27. On the ribbon, click **Model** tab > **Engineering** panel > **Shell** .

28. Press the Ctrl key and click on the flat faces of the model geometry.

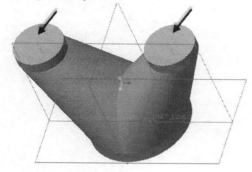

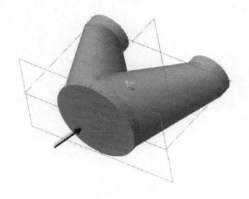

29. On the **Shell** dashboard, type-in 2 in the **Thickness** box.
30. Click **OK**. The part geometry is shelled.

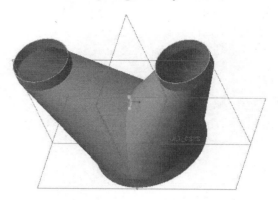

31. Save and close the part file.

Questions

1. Describe the procedure to create a *Blend* feature.

2. List the **Tangency** options.

3. List the type of elements that can be selected to create a *Blend* feature.

Exercises

Exercise 1

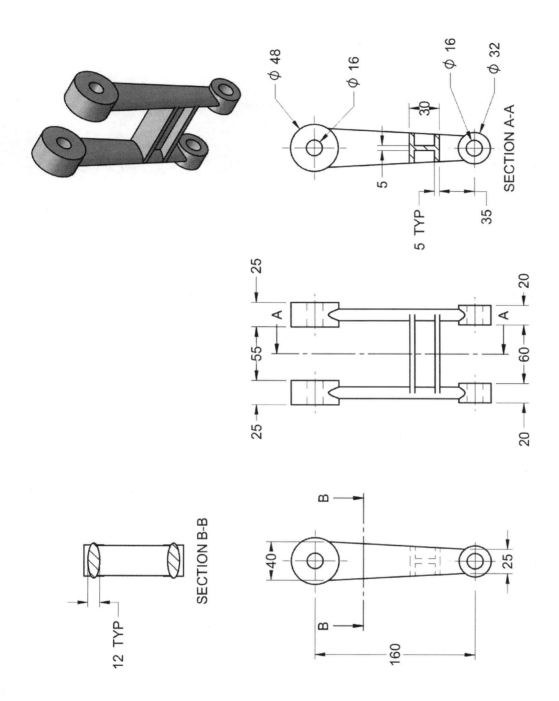

ϕ 48

ϕ 16

ϕ 16

ϕ 32

30

5

5 TYP

35

SECTION A-A

25

20

A

A

55

60

25

20

B

40

25

B

12 TYP

SECTION B-B

160

Chapter 8: Modifying Parts

In design process, it is not required to achieve the final model in the first attempt. There is always a need to modify the existing parts to get the desired part geometry. In this chapter, you will learn various commands and techniques to make changes to a part.

The topics covered in this chapter are:

- *Edit Sketches*
- *Edit Feature Parameters*
- *Edit Feature definition*
- *Suppress and Resume features*

Edit Sketches

Sketches form the base of a 3D geometry. They control the size and shape of the geometry. If you want to modify the 3D geometry, most of the times, you are required to edit sketches.

1. In the Model Tree, expand the feature and click the right mouse on the sketch.

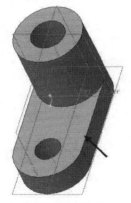

2. Select **Edit Definition** from the menu.

3. Now, modify the sketch and click **OK**. You will notice that the part geometry updates immediately.

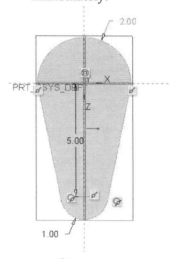

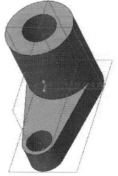

Editing Feature Definition

Features are the building blocks of a model geometry. You can edit a feature by following the steps given next.

1. Select the feature to edit.
2. Click the right mouse button and select **Edit Definition**. The Dashboard related to the feature appears.

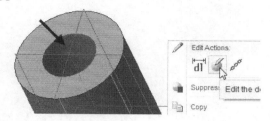

3. On this Dashboard, modify the parameters of the feature and click the green check. The changes take place instantaneously.

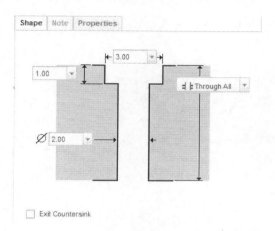

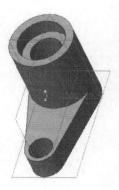

Edit Feature Dimensions

Creo Parametric allows you to modify a feature by editing its parametric dimensions.

1. Select the feature to edit.
2. Click the right mouse button and select **Edit**. The parameters of the feature appear.

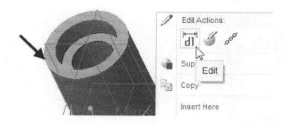

3. To edit a parameter, double-click on it and type-in a new value in the box. Press Enter.

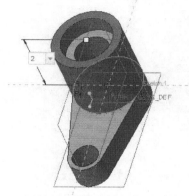

4. Double-click in the graphics window to update the feature.

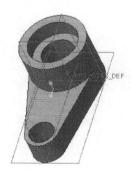

Suppress Features

Sometimes you may need to suppress some features of model geometry.

1. Select the feature to suppress.
2. Click the right mouse button and select **Suppress**.

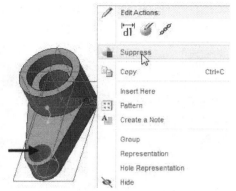

3. Click **OK** to suppress the feature.

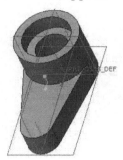

Resume Suppressed Features

1. If you want to resume the suppressed features, then click the **Settings** icon in the Model Tree and select **Tree Filters**.

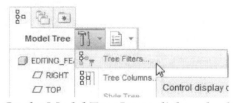

2. On the **Model Tree Items** dialog, check the **Suppressed objects** option in the **Display** section. Click **OK** to close the dialog. The suppressed feature appears with a square dot.

3. In the Model Tree, click on the suppressed feature and select **Resume**. The feature is resumed.

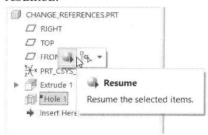

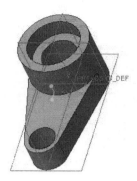

Changing the Feature References

Creo Parametric allows you to change the reference of a feature.

1. In the Model Tree, click the right mouse button on the feature and select **Edit Reference** .

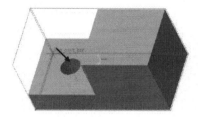

2. Change the first reference of the feature.

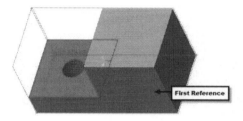

3. Change the second and third reference of the feature.

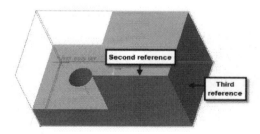

4. On the **Edit References** dialog, click the **Preview** button to view the result. You can also reset the

references by selecting them in the **Edit References** dialog and clicking the **Reset** button.

5. Click **OK** to close the dialog.

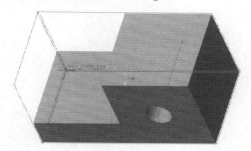

If there are any sketches or features on the geometry, it may show some warnings and error messages. You have to manually solve these problems or avoid changing the sketch support when the model becomes complex. It is recommended that you select correct plane initially based on the design intent.

Examples

Example 1

In this example, you will create the part shown below, and then modify it.

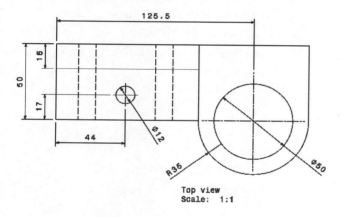

Top view
Scale: 1:1

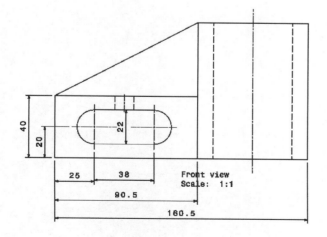

Front view
Scale: 1:1

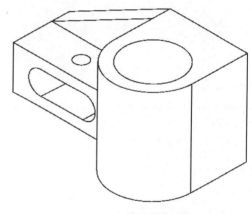

Isometric view
Scale: 1:1

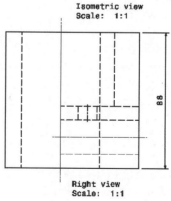

Right view
Scale: 1:1

1. Start **Creo Parametric 4.0**.
2. Create the *Modify Parts* folder and set it as current working folder.

3. On the Quick Access Toolbar, click the **New** button.
4. On the **New** dialog, select **Types > Part**, and then type-in **C08-Example1**.

5. Uncheck the **Use default template** option and click **OK**.
6. On the **New File Options** dialog, select the **solid_part_mmks** template. Click **OK** to start the file.
7. Create the part file, as shown below. If you cannot create it, you can download it from our companion website.

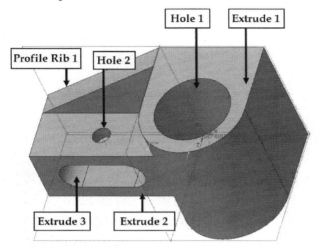

The Model Tree of the part is given next.

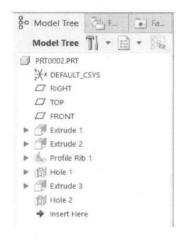

8. Select the 50 mm diameter hole.
9. Select the **Edit definition** icon.

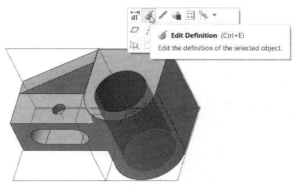

10. On the **Hole** dashboard, click the **Create standard hole** button.
11. Deactivate the **Add tapping** button.
12. Click the **Creates clearance hole** button.
13. Click the **Adds Counterbore** button.
14. Set the screw size to **M36x4**.
15. Click the **Shape** tab and define the parameters, as shown below.

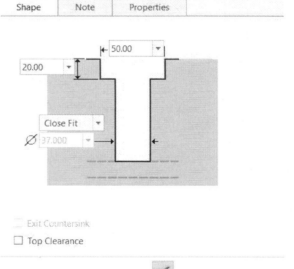

16. Click the green check to complete the modification.

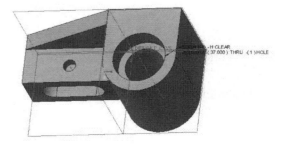

17. Select the rectangular extrude feature from the model.
18. Select **Edit Dimensions** from the shortcut menu.

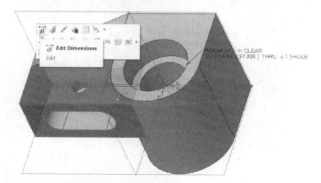

19. Double-click on the horizontal dimension.
20. Type-in 125 in the dimension box and press Enter.

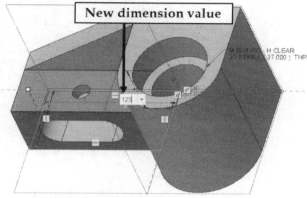

21. Double-click in the graphics window to modify the extrude feature.

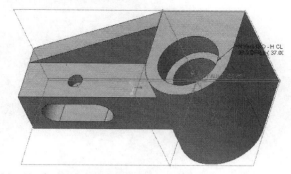

22. In the Model Tree, expand the third extrude feature and click the right mouse button on Section1.
23. Select the **Edit definition** option from the menu. This activates the sketch mode.

24. On the ribbon, click **Sketch** tab > **Setup** panel > **References** .
25. Create a reference by selecting the left face of the first feature.

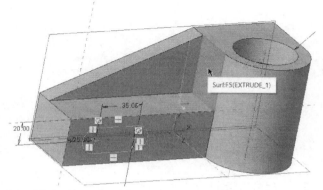

26. Click **Close** on the **References** dialog.
27. Delete the length dimension of the slot, and then add a new dimension between the right-side arc and right vertical edge.

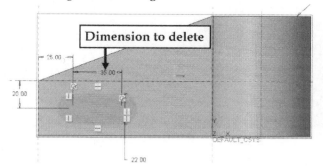

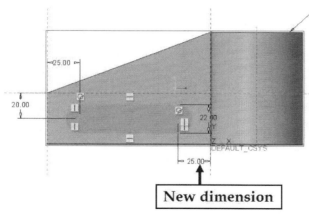

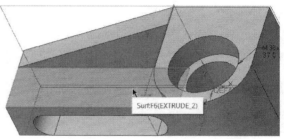

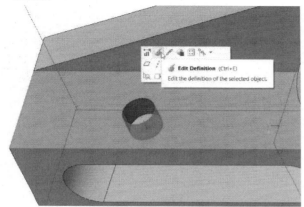

33. Click **Sketch**.

34. Create a line connecting the corners of the top face, as shown.

28. Exit the sketch.

29. Select the small hole from the model geometry.

30. Select the **Edit definition** from the shortcut menu.

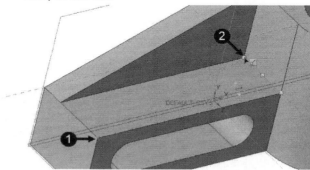

31. On the **Hole** dashboard, click **Datum** drop-down > **Axis**.

35. On the ribbon, click **Sketch** tab > **Datum** panel > **Point**.

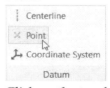

36. Click on the top face of the second extrude feature to place the point.

32. Click on the top face of the second extrude feature.

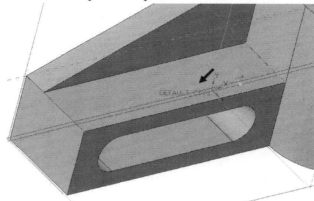

37. Click on the line and select **Toggle Construction**.

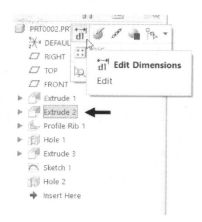

38. On the ribbon, click **Sketch** tab > **Constrain** panel > **Midpoint** .

39. Select the point and the line. The point is made coincident with the midpoint of the line.

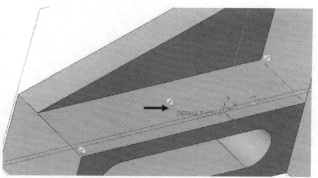

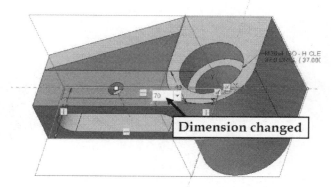

40. Click **OK** on the ribbon.

41. Click the **Resume** icon on the dashboard. The hole is placed on the midpoint of the line.

42. Click the green check to complete the modification.

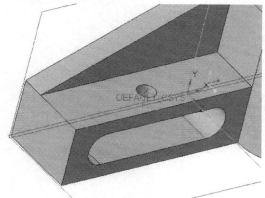

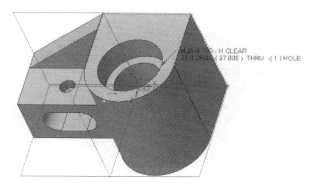

44. Save and close the file.

Questions

1. How do you modify the sketch of a feature?
2. How do you modify a feature directly?
3. How can you change the reference of a feature?

43. Now, change the size of the extrude feature. You will notice that the slot and hole are adjusted automatically.

Exercises

Exercise 1

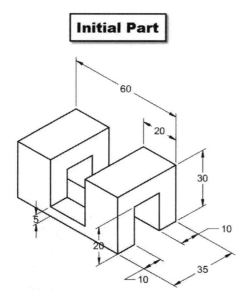

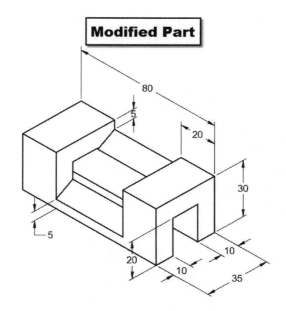

Chapter 9: Assemblies

After creating individual components, you can bring them together into an assembly. By doing so, it is possible to identify incorrect design problems that may not have been noticeable at the part level. In this chapter, you will learn how to bring components into the Assembly environment and position them.

The topics covered in this chapter are:

- *Starting an assembly*
- *Inserting Components*
- *Adding Constraints*
- *Moving components*
- *Collision Detection*
- *Replace Components*
- *Create Subassemblies*
- *Top-down Assembly Design*
- *Create Exploded Views*

Starting an Assembly

To begin an assembly file, you can use the **New** icon and select the **Type > Assembly**. Select **Sub-type > Design** and type-in the name of the file. Click **OK**.

Inserting Components

There are two different methods to insert an existing part into an assembly. The first one is to insert using the **Assemble** command.

1. On the ribbon, click **Model > Component > Assemble** .
2. Browse to the location of the component and select it.

Assemblies

157

3. Click **Open**. The component appears inside the assembly.

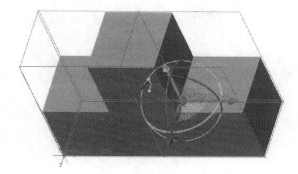

You can also insert a component into the Assembly by dragging it from the windows explorer into the assembly window.

Fixing the first Component

After inserting components into an assembly, you have to define constraints between them. By applying constraints, you can make components to flush with each other or two cylindrical faces concentric with each other, and so on. As you add constraints between components, the degrees of freedom will be removed from them. By default, there are six degrees of freedom for a part (three linear and three rotational). Eliminating degrees of freedom will make components attached and interact with each other as in real life. Now, you will learn to add constraints between components.

After placing the component at the origin, it is free to move. You can check the degrees of freedom by clicking and dragging the 3D Dragger.

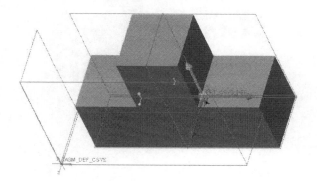

1. In order to remove the degrees of freedom of the first component, click **Automatic > Default** on the **Component Placement** dashboard.

The component is positioned at its default location.

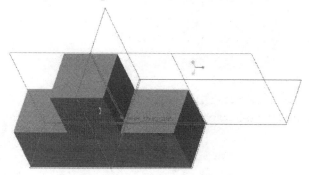

You can also use the **Fix** constraint to position it at its current location.

2. Click the green check.

Inserting the Second Component

1. On the ribbon, click **Model > Component > Assemble** .
2. Go to the location of the second component.
3. Select the component and click **Open**.

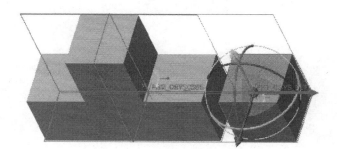

Moving and rotating components

After inserting components into the assembly, you can move or rotate them.

1. On the 3D Dragger, click the **X axis**, and then drag the component along the x-axis.

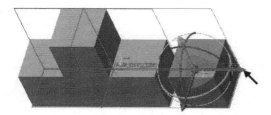

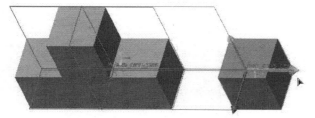

2. Likewise, use the **Y axis**, **Z axis** to drag the component along Y and Z axes, respectively.

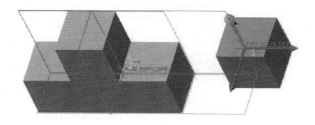

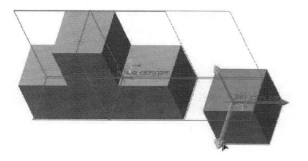

3. Use the **XY plane**, **YZ plane**, or **XZ plane** to move the component on three different planes.

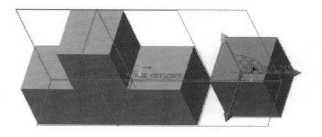

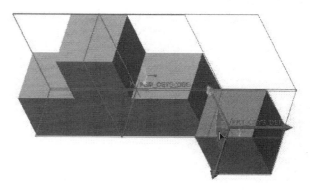

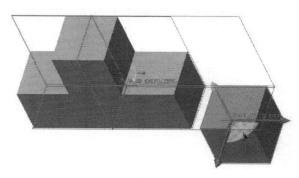

4. Click the sphere of the 3D Dragger and drag the pointer to move the component randomly.

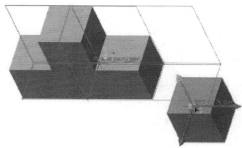

5. Use the torus displayed around the x-axis to rotate the component about the x-axis.

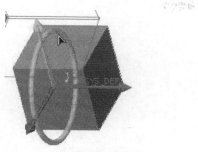

6. Likewise, rotate the component about the Y and Z axis.

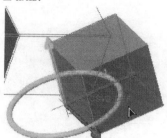

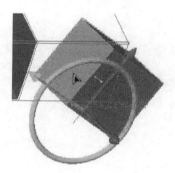

Coincident Constraint

The **Coincident** constraint makes two faces coincident with each other. The selected faces can flush with each other or positioned opposite to each other.

1. Insert the component into the assembly.
2. Select a face of the first part.
3. Click on a face of the second part.
4. On the Dashboard, click **Automatic > Coincident**. This creates a coincident constraint between the two faces.

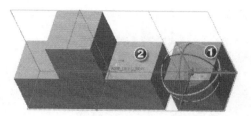

5. On the dashboard, click the **Change orientation** icon to change the orientation of the component.

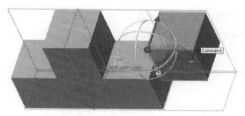

The **Coincident Constraint** also makes the axes of two cylindrical faces coincide with each other.

1. Click on a cylindrical face or axis of the first part.
2. Click on a cylindrical face, or axis of the target part.
3. On the Dashboard, click **Automatic > Coincident** . The two cylindrical axes are aligned together.

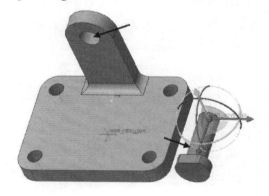

⊓⊓ Distance Constraint

The **Distance** constraint creates a distance between two faces. In addition, the faces will be parallel to each other.

1. Select a face of the first part.
2. Click on a face of the second part.
3. On the Dashboard, click **Automatic > Distance**.

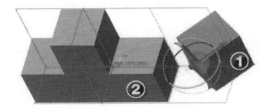

4. On the dashboard, click the **Change orientation** icon to make the selected faces point in opposite direction.

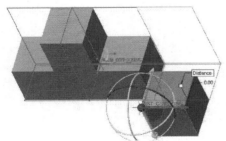

5. Type-in a value in the **Offset** box (or) drag the distance handle to add a distance between the selected faces.

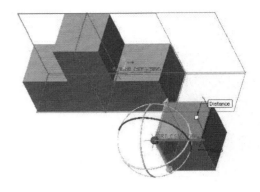

⬖ Angle Offset

The **Angle Offset** constraint is used to position faces at a specified angle.

1. Click on a plane or face of the first part.
2. Click on a plane or face of the second part.

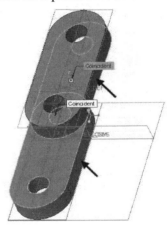

3. On the Dashboard, click **Automatic > Angle Offset**.
4. Type-in a value in the **Angle** box on the dashboard.

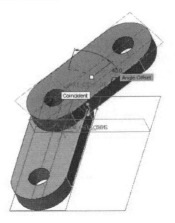

⃝⃝ Parallel Constraint

The **Parallel** constraint makes an edge or face of one part parallel to that of another part.

1. Select a planar face, or linear edge of the first part.
2. Click on an element of the second part.

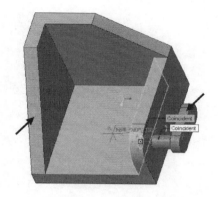

3. On the Dashboard, click **Automatic > Parallel**. Two selected elements will be parallel to each other.

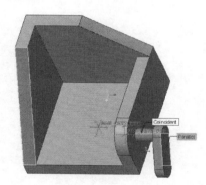

4. On the dashboard, click the **Change orientation** ⁄ icon to change the orientation of the component.

⃝ Normal Constraint

The **Normal** constraint makes a face or edge of one part perpendicular to that of another part.

1. Select a planar face or linear edge of the first part.
2. Click on an element of the second part.

3. On the Dashboard, click **Automatic > Normal**. Two selected elements will be perpendicular to each other.

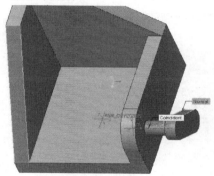

Copying Components with Constraints

If you have an assembly in which you need to assemble the same part multiple times, it would be a tedious process. In such cases, the **Copy** and **Paste** commands will drastically reduce or even eliminate the time used to assemble commonly used parts. To copy and paste a component, first you need to define a constraint or set of constraints between two parts. For example, define the **Coincident** constraint between the screw axis and the hole, and then make the bottom flat face of the screw head coincident with the top face.

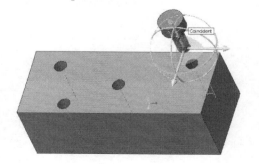

1. Select the screw and click **Model > Operations > Copy** on the ribbon (or) Press Ctrl+C on your keyboard.
2. On the ribbon, click **Model > Operations > Paste** (or) Press Ctrl+V on your keyboard.
3. Select the cylindrical face of another hole and its top face. The screw is pasted into it.

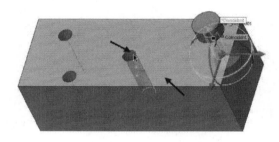

4. Click the green check.

Repeating Components with Constraints

The **Repeat** ↺ command provides a more convenient way to insert the repeated components.

1. Select the component to repeat and click **Model > Component > Repeat**.

The **Repeat Component** dialog shows the list of constraints that can be added.

2. On the dialog, select the first Coincident reference and click **Add**.

3. Select the axes of the two holes.

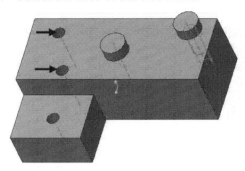

The screw is positioned in both the holes.

4. Press hold the Ctrl key and select both the **Coincident** references from the dialog. Click **Add**.
5. Select the axis and top face of the hole as shown.

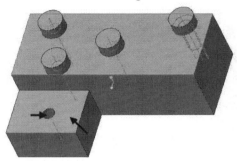

The screw is positioned in the hole as shown.

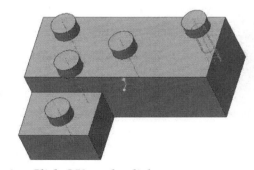

6. Click **OK** on the dialog.

Collision Detection

In an assembly, two or more components can overlap or occupy the same space. However, this would be physically impossible in the real world. When you add constraints between components, Creo Parametric develops real-world contacts and movements between them. However, sometimes clashes can occur. To check such errors, Creo

Parametric provides you with an option to identify collision.

1. Insert two components into the assembly, leave the second component unconstrained, and click the green check on the dashboard.

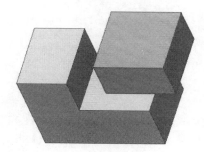

2. Click **File > Prepare > Model Properties**.
3. On the **Model Properties** dialog, under the **Assembly** section click the **change** option next to **Collision detection**.
4. On the **Collision Detection Settings** dialog, select **Global collision detection** and check the **Sound warning upon collision** option.
5. Click **OK** and close the **Model Properties** dialog.
6. On the ribbon, click **Model > Component > Drag Components**.
7. Select the unconstrained component and move the pointer. The collision between the two components is detected along with a sound.

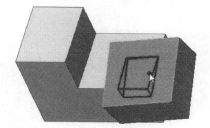

8. Click **Close** on the **Drag** dialog.

Again, you can use the **Drag Components** command to detect the collision between the components.

Editing and Updating Assemblies

During the design process, the correct design is not achieved on the first attempt. There is always a need to go back and make modifications. Creo Parametric, allows you to accomplish this process very easily.

1. To modify a part in an assembly, select it from the graphics window.
2. Click the right mouse button and select **Activate** ◈ . This activates the **Part** environment. You can also select **Open** to open the part in a separate window.

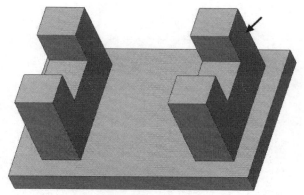

3. Select the feature to edit, click the right mouse button and select **Edit Definition**.

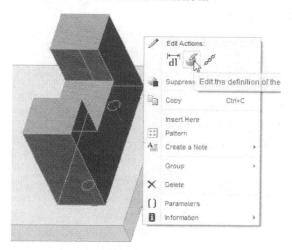

4. To edit the sketch, click the **Placement** tab, and then select the **Edit** button.
5. Click **OK** after editing the sketch.
6. Modify the feature parameters, and then click the green check.

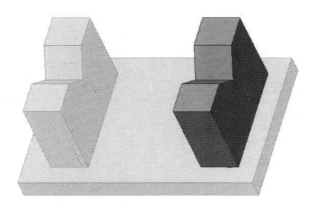

7. In the Model Tree, right-click on **Assembly** and select **Activate** ◈ to return to the **Assembly** environment.
8. Right-click in the graphics window and select **Regenerate**.

Redefining Constraints

You can also redefine the existing constraints in an assembly. For example, if you want to change the faces that coincide with each other, then follow the steps given next.

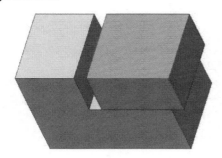

1. In the Model Tree, click the right mouse button on the component to modify, and then select **Edit Definition** 🖱. The constraints related to the component appear on the model.
2. Click the right mouse button on the constraint and select **Edit References**.

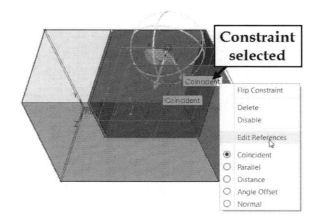

A palette appears on the constraint. You can change the constraint type, orientation, references using this palette.

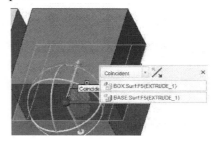

3. Click on the right face of the component.

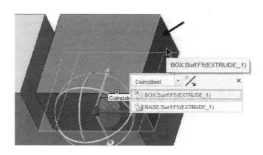

The Coincident constraint is redefined.

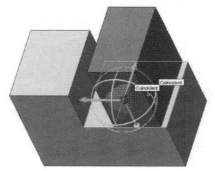

Change Constraint

You can also convert an existing constraint into another type of constraint. For example, if you want to convert the **Coincident** constraint into **Distance** constraint, then follow the steps given next.

1. Click the right mouse button on the **Coincident** constraint and select **Distance**.

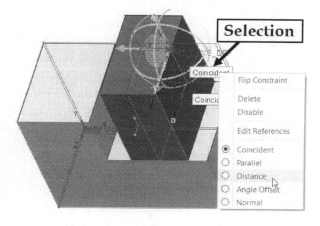

2. Now, drag the Distance handle to change the distance value.

3. Click the green check ✓ on the dashboard.

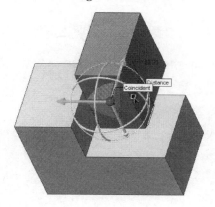

⟲ Replace Component

Creo Parametric allows you to replace any component in an assembly. To do this, follow the steps given next.

1. Select the component to replace.
2. Right-click and select **Replace**.

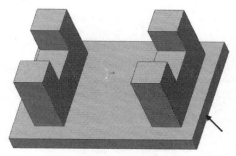

3. On the **Replace** dialog, select **Replace By > Unrelated Component**.

4. Click the folder 📂 icon on the dialog and go to the location of the replacement component.

5. Select the component and click **Open**.

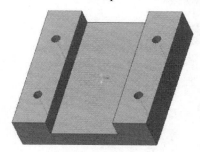

6. Click **OK** to replace the component.

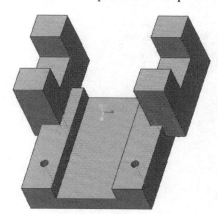

7. Now, you can redefine the existing constraints or delete them and define new constraints. In this case, you can redefine the existing constraints. In the Model Tree, click the right mouse button on the affected component and select **Edit Definition**.

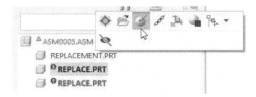

8. Select the references on the replacement part.

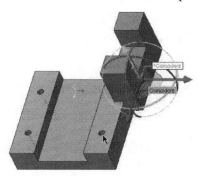

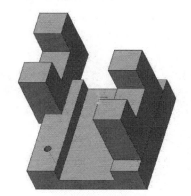

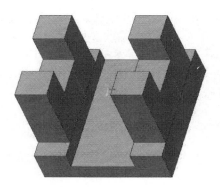

Top Down Assembly Design

In Creo Parametric, there are two methods to create an assembly. The method you are probably familiar with is to create individual components, and then insert them into an assembly. This method is known as Bottom-Up Assembly Design. The second method is called Top Down Assembly Design. In this

method, you will create individual components within the Assembly environment. This allows you to design an individual part while taking into account how it will interact with other components in an assembly. There are several advantages in Top-Down Assembly Design. As you design a part within the assembly, you can be sure that it will fit properly. You can also use reference geometry from the other components.

Creating a New Part in the Assembly

Top-down assembly design can be used to add new parts to an already existing assembly.

1. To create a part at the assembly level using the Top down Design, activate the **Create** command (click the **Create** button on the **Component** panel).
2. In the **Create Component** dialog, click **Type > Part**.
3. Type the name of the component and click **OK**.
4. On the **Creation Options** dialog, select **Creation Method > Locate default datums**.
5. Select **Locate Datums Method > Three planes** and click **OK**.
6. Select the Front, Top, and right planes. A part file is created.
7. Now, use the part modeling commands and create the part geometry.

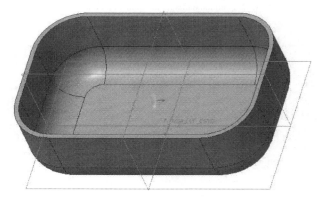

8. In the Model Tree, right-click on the **Assembly** and select **Activate**.
9. To create the second component, activate the **Create** command and select **Part** on the **Create Component** dialog.

10. Type-in the component name and click **OK**.
11. On the **Creation Options** dialog, select **Create features** and click **OK**.
12. Now, you can create the part by using the faces and edges of the first part as reference. For example, activate the **Sketch** command and select the top face of the first part.

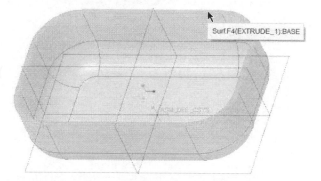

13. Select the Front and Right planes are references and click the **Sketch** button.
14. Activate the **Project** command and project the outer edges of the first component.

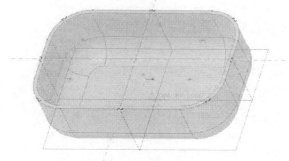

15. Use the sketch to create an *Extrude* feature.

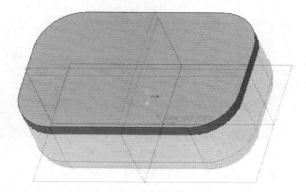

16. Activate the first component and modify the model.

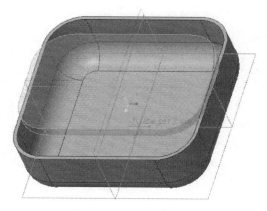

17. At the bottom of the window, click the yellow circular dot to open the **Regeneration Manager**.
18. Click the **Regenerate** button on the dialog.
19. Return to the **Assembly** environment to see the updated second component.

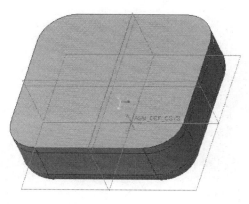

20. To save the assembly and its components, click **Save** on the Quick Access Toolbar.
21. Define the location and file name of the assembly, and then click **OK**. The assembly and its components are saved.

Sub-assemblies

The use of sub-assemblies has many advantages in Creo Parametric. Sub-assemblies make large assemblies easier to manage. They make it easy for multiple users to collaborate on a single large assembly design. They can also affect the way you document a large assembly design in 2D drawings. For these reasons, it is important for you to create sub-assemblies in a variety of ways. The easiest way to create a sub-assembly is to insert an existing assembly into another assembly. Next, apply

constraints to constrain the assembly. The process of
applying constraints is also simplified. You are
required to apply constraints between only one part
of a sub-assembly and a part of the main assembly.
In addition, you can easily hide a group of
components with the help of sub-assemblies. To do
this, right-click on a sub-assembly in the Model Tree,
and then select **Hide** .

Subassembly

Main Assembly

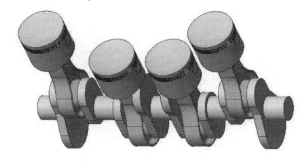

Mirroring Components

When designing symmetric assemblies, Creo
Parametric has an option to help you in saving time
and capture design intent. For example, you can
mirror the component as shown instead of inserting
it again.

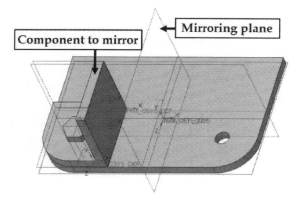

1. On the ribbon, click **Model > Component > Mirror Component** .
2. Select the component to mirror.
3. Select the mirroring plane.
4. On the **Mirror Component** dialog, select **New Component > Create a new model**.
5. Type-in **Mirrored_bracket** in the **Name** box and click **OK**.
6. Select **Mirror > Geometry with features**.
7. Check the **Preview** option to preview the mirrored component.
8. Click **OK** to mirror the component.

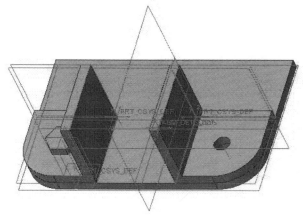

Creating Sub-assemblies from individual parts

In addition to creating sub-assemblies and inserting
them into another assembly, you can also take
individual parts that already exist in an assembly
and convert them into a sub-assembly.

1. Press and hold the **Shift** key and select parts from the assembly from the Model Tree.
2. Click the right mouse button and select **Move to sub-assembly**.

3. On this dialog, type-in the name of the sub-assembly and click **OK**.

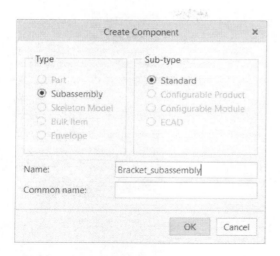

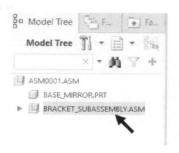

4. On the **Creation Options** dialog, select **Locate default datums** and **Align csys to csys**.

Mirroring Sub-assemblies

Similar to mirroring components, you can also mirror sub-assemblies of an assembly.

1. On the ribbon, click **Model > Component > Mirror Component**.
2. On the **Mirror Component** dialog, type-in the name of the assembly and click **OK**.
3. Check the **Geometry dependent** and **Placement dependent** options, and select the sub-assembly.

5. Click **OK**.
6. Select the Coordinate system of the assembly. The selected components are moved to the sub-assembly.

4. Select the right plane.
5. Check the **Preview** option and click **OK** to mirror the subassembly.

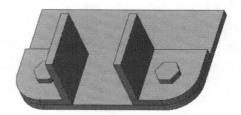

Examples

Example 1 (Bottom Up Assembly)

In this example, you will create the assembly shown next.

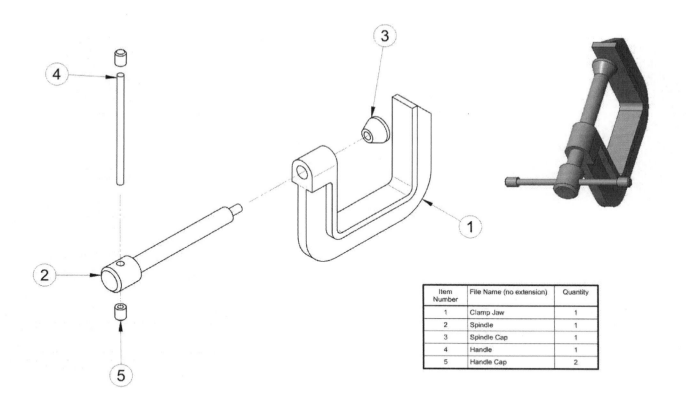

Item Number	File Name (no extension)	Quantity
1	Clamp Jaw	1
2	Spindle	1
3	Spindle Cap	1
4	Handle	1
5	Handle Cap	2

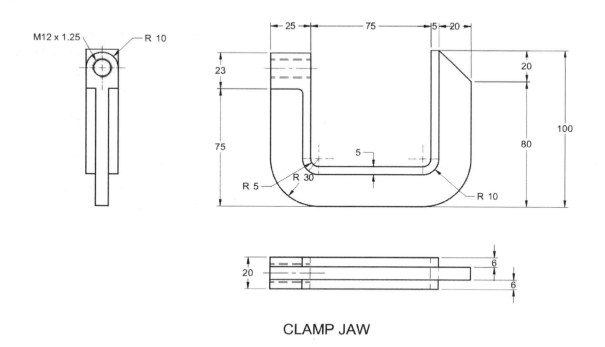

CLAMP JAW

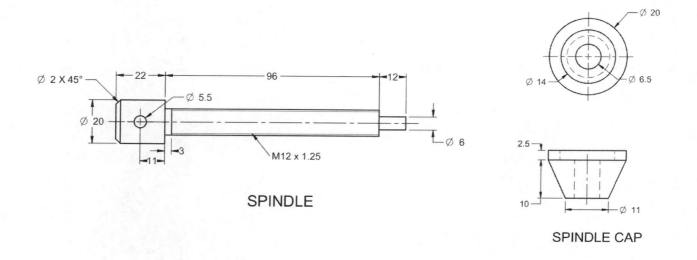

SPINDLE

SPINDLE CAP

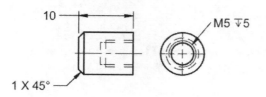

HANDLE CAP

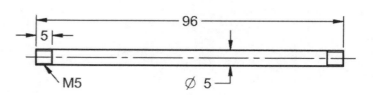

HANDLE

1. Create and save all the components of the assembly in a single folder. Name this folder as *G-Clamp*. Close all the files.

If you cannot create the components, you can download them from the companion website.

2. Start **Creo Parametric 4.0**.
3. Set *G-Clamp* folder as the current working directory.
4. On the Quick Access Toolbar, click the **New** button.
5. On the **New** dialog, select **Type > Assembly**.
6. Select **Sub-Type > Design**.
7. Type-in *G-Clamp* in the **Name** box and uncheck the **Use default template** option.
8. Click **OK**.
9. On the **New File Options** dialog, select **mmks_asm_design** option and click **OK**.
10. On the ribbon, click **Model** tab > **Component** panel > **Assemble** drop-down > **Assemble** .

11. Select *Clamp-Jaw.prt* and click **Open**.
12. On the **Component Placement** dashboard, select the **Default** option from the Component reference drop-down.

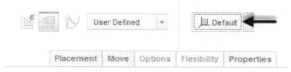

13. Click the green check on the dashboard. This fixes the component at the origin.

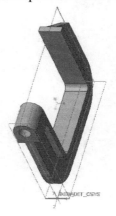

14. On the ribbon, click **Model** tab > **Component** panel > **Assemble** drop-down > **Assemble** .
15. Select *Spindle.prt*, and then click **Open**.
16. Select the axes of the spindle and clamp jaw.

17. On the **Component Placement** dashboard, select the **Coincident** constraint.

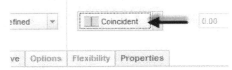

18. Click and drag the blue arrow displayed on the spindle. This will move the spindle forward.

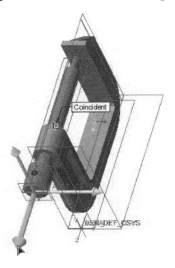

19. Zoom in to the back portion of the spindle and select its horizontal plane.
20. Select the vertical plane of the clamp jaw.

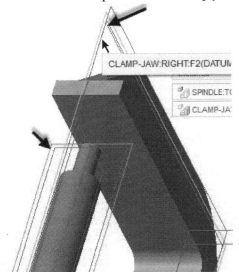

21. On the **Component Placement** dashboard, select the **Parallel** constraint.

22. Zoom in to the front portion of the spindle and select its front face.
23. Select the front face of the clamp jaw. You will notice that the Coincident constraint is applied between the two faces.

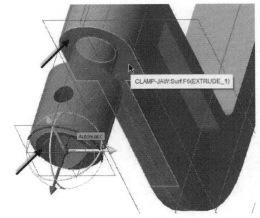

24. Double-click on the **Coincident** constraint.
25. Select the **Distance** option from the drop-down.

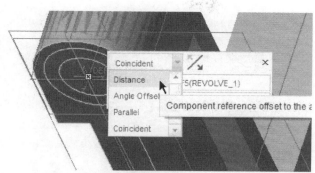

26. On the **Component Placement** dashboard, type-in 40 in the offset box.

You will notice that the Status on the dashboard changes to Fully Constrained.

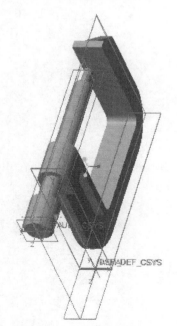

27. Click the green check ✓ to apply the coincident constraint.

28. On the ribbon, click **Model** tab > **Component** panel > **Assemble** drop-down > **Assemble** 🗗.

29. Select *Spindle-Cap.prt*, and then click **Open**.

30. Select the axes of the spindle-cap and spindle.

31. On the **Component Placement** dashboard, select the **Coincident** constraint.

32. Click and drag the blue handle of the spindle-cap. This moves the spindle-cap.

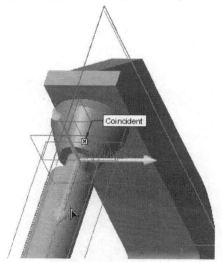

33. Select the flat face of the spindle-cap, as shown below.

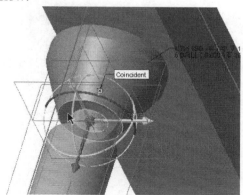

34. Press and hold the middle mouse button and drag the pointer. This rotates the assembly.

35. Select the flat face of the spindle, as shown.

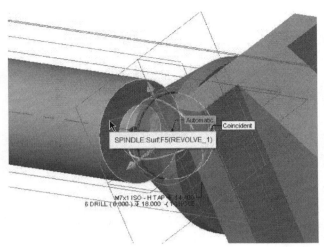

36. On the **Component Placement** tab, select the **Coincident** constraint. This fully-constrains the spindle-cap.

37. Click the green check ✓ on the dashboard.

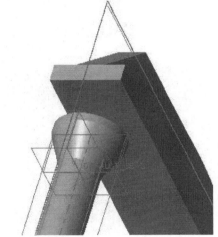

38. Insert the *Handle.prt* into the assembly.

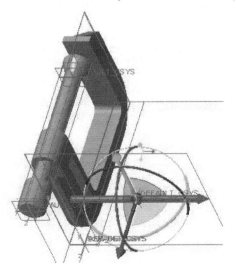

39. Select the axes of the handle and the hole on the spindle.

40. Apply the **Coincident** constraint.

41. Zoom in to the handle and select the vertical plane located at the middle of the handle.

42. Select the vertical plane of the spindle.

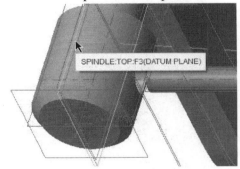

43. Apply the **Coincident** constraint. This fully-constrains the handle.

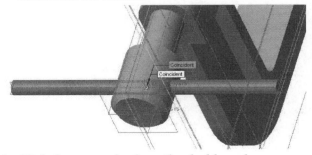

44. Click the green check on the dashboard.

45. Insert the *Handle-cap.prt* into the Assembly window.

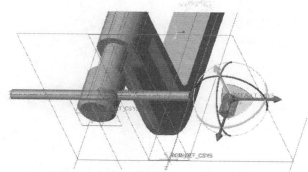

46. Select the axes of the handle and handle-cap and apply the **Coincident** constraint.

47. Apply the **Distance** constraint between the flat faces of the handle-cap and handle. The offset distance is -5.

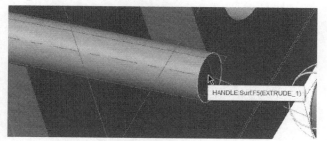

48. Click the **Change orientation of constraint** icon, if required.
49. Click the green check on the dashboard.

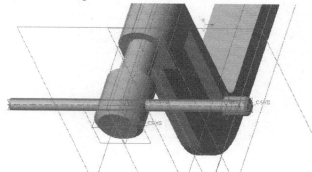

50. Likewise, assemble another instance of the handle cap.

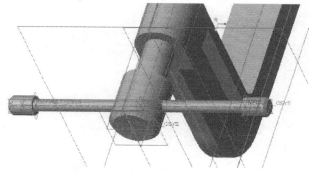

51. Save and close the assembly.

Example 2 (Top Down Assembly)

In this example, you will create the assembly shown next.

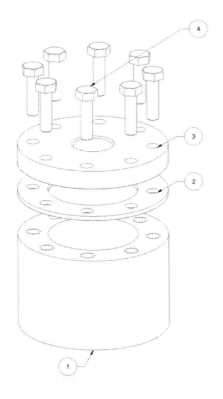

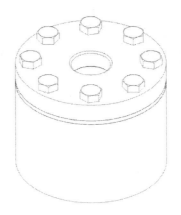

4	HEX BOLT AM,M8X1.25X30	8
3	COVER PLATE	1
2	GASKET	1
1	CYLINDER BASE	1
PC NO	PART NAME	QTY

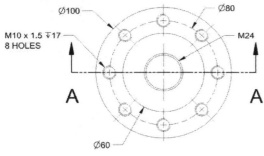

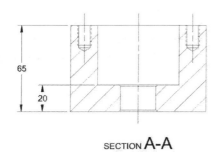

SECTION A-A

Cylinder Base

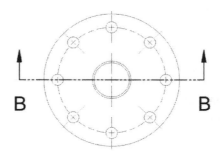

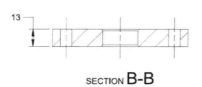

SECTION B-B

Cover Plate

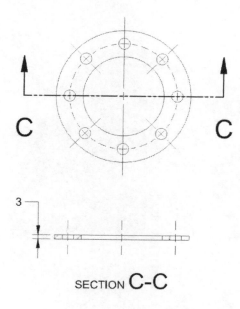

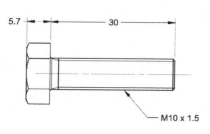

SECTION C-C

Gasket

1. Start **Creo Parametric 4.0**.
2. Create a folder with the name *Pressure Cylinder* and set it as current working folder.
3. On the Quick Access Toolbar, click the **New** button.
4. On the **New** dialog, select **Type > Assembly**.
5. Select **Sub-Type > Design**.
6. Type-in *Pressure_Cylinder* in the **Name** box and uncheck the **Use default template** option.
7. Click **OK**.
8. On the **New File Options** dialog, select the **mmks_asm_design** template and click **OK**.
9. On the ribbon, click **Model** tab > **Component** panel > **Create** .
10. Select **Type > Part** from the **Create Component** dialog.
11. Type-in *Cylinder_Base* in the **Name** box and click **OK**.
12. On the **Creation Options** dialog, select **Creation method > Locate default datums**.
13. Select **Locate Datums Method > Align csys to csys**.

Screw

14. Click **OK** and select the default coordinate system.

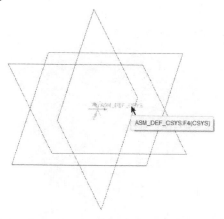

This creates a new part file inside the assembly.

15. Draw a sketch on the zx plane and revolve it.

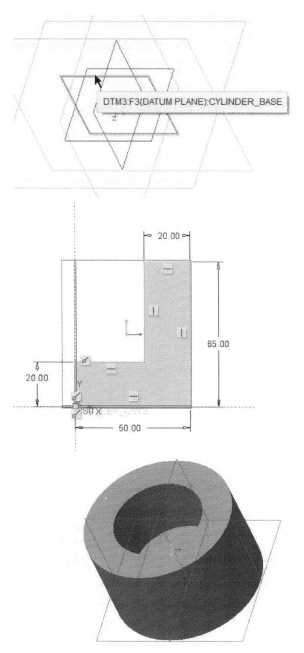

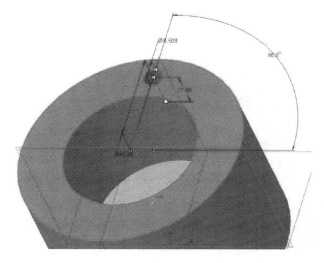

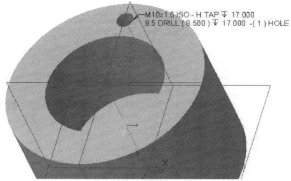

17. Create a circular pattern of the hole.

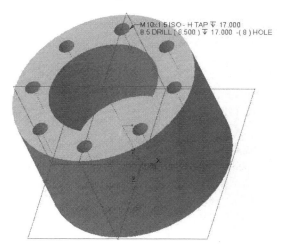

16. Create a threaded hole on the top face of the model.

18. In the Model Tree, click on **PRESSURE_CYLINDER.ASM** and select **Activate**. This switches back to the Assembly mode.

19. Activate the **Create** ⬓ command (On the ribbon, click **Model** tab > **Component** panel > **Create**).

20. On the **Create Component** dialog, select the **Part** option and type-in *Gasket* in the **Name** box. Click **OK**.

21. On the **Creation Options** dialog, set the **Creation method** to **Locate default datums**.

22. Set **Locate Datums Method** to **Three planes**, and click **OK**.

23. Select the front plane of the assembly to define the first plane of the Gasket.

24. Select the top face of the Cylinder base to define the top plane of the Gasket.

25. Select the right plane of the assembly to define the right plane of the Gasket.

26. Activate the **Extrude** command and click on top plane of the gasket.

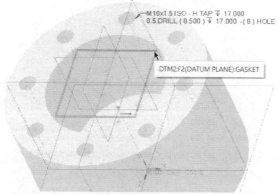

27. On the ribbon, click **Sketch** tab > **Sketching** panel > **Project** ☐.

28. Click on the outer edges of the top face of the model geometry.

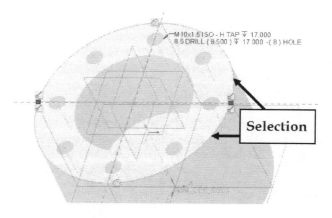

29. Zoom in to anyone of the holes and click its thread edges.

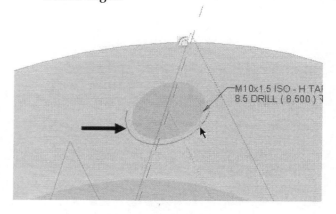

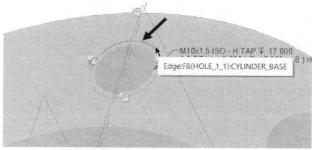

30. Likewise, select the thread edges of other holes, as shown.

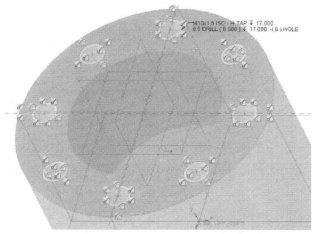

31. Click on the inner circular edges of the top face.

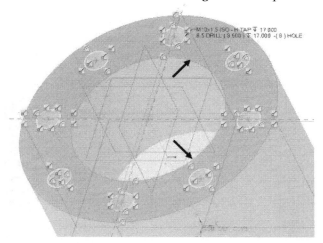

32. Click **Close** on the **Type** dialog.
33. Click **OK** on the **Sketch** tab of the ribbon.
34. Extrude the sketch up to 3 mm length in the upward direction.

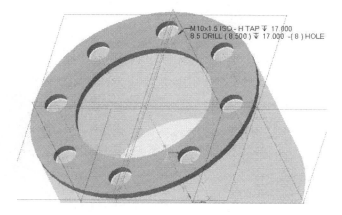

35. In the Model Tree, click on **PRESSURE-CYLINDER.ASM** and select **Activate**. This switches you back to the Assembly mode.
36. Activate the **Create** command.
37. On the **Create Component** dialog, select the **Part** option and type-in *Cover-plate* in the **Name** box. Click **OK**.
38. On the **Creation Options** dialog, set the **Creation method** to **Locate default datums**.
39. Set **Locate Datums Method** to **Three planes**, and click **OK**.
40. Select the front plane of the assembly to define the first plane of the Cover-plate.
41. Select the top face of the gasket to define the top plane of the Cover-plate.
42. Select the right plane of the assembly to define the right plane of the Cover-plate.
43. Activate the **Extrude** command and click on top plane of the gasket.

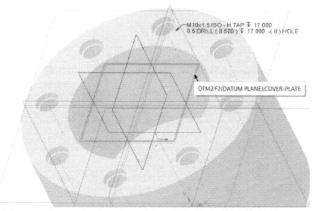

44. On the ribbon, click **Sketch** tab > **Sketching** panel > **Project**.
45. Click on the outer edges of the top face of the gasket.

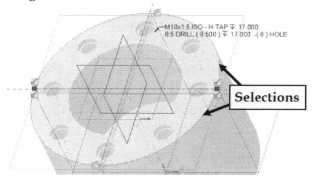

46. Click on the edges of the circular hole pattern of the gasket.

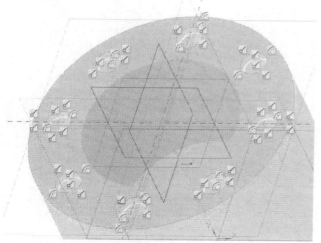

47. Click **Close** on the **Type** dialog.
48. Click **OK** on the **Sketch** tab of the ribbon.
49. Create an extruded feature of the 13 mm depth.

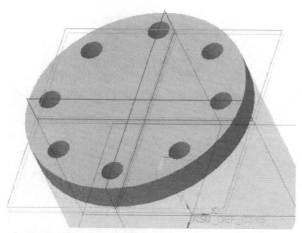

50. Activate the **Assembly** mode.
51. Activate the **Create** command.
52. On the **Create Component** dialog, select the **Part** option and type-in *Screw* in the **Name** box. Click **OK**.
53. On the **Creation Options** dialog, set the **Creation method** to **Locate default datums**.
54. Set **Locate Datums Method** to **Axis normal to plane**, and click **OK**.
55. Select the top face of the cover plate.
56. Select the axis of the hole, as shown below.

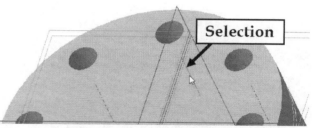

57. Start a sketch on the top plane of the screw.

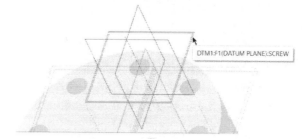

58. Activate the **Project** command.
59. Zoom hole and select it edges.

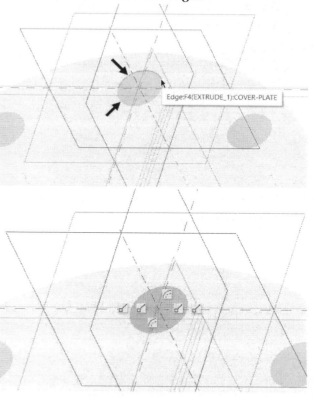

60. Click **Close** on the **Type** dialog.
61. Click **OK** on the **Sketch** tab of the ribbon.
62. Extrude the sketch up to 30 mm length in the downward direction.

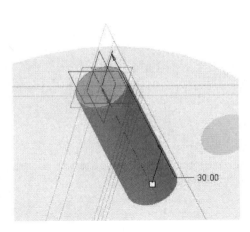

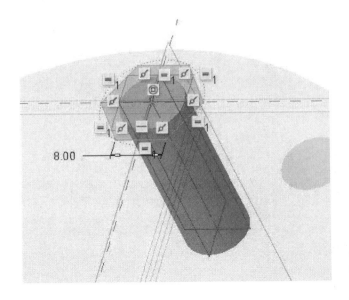

63. Start a sketch on the top face of the extruded feature.

64. On the ribbon, click **Sketch** tab > **Sketching** panel > **Palette** .

65. On the **Sketcher Palette** dialog, click the **Polygons** tab and drag the **6-sided Hexagon** into the sketch.

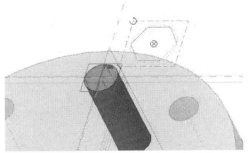

66. Click and drag the center point of the hexagon on to the axis of the extruded feature. Click the green check on the dashboard.

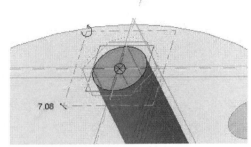

67. Modify the dimension to 8.

68. Make the center point of the hexagon coincident with the sketch origin.

69. Exit the sketch and extrude it up to 5.7 mm length.

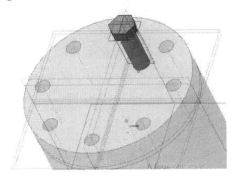

70. Apply Cosmetic Thread M10 x 1.5 to the cylindrical portion of the screw (refer to the **Cosmetic Thread command** section in Chapter 4).

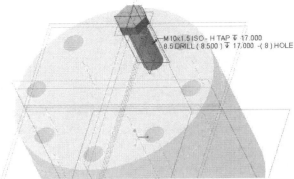

71. Activate the **Assembly** mode.

72. Select the screw from the Model Tree.

73. On the ribbon, click **Model** tab > **Modifiers** panel > **Pattern** drop-down > **Pattern**.
74. On the **Pattern** dashboard, select the **Axis** option from the drop-down located at the left side.
75. Select the axis passing through the center of the assembly.
76. Specify the parameters on the dashboard such that the 8 screws are created throughout 360.
77. On the **Pattern** dashboard, click the **Options** tab and select **Regeneration option** > **Variable**.
78. Click the green check on the dashboard to complete the pattern feature.

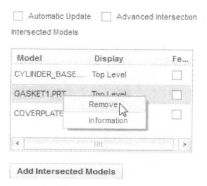

89. Select the cover plate and cylinder base, and then click **OK** on the **Select** dialog.
90. Click the **Shape** tab and type-in 81 as the thread distance.
91. Click the green check to create the hole.

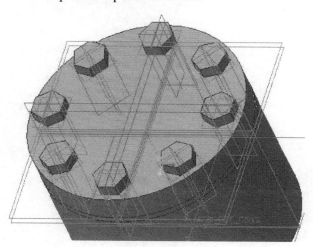

79. On the ribbon, click **Model** tab > **Cut & Surface** panel > **Hole**.
80. Click on the top face of the Cover plate.
81. On the **Hole** dashboard, click **Datum** drop-down >**Axis**.
82. Select the circular edge of the Cover plate, and click **OK** on the **Datum Axis** dialog.
83. On the dashboard, click the **Resume** ▶ icon. The hole will be placed at the center.
84. Click the **Create standard hole** icon on the **Hole** dashboard.
85. Select the **Through All** option.
86. Set the **Screw size** to **M24x1.5**.
87. Click the **Intersection** tab and uncheck the **Automatic Update** option.
88. Click the right mouse button on GASKET and select **Remove**.

92. On the **Graphics** toolbar, click the **View Manager** button.
93. On the **View Manager** dialog, click the **Explode** tab and click the **New** button.
94. Type-in the name of the explosion and press Enter.
95. Click **Close**.
96. On the ribbon, click **Model** tab > **Model Display** panel > **Edit Position** .
97. On the **Explode Tool** dashboard, make sure that the **Translate** icon is activated.

98. Press and hold the Ctrl key and select all the screws.

99. Click and drag the vertical arrow upward. All the screws will be move up.

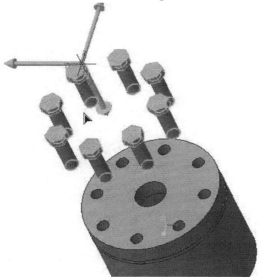

100. Likewise, move the cover plate and gasket upward.

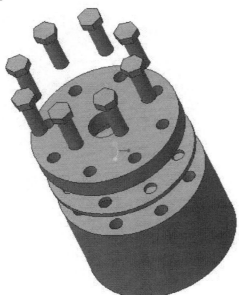

101. On the **Explode Tool** dashboard, click the

    Explode Lines icon.

102. Select the cylindrical face of anyone of the screws.

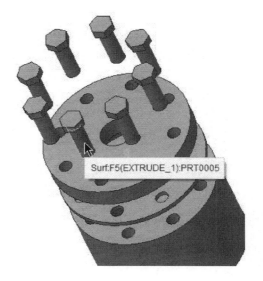

Surf:F5(EXTRUDE_1):PRT0005

103. Select the cylindrical face of the corresponding hole on the Cylinder base.

104. On the **Cosmetic Offset Line** dialog, select the **Use cylinder axis** option under the **Reference 1** and **Reference 2** sections.

105. Click **Apply** to create the exploded line between the screw and hole.

106. Likewise, create exploded lines between the other screws and holes.

107. Close the **Cosmetic Offset Line** dialog.

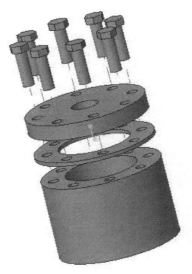

108. Click the green check on the dashboard to complete the explosion.

109. On the **Graphics** toolbar, click the **View**

    Manager button.

110. On the **View Manager** dialog, click the **Explode** tab.

111. Click the right mouse button on the Exploded view and select **Save**.

112. Click **OK** on the **Save Display Elements** dialog.

113. Close the **View Manager** dialog.

114. On the ribbon, click **Model** tab > **Model Display** panel > **Exploded View** . This collapses the explosion.

115. On the ribbon, click **File > Options**.

116. On the **Options** dialog, click the **Entity Display** category at the left side.

117. Under the **Assembly display Settings** section, check the **Show animation while exploding the assembly** and **Follow explode sequence** options.

118. Type-in 10 in the **Maximum seconds an animation takes place between explode states** box.

119. Click **OK** and **NO**.

120. On the ribbon, click **Model** tab > **Model Display** panel > **Exploded View**. You will notice that the components of the assembly are exploded in a sequence.

121. Click the **Exploded View** icon to un explode the assembly.

122. Save and close the assembly.

Questions

1. How do you start an assembly?
2. What is the use of the **Repeat** command?
3. List the advantages of Top-down assembly approach.
4. How do you create a sub-assembly in the Assembly environment?
5. Briefly explain how to edit components in an assembly.
6. What are the results that can be achieved using the **Create** command?
7. How do you redefine constraints in Creo Parametric?
8. What is the use of the **Angle Offset** constraint?

Exercise 1

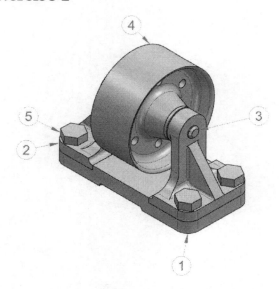

Item Number	File Name (no extension)	Quantity
1	Base	1
2	Bracket	2
3	Spindle	1
4	Roller-Bush assembly	1
5	Bolt	4

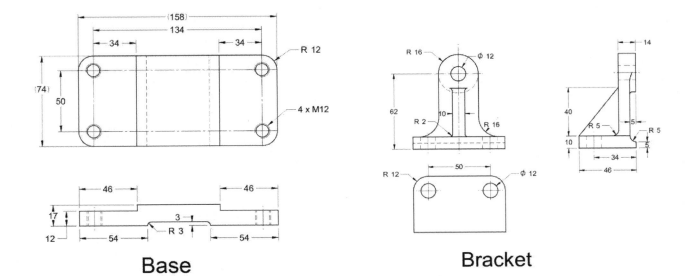

Base

Bracket

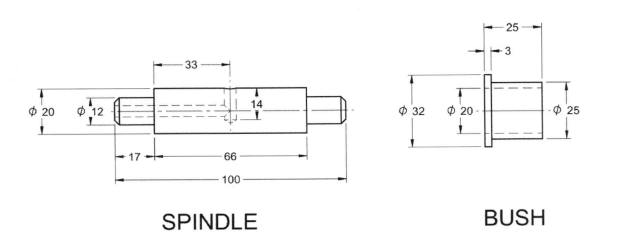

SPINDLE

BUSH

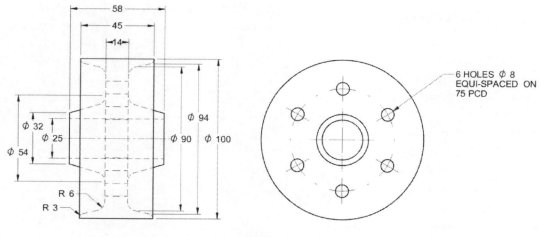

Roller

6 HOLES ⌀ 8
EQUI-SPACED ON
75 PCD

58
45
14
⌀ 32
⌀ 25
⌀ 54
⌀ 94
⌀ 90
⌀ 100
R 6
R 3

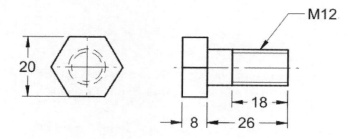

M12

20
18
8
26

Bolt

Chapter 10: Drawings

Drawings are used to document your 3D models in the traditional 2D format including dimensions and other instructions useful for the manufacturing purpose. In Creo Parametric, you first create 3D models and assemblies, and then use them to generate the drawing. There is a direct association between the 3D model and the drawing. When changes are made to the model, every view in the drawing will be updated. This relationship between the 3D model and the drawing makes the drawing process fast and accurate. Because of the mainstream adoption of 2D drawings of the mechanical industry, drawings are one of the three main file types you can create in Creo Parametric.

The topics covered in this chapter are:

- *Create General views*
- *Projection views*
- *Auxiliary views*
- *Sections views*
- *Detail views*
- *Break-out Section views*
- *Broken view*
- *Exploded views*
- *Parts List and Balloons*
- *Generate Dimensions*
- *Dimensions*
- *Axis*
- *Notes*

Starting a Drawing

Follow the steps given next to start a new drawing.

1. On the Quick Access Toolbar, click the **New** icon.
2. On the **New** dialog, select **Type > Drawing**.
3. Type-in the drawing name and click **OK**.
4. On the **New Drawing** dialog, click the **Specify Template > Empty** to the start a drawing with an empty sheet.

You can select **Use template**, and then select a standard template to start a drawing. The standard drawing views are placed on the sheet, automatically.

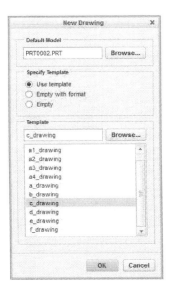

The **Empty with format** option starts a drawing using a standard or user-defined format.

5. Set the drawing orientation to **Portrait** or **Landscape** or **Variable**.
6. Select the sheet size from the **Standard Size** drop-down. The drawing units are defined automatically based on the standard size. You can manually define the units and sheet size by selecting **Variable** orientation.
7. Click the **Browse** button under the **Default Model** section and select the reference 3D model.
8. Click **OK** to start the drawing.

Setting the Drawing Model

A drawing is a 2D representation of a 3D model (part or assembly). You need to associate a 3D model with the drawing file. At the beginning, you have selected a 3D model while creating the drawing file. However, you can add more models to the drawing after creating the drawing. The **Drawing Model** command helps you to add, remove, and set the model for creating drawing views. On the ribbon, click **Layout** tab > **Model Views** panel > **Drawing Models**. The **DWG MODELS** menu pops up on the top right corner of the screen.

The options on this menu helps you add, remove, or set current drawing model.

Drawing Properties

Before creating the drawing, you have to check the sheet properties, and modify them as per your requirement.

1. Click **File > Prepare > Drawing Properties**.
2. On the **Drawing Properties** dialog, click the **change** link next to **Detail Options**. The **Options** dialog appears.

On this dialog, you can modify the properties such as angle of projection, units, and so on. For example, if you want to change the angle of projection, type-in projection in the **Option** box and click **Find**. On the **Find Option** dialog, select a value from the **Set value** drop-down, and click **Add/change**. Click **Close** on the **Find Option** dialog. Click **OK** on the **Options** dialog, and then close the **Drawing Properties** dialog.

 General View

There are different standard views available in a 3D part such as front, right, top, and isometric. In Creo Parametric, you can create these views using the **General View** command.

1. On the ribbon, click **Layout > Model Views > General View**.

2. On the **Select Combined State** dialog, click **No combined state**, and click **OK**.
3. Click on the drawing sheet to define the view location.

4. On the **Drawing View** dialog, select **Model view names > FRONT**, and then click **Apply**.
5. On the dialog, click **Categories > Scale** and define the view scale. You use the default scale or define a custom scale. Click **Apply** after making changes.
6. Click **Categories > View Display** and set the **Display Style**.
7. Click **OK** to create the view.

Projection View

After you have created the first view in your drawing, a projection view is one of the simplest views to create.

1. On the ribbon, click **Layout > Model Views > Projection View**.
2. After activating this command, move the pointer in the direction you wish to have the view projected.

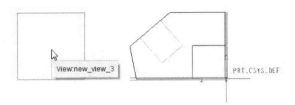

3.   Next, click on the sheet to specify the location.

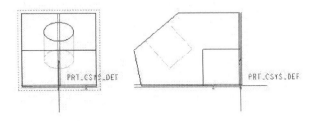

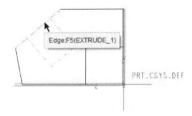 Auxiliary View

Most of the parts are represented by using orthographic views (front, top and/or side views). However, many parts have features located on inclined faces. You cannot get the true shape and size for these features by using the orthographic views. To see an accurate size and shape of the inclined features, you need to create an auxiliary view. You create an auxiliary view by projecting the part onto a plane other than horizontal, front or side planes.

1.   On the ribbon, click **Layout > Model Views > Auxiliary View**.
2.   Click the angled edge of the model to establish the direction of the auxiliary view.
3.   Move the pointer and click.

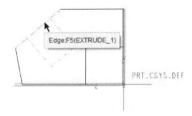

4.   Drag the mouse to the desired location. Click to locate the view.

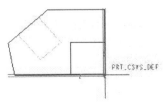

Section Views

One of the common views used in 2D drawings is the section view. Creating a section view in Creo Parametric is very simple.

1.   Create the base view and side view of the model as shown.
2.   On the Graphics toolbar, click **Display Style drop-down > Hidden Line** .

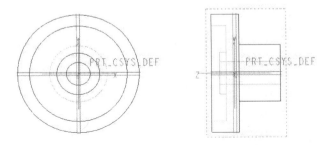

3.   Select the side view and click the right mouse button.
4.   Select **Properties** to open the **Drawing View** dialog.
5.   Select **Categories > Sections**, and click **2D cross-section**.
6.   Click the **Add cross-section to view** button.
7.   On the **Menu Manager**, select **Planar** and **Single**, and then click **Done**.
8.   Enter **A** as the name of the cross-section and click the green check.
9.   Select the cutting plane from the base view.

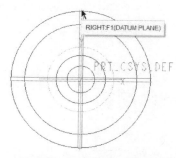

10. On the **Drawing View** dialog, set the **Section Area** to **Full**.

11. Click **OK** to create the section view.

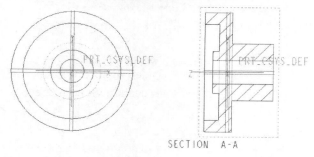

12. On the ribbon, click **Layout > Edit > Arrows** ⬚.

13. Select the cross-section and base views.

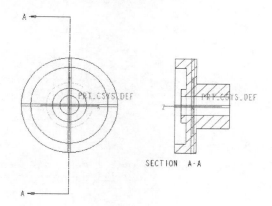

14. Click the middle mouse button to exit the command.

15. Select the section arrows.

16. Drag the arrows to reduce their length.

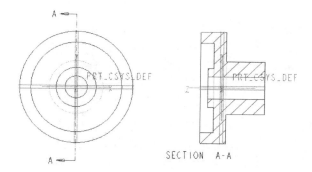

You can flip the direction of the arrows by selecting them, right clicking and selecting **Flip Material Removal Side**.

You can change the spacing between the hatch lines of the section view by following the steps given next.

1. Deselect the section view.

2. Select the hatching of the section view and click the right mouse button.

3. Select **Properties** to open the **Menu Manager**.

4. Click **Spacing** on the Menu Manager.

5. On the Menu Manager, under **Modify Mode**, select **Half**.

6. Click **Done** and click in the graphics window.

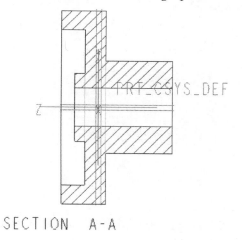

Likewise, you can modify the angle, line style and other properties of the section view.

Offset Section View

If you want to create a section view by using a multi-segment section line, then follow the steps given next.

1. Create the base and projected views as shown.

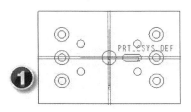

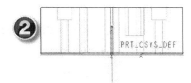

2. Click the right mouse button on the projected view and select **Properties**.
3. Select **Categories > Sections**, and click **2D cross-section**.
4. Click the **Add cross-section to view** ![+] button.
5. On the **Menu Manager**, select **Offset** and **Single**, and then click **Done**.
6. Enter **A** as the name of the cross-section and click the green check. A new window appears with the 3D model.
7. Click on the top surface of the model to define the sketching plane.

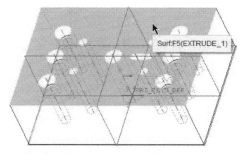

8. Click **Okay** and **Default** on the **Menu Manager**.
9. In the 3D model window, click **View > Orientation > Sketch Orientation**.

10. Click **Sketch > Line > Line** and draw the cutting plane as shown.

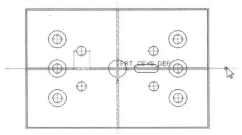

11. Click **Sketch > Done** to close the 3D Model window.
12. On the **Drawing View** dialog, drag the horizontal scroll bar and click in the **Arrow Display** field.
13. Select the base view and click **OK**.

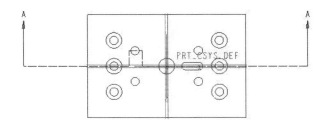

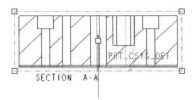

Half Section View

Follow the steps given below to create a half section view.

1. Create the base and projected views as shown.

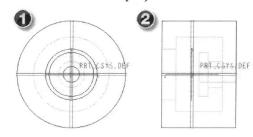

2. Click the right mouse button on the projected view and select **Properties**.
3. Select **Categories > Sections**, and click **2D cross-**

section.

4. Click the **Add cross-section to view** button.

5. On the **Menu Manager**, select **Planar** and **Single**, and then click **Done**.

6. Enter **A** as the name of the cross-section and click the green check.

7. Select the cutting plane from the base view.

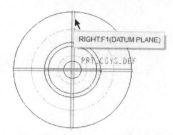

8. On the **Drawing View** dialog, set the **Section Area** to **Half**.

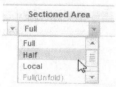

9. Select a plane on the base view to define the half section.

10. Pick a side to display the hatch lines.
11. Click **OK** to create the half section view

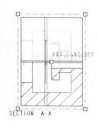

Aligned Section View

Follow the steps given next to create the aligned section view.

1. Create the base and projected views as shown.

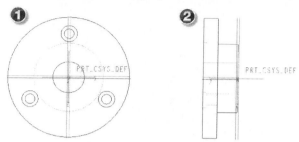

2. Click the right mouse button on the projected view and select **Properties**.

3. Select **Categories > Sections**, and click **2D cross-section**.

4. Click the **Add cross-section to view** button.

5. On the **Menu Manager**, select **Offset** and **Single**, and then click **Done**.

6. Enter **A** as the name of the cross-section and click the green check. A new window appears with the 3D model.

7. Click on the top surface of the model to define the sketching plane.

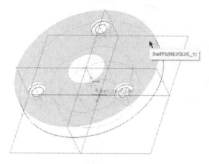

8. Click **Okay** and **Default** on the **Menu Manager**.
9. In the window, click **View > Orientation > Standard Orientation**.
10. Select the axes of the center hole and counterbore hole as the reference.
11. Close the **References** dialog.
12. In the 3D model window, click **View > Orientation > Sketch Orientation**.

13. Click **Sketch > Line > Line** and draw the cutting plane as shown.

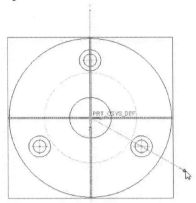

14. Click **Sketch > Done** to close the 3D Model window.
15. On the **Drawing View** dialog, set the **Section Area** to **Full(Aligned)**.

16. Select the axis of the revolved solid as shown.

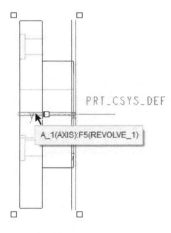

17. On the **Drawing View** dialog, drag the horizontal scroll bar and click in the **Arrow Display** field.
18. Select the base view and click **OK**.

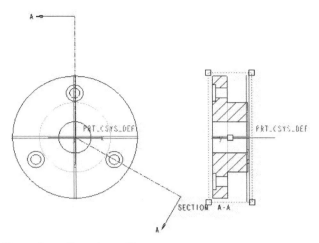

Creating Section Cuts

A section cut displays the surface that is exposed after sectioning. It hides the edges. You can create section cuts by selecting **Model edge visibility > Area** on the **Drawing View** dialog while creating the section view.

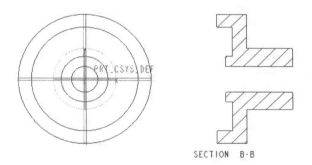

Detailed View

If a drawing view contains small features that are difficult to see, a detailed view can be used to zoom in and make things clear. To create a detailed view, follow the steps given next.

1. On the ribbon, click **Layout > Model Views > Detailed View**.
2. Click on the edge of the model to define the center of the detailed view as shown.

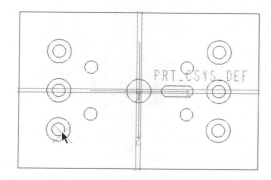

3. Draw a spline to identify the area that you wish to zoom in. It should enclose the center point.

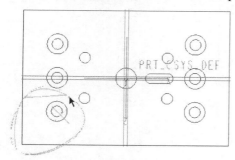

4. Click the middle mouse button once the spline is drawn.
5. Move the pointer and click to locate the view. The detail view will appear with a label.

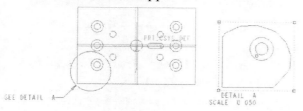

If you want to change the scale value, then click the right mouse button on the detail view and select **Properties**. On the **Drawing View** dialog, select **Categories > Scale**, type-in a new value in the **Scale** box, and click **OK**.

Partial View

Follow the steps given next to create the partial view.

1. Select the view, right-click and select **Properties**.
2. On the **Drawing view** dialog, click **Categories > Visible Area** and select **View visibility > Partial**

View.

3. Select an edge on the view to define the reference point.

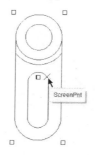

4. Draw a spline enclosing the center point, and then click the middle mouse button.
5. Click **OK**.

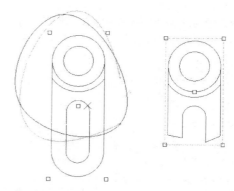

Broken View

You can add break lines to a drawing view, which is too large to fit on the drawing sheet. They break the view so that only important details are shown.

1. Select the view, right-click and select **Properties**.
2. On the **Drawing view** dialog, click **Categories > Visible Area** and select **View visibility > Broken View**.
3. Click the **Add break** button on the dialog.
4. Click on an edge to locate the beginning of the break.

5. Move the pointer in the direction perpendicular to the selected edge.

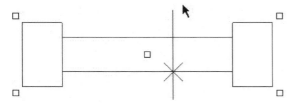

6. Select a point to define the end of the break.

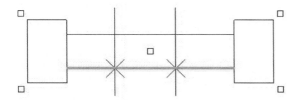

7. Click **OK** to create the broken view.
8. Drag the views closer to each other.

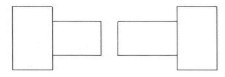

If you want to change the line type of the break lines, then click the right mouse button on view and select **Properties**. On the **Drawing View** dialog, click **Categories > Visible Area**. Drag the scroll bar and select a new line type to be applied from the **Break Line Style** drop-down menu. Click **OK** to close the dialog.

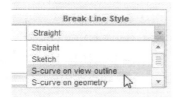

Breakout View

The Breakout View alters an existing view to show the hidden portion of a part or assembly. This view is very useful to show the parts, which are hidden in an

assembly. You need to create a closed profile to breakout a view.

1. Create the base and projected views as shown.

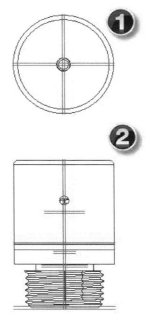

2. Select the view to be broken, click the right mouse button and select **Properties**.
3. Select **Categories > Sections**, and click **2D cross-section**.
4. Click the **Add cross-section to view** button.
5. On the **Menu Manager**, select **Planar** and **Single**, and then click **Done**.
6. Enter **A** as the name of the cross-section and click the green check.
7. Select the cutting plane from the base view.

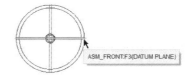

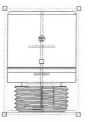

8. On the **Drawing View** dialog, set the **Section Area** to **Local**.

9. Select an edge on the view to define the center point.

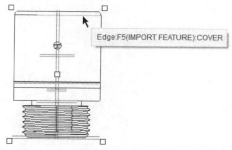

6. Draw a spline enclosing the center point, and then click the middle mouse button.

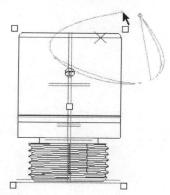

7. Click **OK**.

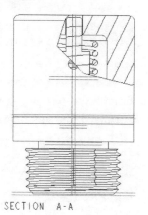

SECTION A-A

Exploded View

You can display an assembly in an exploded state as long as the assembly already has an exploded view defined. Follow the steps given next to define the exploded view in an assembly.

1. Open the assembly file.
2. On the **Graphics** toolbar, click the **View Manager** icon.
3. On the **View Manager** dialog, click the **Explodes** tab and create a new exploded view with the name **Explosion**.
4. Explode the components of the assembly using the **Edit Position** command.
5. On the **View Manager** dialog, click **Edit > Save**.
6. Click OK.
7. Close the **View Manager** dialog.
8. Save the assembly file.

Follow the steps given next to insert the exploded view in a drawing.

1. Open a drawing file.
2. On the ribbon, click **Layout > Model Views > General View**.
3. Select **No Combined state** and click **OK**.
4. Click on the drawing sheet to position the view.
5. In the **Drawing View** dialog, click **Categories > View States** and check the **Explode components in view** option.
6. Select **Assembly explode state > EXPLOSION**.
7. Click **OK** to generate the exploded view of the assembly.

View Display

When working with Creo Parametric drawings, you can control the way a model view appears by using the **Drawing View** dialog. For example, if you want to show or hide the hidden lines, then follow the steps given next.

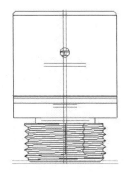

1. Click the right mouse button on the view and select **Properties**.
2. On the **Drawing View** dialog, under the **View Display** section, select **Display Style > Hidden**.
3. Click **OK** to apply the changes.

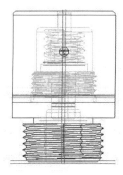

View Movement

Creo Parametric locks the drawing views to their original positions and restricts from moving them. If you want to move a drawing view, click the right mouse button on it and deactivate **Lock View Movement**.

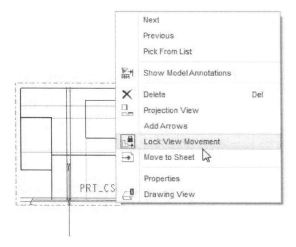

Now, you can move the drawing view.

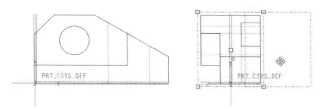

View Alignment

There are several types of views that are automatically aligned to a parent view. These include projected views, auxiliary views, and section views. For example, if you want to move any view, the movement is constrained along the parent view. You can make the view independent of its parent view by breaking the link between them. To do this, click the right mouse button on the view. Select **Properties**.

On the **Drawing View** dialog, click **Categories > Alignment**. Uncheck the **Align this view to other view** option and click **OK**. Now, you can move the view independently.

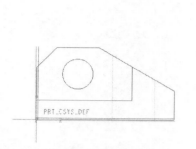

I	COVER	I	cover.prt	
2	GASKET	I	gasket.prt	
3	GASKET2	I	prt0002.prt	
4	NIPPLE	I	prt0003.prt	
5	PUSHER	I	pusher.prt	
6	SPRING	I	spring.prt	

SCALE I 000

Bill of Material

Creating an assembly drawing is very similar to creating a part drawing. However, there are few things unique in an assembly drawing. One of them is creating parts list. A parts list identifies the different components in an assembly. Generating a parts list is very easy in Creo Parametric. First, you need to have a view of the assembly.

1. On the ribbon, click **Table > Table > Table > Quick Tables >Assembly > bom description down**.

2. Click on the drawing sheet to position the bill of materials.

If you want to modify the bill of material, then click the right mouse button on the bill of material. Select **Properties** to open the **Table Properties** dialog. On the **Table Properties** dialog, click on the tabs and modify the properties. Click **OK** to apply the changes.

⑤ Balloons

To add balloons to the assembly drawing, click **Table > Balloons > Create Balloons > Create Balloons – All** on the ribbon.

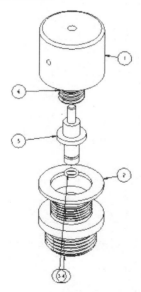

Select the overlapping balloon and drag it to a new location.

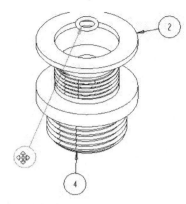

Centerlines

Centerlines are used in engineering drawings to denote hole centers and lines. If you want to display the centerlines of a drawing view, then follow the steps given next.

1. On the ribbon, click **Annotate > Annotations > Show Model Annotations** .
2. Select a drawing view having holes by clicking on the view boundary. Press the Ctrl key to select multiple views.

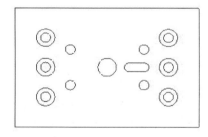

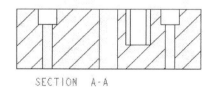

SECTION A-A

3. On the **Show Model Annotations** dialog, click the **Datums** tab and select **Type > Axes**. The axes appear on the drawing view(s).
4. Select the axes to include and click **OK**.

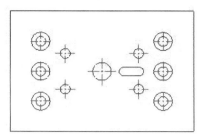

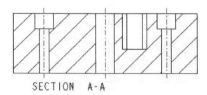

SECTION A-A

Dimensions

Creo Parametric provides you with different types of commands to add dimensions to the drawing.

 Show Model Annotations

One of the methods to add dimensions to the drawing is to retrieve the dimensions that are already contained in the 3D part file. The **Show Model Annotations** command helps you to do this.

1. On the ribbon, click **Annotate > Annotations > Show Model Annotations**.
2. On the **Show Model Annotations** dialog, click the **Dimension** tab and select **Type > All**.
3. Select the drawing view by clicking on its view boundary.

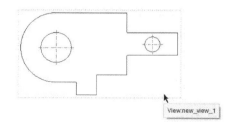

4. Click the **Select All** icon on the **Show Model Annotations** dialog, and then click **OK**.

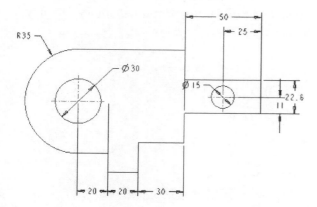

You can erase a dimension by selecting it, right-clicking, and selecting **Erase**.

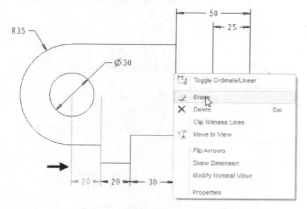

To unerase the erased dimension, expand **Annotations** in the Drawing Tree. Click the right mouse button on the erased dimension and select **Unerase**.

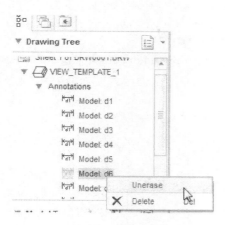

You can delete the dimension permanently by selecting it and pressing **Delete**.

Move to View

The **Move to View** command moves a dimension from one view to another.

1. Select the dimension to move.
2. On the ribbon, click **Annotate > Edit > Move to View**.
3. Select the destination view.

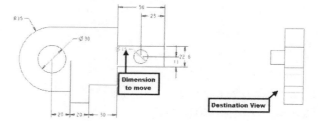

The dimension is moved to the destination view.

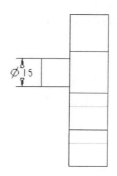

Adding Dimensions

If you want to add some more dimensions, which are necessary to manufacture a part, use the

Dimension command (on the ribbon, click **Annotate > Annotations > Dimension**) to create linear, radial or any type of dimension. As you activate this command, the **Select Reference** dialog appears.

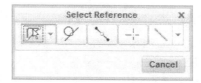

You can use the options on this dialog to define the type of dimension reference. For example, click the

Tangent icon, press the Ctrl key and select two

arcs. A dimension appears between the tangent points of the arcs. Move the pointer and middle-click to position the dimension.

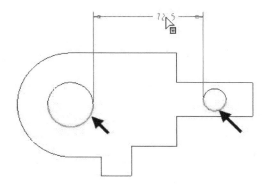

Linear Dimensions

To create a linear dimension, activate the **Dimension** command and select a linear edge of the drawing view. Move the pointer and middle-click to position the dimension.

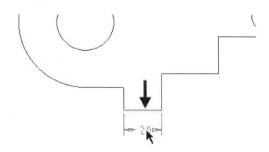

Radial Dimensions

To add a radial dimension, activate the **Dimension** command and select a circular edge. Click the right mouse button to view a menu. Use the options on this menu to create four different types of radial dimensions

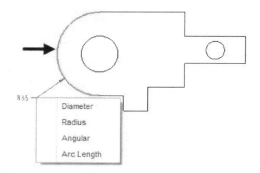

Move the pointer and middle-click to position the dimension. You can change the dimension type

using the **Orientation** drop-down on the **Display** panel of the **Dimension** tab.

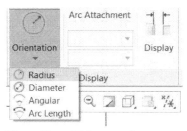

Baseline Dimensions

The **Dimension** command can also be used to create baseline dimensions.

1. Activate the **Dimension** command.
2. Press the Ctrl key and select the parallel edges as shown.
3. Move the pointer and middle-click to create the baseline dimensions.

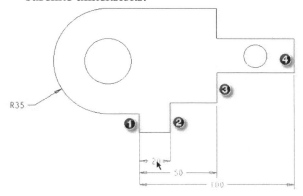

Align Dimensions

This command aligns the dimensions horizontally or vertically.

1. Press the Ctrl key and select two or more dimensions.

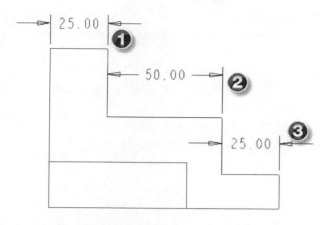

2. On the ribbon, click **Annotate > Edit > Align Dimensions**.

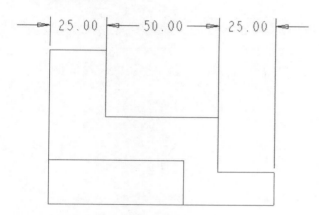

Ordinate Dimension

Ordinate dimensions are another type of dimensions that you can add to a drawing.

1. On the ribbon, click **Annotate > Annotations > Ordinate Dimension**.
2. Click on any edge of the drawing view to define the zero reference.
3. Now, press the Ctrl key and click on an edge of the drawing view.
4. Likewise, click on other edges parallel to the zero reference.

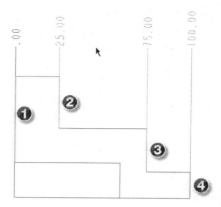

5. Move the pointer and middle-click to place the ordinate dimension.

Auto Ordinate Dimension

This command creates ordinate dimensions, automatically.

1. On the ribbon, click **Annotate > Annotations > Ordinate Dimension > Auto Ordinate Dimension**.
2. Select the surface that has the edges to be dimensioned.

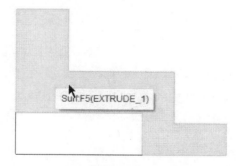

3. Click **OK** on the **Select** dialog.
4. Select the zero reference of the ordinate dimensions.

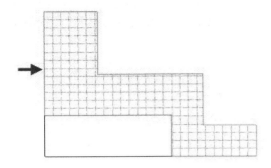

5. Click **Done/Return** on the **Menu Manager**.

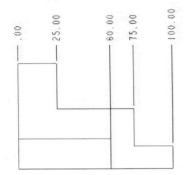

You can also convert baseline dimensions into ordinate dimensions. Press the Ctrl key and select the baseline dimensions. Click the right mouse button and select **Toggle Ordinate/Linear**.

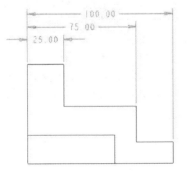

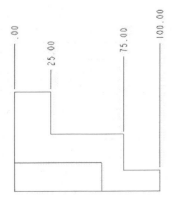

Angle Dimensions

The **Dimension** command can be used to create angle dimensions.

1. On the ribbon, click **Annotate > Annotations > Dimension**.
2. Press the Ctrl key and select two lines, which are positioned at an angle to each other.

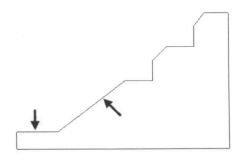

3. Click the right mouse and select any angle sector.

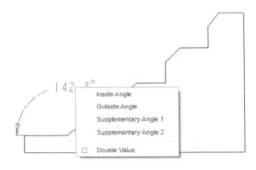

4. Middle-click to position the dimension.

Unattached Note

Notes are important part of a drawing. You add notes to provide additional details, which cannot be done using dimensions and annotations.

1. On the ribbon, click **Annotate > Annotations > Note > Unattached Note**.
2. Click on the drawing sheet to define the location of the note.
3. Type-in the text and click the middle mouse button.

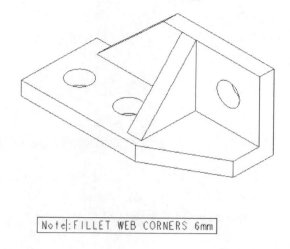

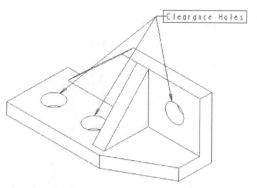

4. Type-in the leader text and middle-click. You can also use the option on the **Format** tab of the ribbon to format the text.

⌐ᴬ Leader Note

Leader notes are an essential element in creating drawings.

1. On the ribbon, click **Annotate > Annotations > Note > Leader Note**.
2. Click on the edge to add a leader. Press the Ctrl key and select multiple edges to add a single leader to multiple edges.

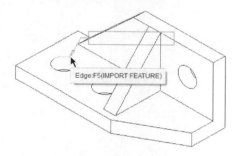

3. Move the pointer and middle-click to position the leader.

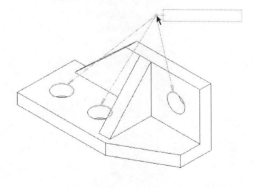

Examples
Example 1
In this example, you will create drawing format file.

1. Start **Creo Parametric 4.0**.
2. Create the *Drawings* folder and set it as current working folder.
3. On the **Home** tab, click the **New** button.
4. On the **New** dialog, select **Type > Format**.
5. Type-in *Sample-Format* in the **Name** box and click **OK**.
6. Select **Empty** from the **Select Template** section.
7. Set the **Orientation** to **Landscape**.
8. Set the **Standard Size** to **A3**.
9. Click **OK**.
10. On the ribbon, click **Table** tab > **Table** panel > **Table** drop-down > **Quick Table** > **title block**. The table is attached to the pointer.

11. On the **Select Point** dialog, click the **Select a point on drawing object or entity** button.

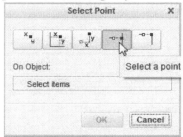

12. Select the lower right corner point of the sheet.

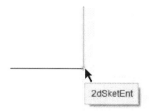

13. Click **OK**. The title block is placed at the selected point.
14. Double-click in the top row of the title block, and then type-in the company name.
15. Save and close the format file.

Example 2

In this example, you will create the 2D drawing of the part as shown.

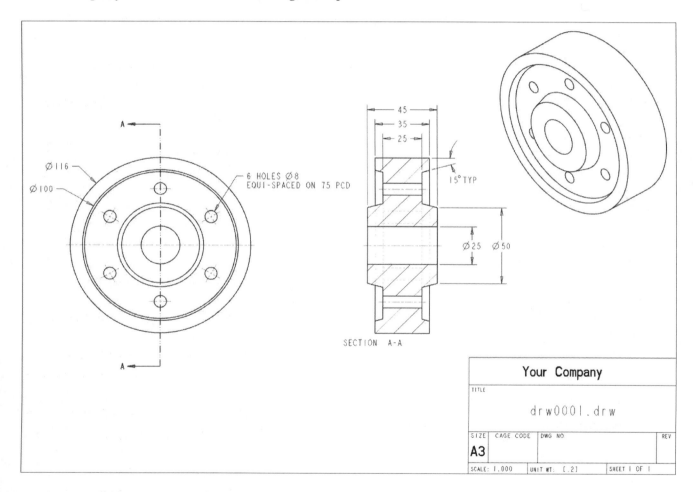

Starting a New Drawing

1. Start **Creo Parametric 4.0**.
2. Set the *Drawings* folder as current working folder.
3. Copy the Exercise1.prt file created in Chapter 5 to the *Drawings* folder.
4. On the **Home** tab, click the **New** button.
5. On the **New** dialog, select **Type > Drawing**.

6. Type-in *Example2* in the **Name** box and uncheck the **Use default template** option.

7. Click **OK**.

8. On the **New Drawing** dialog, click the **Browse** button in the **Default Model** section and select the *C05-Exercise1.prt* file.

9. Under the **Select Template** section, select the **Empty with Format** option.

10. Click the **Browse** button in the **Format** section.

11. Go to the Drawings folder and select the *Sample-Format.frm* file.

12. Click **Open**, and then click **OK**. The dialog appears, as shown below.

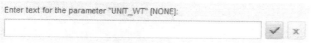

13. Click the green checks to accept the default values.

Generating Drawing Views

1. On the ribbon, click **Layout** tab > **Model Views** panel > **General View**.

2. On the **Select Combined State** dialog, select the **No combined State** option and click **OK**.

3. Click on the left side of the drawing sheet to position the view.

4. On the **Drawing View** dialog, select **FRONT** from the **Model view names** list.

5. Type-in **Front** in the **View name** box and click **Apply**.

6. Click **Categories > View Display**, and set the **Display style** to **Hidden**.

7. Click **OK**.

8. Select the view and deactivate the **Lock view Movement** icon on the Document panel of the ribbon.

9. Move the view to the position, as shown below.

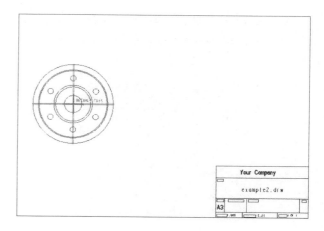

Now, you have to create the projected view.

10. On the ribbon, click **Layout** tab > **Model Views** panel > **Projection View**.

11. Move the pointer rightward and click to position the projected view.

12. On the **Graphics** toolbar, click **Display style** drop-down > **Hidden Line**.

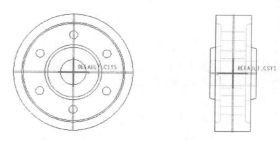

Now, you have to create the section view.

13. Select the right view and click the right mouse button.

14. Select **Properties** from the shortcut menu.

15. On the **Drawing view** dialog, select **Categories > Sections**.

16. Under **Section Options**, select **2D cross-section** and click the **Add cross-section to view** button.

17. Click **Done** on the **Menu Manager**.

18. Enter **A** as the name of the cross-section and click the green check.

19. Select the right plane from the Front view.

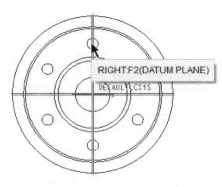

20. Click **OK** to create the section view.

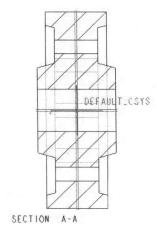

SECTION A-A

Now, you need to add arrows to the front view.

21. Select the section view and click right mouse button.
22. Select **Add arrows** from the shortcut menu.
23. Select the Front view to add arrows to it.

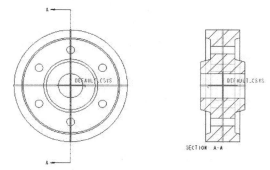

SECTION A-A

Now, you have to create the Isometric view.

24. On the ribbon, click **Layout** tab > **Model Views** panel > **General View** .
25. Select the **No Combined state** option and click **OK**.

26. Click on the top right corner of the drawing sheet to position the view.
27. On the **Drawing View** dialog, select **Standard Orientation** from the **Model view names** list.
28. Set the **Default Orientation** to **Isometric**.
29. Type-in **Isometric** in the **View name** box and click **Apply**.
30. Select the **View Display** option from the **Categories** list.
31. Set the **Display Style** to **No Hidden**.
32. Click **OK** on the **Drawing View** dialog.
33. Drag the Isometric view and position it, as shown below.

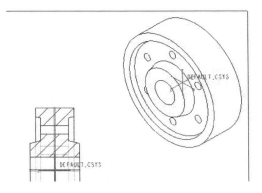

Add Axis lines

1. On the ribbon, click **Annotate** tab > **Annotations** panel > **Show Model Annotations** .
2. On the **Show Model Annotations** dialog, click the **Show Model datums** tab and select **Type > Axes**.
3. Press and hold the Ctrl key and select the holes and revolved feature of the section view.

SECTION A-A

4. Click the **Select All** ⊠̄ button located at the bottom-left corner on the **Show Model Annotations** dialog.
5. Click **Apply**.
6. Select the Front view by clicking on its view boundaries.
7. Select the axis lines to be included in the drawing view. Click **OK**.

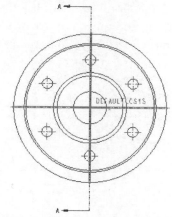

8. Select the center mark of the hole in the first quadrant.
9. Right-click and select **Edit Attachment**.
10. On the **Menu Manager**, click **Through Geometry** and select the select the axis line passing through the center.

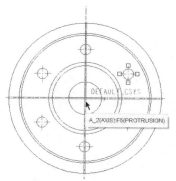

11. Click **Done/Return** on the **Menu Manager**. The orientation of the center mark is changed.

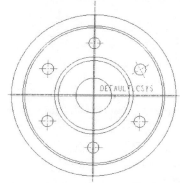

12. Likewise, change the orientation of the other center marks, as shown below.

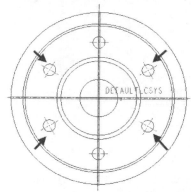

Showing Dimensions of the Geometry

1. On the ribbon, click **Annotate** tab > **Annotations** panel > **Show Model Annotations** ⊠̄.
2. On the **Show Model Annotations** dialog, click the **Show the model dimensions** ⊢⊣ tab.
3. Select the section view from the drawing sheet. You will notice that the model dimensions appear.
4. Select the dimensions from the section view, as shown below.

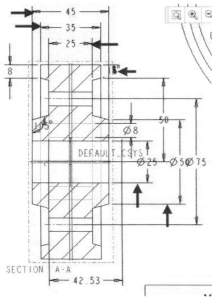

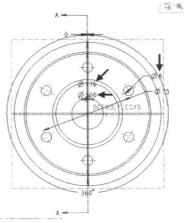

5. Click **OK** on the dialog.
6. Click and drag the diameter 50 dimension.

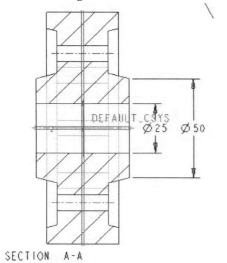

11. Click and drag the diameter dimensions.
12. Select the diameter dimension of the small hole.
13. Click the right mouse and select **Properties**.
14. On the **Dimension Properties** dialog, click the **Display** tab.
15. Type-in **6 HOLES** in the **Prefix** box.
16. Type-in **EQUI-SPACED ON 75 PCD** below @D.
17. Click **OK** and drag the dimension.
18. Select the hole diameter dimension, click the right mouse button, and select **Flip Arrows**.
19. Likewise, flip the arrows of the other diameter dimensions.

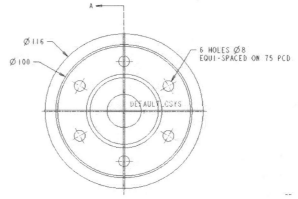

7. Activate the **Show Model Annotations** command.
8. Select the front view.
9. Select the dimensions of the front view, as shown below.
10. Click **OK**.

20. Select the angular dimension on the section view.
21. Right-click and select **Properties**.
22. On the **Dimension Properties** dialog, click the **Display** tab and type-in **TYP** in the **Suffix** box.
23. Click **OK** and drag the dimension.
24. Select the angular dimension.
25. Right-click and select **Flip Arrows** from the shortcut menu.

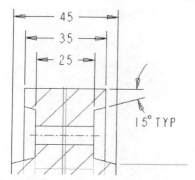

26. Save and close the drawing.

Example 3

In this example, you will create an assembly drawing shown below

.

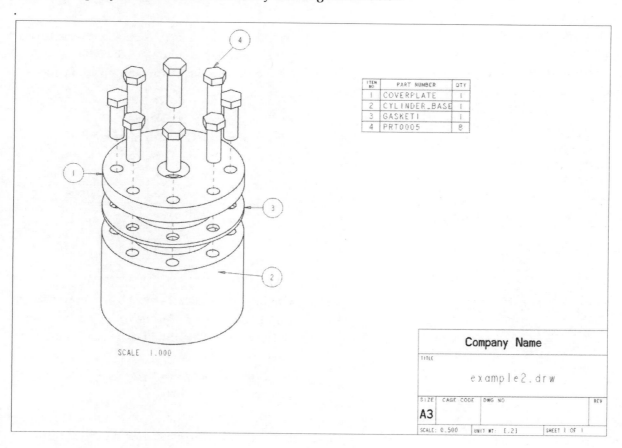

ITEM NO	PART NUMBER	QTY
1	COVERPLATE	1
2	CYLINDER_BASE	1
3	GASKET1	1
4	PRT0005	8

Company Name

TITLE

example2.drw

SIZE	CAGE CODE	DWG NO		REV
A3				
SCALE: 0.500	UNIT WT: [.2]	SHEET 1 OF 1		

SCALE 1.000

Starting the Drawing

1. Start **Creo Parametric 4.0**.
2. Set the *Drawings* folder as current working folder.
3. Copy the Pressure-Cylinder.prt file created in Chapter 10 to the *Drawings* folder.
4. On the **Home** tab, click the **New** button.
5. On the **New** dialog, select **Type > Drawing**.
6. Type-in *Example3* in the **Name** box and uncheck the **Use default template** option.
7. Click **OK**.
8. On the **New Drawing** dialog, click the **Browse** button in the **Default Model** section and select the Pressure-Cylinder.asm file.
9. Click **OK**, and the keep clicking the green check to accept the default values.

Generating Exploded View

1. On the ribbon, click **Layout** tab > **Model Views** panel > **General View** ⬔ .
2. On the **Select Combined State** dialog, select the **No combined State** option and click **OK**.
3. Click on the center of the drawing sheet to position the view.
4. On the **Drawing View** dialog, select **Standard Orientation** from the **Model view names** list.
5. Set the **Default Orientation** to **Isometric**.
6. Type-in **Exploded View** in the **View name** box and click **Apply**.
7. Under the **Categories** section, click the **View States** option.
8. Under the **Explode view** section, check the **Explode components in view** option.
9. Select the name from the **Assembly explode state** drop-down and click **Apply**.
10. In the **Categories** section, click the **Scale** option.
11. Select **Custom Scale** and type-in **1** in the box next to it.
12. Click **OK**.
13. Change the **Display Style** to **No Hidden**.

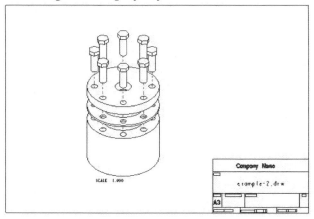

Adding Bill of Materials and Balloons

1. On the ribbon, click **Table** tab > **Table** panel > **Table** drop-down > **Quick Tables** > **Assembly** > **bom description down**.

2. Position the table at the top right corner on the drawing sheet.

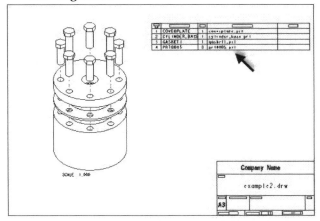

3. Click in the Notes column of the table.
4. On the ribbon, click **Table** tab > **Table** panel > **Select Table** drop-down > **Select Column** ⊞ .
5. Right-click and select **Delete**.
6. Click **Yes** on the **Confirm** message box.
7. Likewise, delete the **Description** column.

ITEM NO	PART NUMBER	QTY
1	COVERPLATE	1
2	CYLINDER_BASE	1
3	GASKET1	1
4	PRT0005	8

8. On the ribbon, click **Table** tab > **Balloons** panel > **Create Balloons** drop-down > **Create Balloons-All**. This automatically generates the balloons.
9. Select the balloons one-by-one, and then drag to arrange them properly.

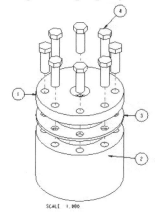

10. Save and close the drawing.

Questions

1. How to create drawing views using **General View** command?
2. How do you show or hide hidden edges of a drawing view?
3. How do you retrieve dimensions of the 3D part model?
4. How do you control the properties of dimensions and annotations?

5. Describe the procedure to create centerlines and center marks.
6. How do you add symbols and texts to a dimension?
7. How do you add break lines to the drawing view?
8. How do you create aligned section views?
9. How do you create the exploded view of an assembly?

Exercises

Exercise 1

Create orthographic views of the part model shown next. Add dimensions and annotations to the drawing.

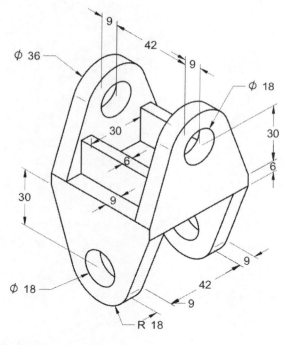

Exercise 2

Create orthographic views and an auxiliary view of the part model shown below. Add dimensions and annotations to the drawing.

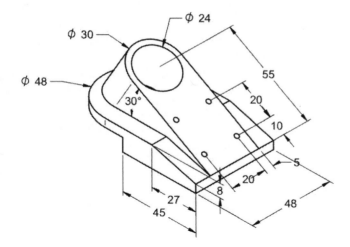

Chapter 11: Sheet Metal Design

You can make sheet metal parts by bending and forming flat sheets of metal. In Creo Parametric, sheet-metal parts can be folded and unfolded enabling you to show them in the flat pattern as well as their bent-up state. There are two ways to design sheet-metal parts in Creo Parametric. Either you can start the sheet-metal part from scratch using sheet-metal features throughout the design process or you can design it as a regular solid part and later convert it to a sheet-metal part. Most commonly, you design sheet-metal parts in the **Sheetmetal Part** environment from the beginning. In this chapter, you will learn both the approaches.

The topics covered in this chapter are:

- *Planar Walls*
- *Flat Walls*
- *Flanges*
- *Extrusions*
- *Bends*
- *Unbend*
- *Bend back*
- *Flat Pattern*
- *Punch and Die Forms*
- *Conversion to Sheet Metal*

Starting a Sheet Metal part

To start a new sheet metal part, follow the steps given next.

1. Click **Home > Data > New** on the ribbon.
2. On the **New** dialog, select **Type > Part** and **Subtype > Sheetmetal**.
3. Type the name of the part, and uncheck the **Use template** option.
4. On the **New File Options** dialog, select the required template and click **OK**.

Sheetmetal Model Properties

Sheetmetal Model Properties define the bend allowance, bend size, relief, and bend orders and other design rules. You can define these properties by using the **Model Properties** dialog.

1. On the File menu, click **Prepare > Model Properties**.
2. On the **Model Properties** dialog, click the **change** option next to **Thickness**. The **Material Thickness** dialog appears.
3. On the **Material Thickness** dialog, type-in the **Material Thickness** value and click **Regenerate**.
4. On the **Model Properties** dialog, click the **change** option next to **Bend Allowance**.
5. On the **Sheetmetal Preferences** dialog, type-in the K-factor/Y-factor value in the **Factor value** box.

The **K Factor** is the ratio that represents the location of neutral sheet measured from the inside face with respect to the thickness of the sheet metal part. The Neutral Factor defines the bend allowance of the sheet metal part. The standard formula that calculates the bend allowance is given below.

$$BA = \frac{\pi(R + KT)A}{180}$$

BA = Bend Allowance

R = Bend Radius

K = Neutral Factor = t/T

T = Material Thickness

t = Distance from inside face to the neutral sheet

A = Bend Angle

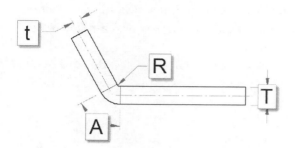

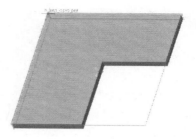

You can also define the bend allowance by using your own bend allowance table. Click the **Part Bend Allowances Table** button. On the **Bend Allowances Tables** dialog, select a table from the list and click the arrow pointing ⇒ towards right. Click **OK** to close the dialog.

6. Click **OK**.
7. Click the **Close** button on the **Model Properties** dialog.

Planar Wall

The planar wall is a basic type of sheet metal feature.

1. To create a wall, create a closed sketch on a plane.

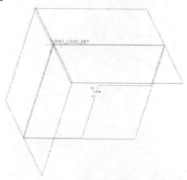

2. On the ribbon, click **Model > Shapes > Planar**.
3. Click on the sketch.
4. On the **Planar** dashboard, type-in a value in the **Thickness** box.
5. Click the **Change Direction** button to reverse the direction of the wall.
6. Click **OK**.

Flat Wall

The second feature after creating a planar wall is flat wall. You can create this feature using a linear edge of a sheet metal part.

1. On the ribbon, click **Model > Shapes > Flat Wall**.
2. Click an edge of the planar wall feature. The wall preview appears on the selected edge.

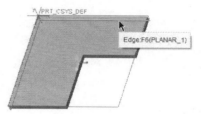

3. On the dashboard, select the wall shape from the drop-down available on the left side.

4. On the dashboard, click the **Shape** tab and set the shape dimensions. Double-click on the dimension values to edit them.

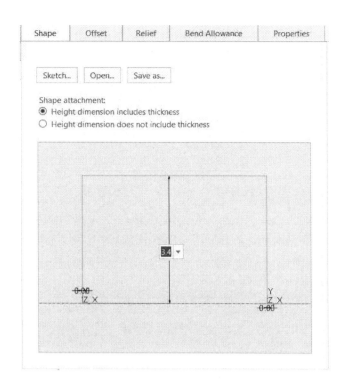

5. Set the method to dimension the radius. The options to dimension radius are given next.

This option creates the bend by specifying the outer bend radius.

This option creates the bend by specifying the inner bend radius.

This option creates the bend by using the default bend side that you have specified on the **Model Properties** dialog.

6. Type-in a value in the **Angle** box.
7. Type-in the bend radius or select the **Thickness** or **2.0*Thickness** option.

8. Click the **Change Thickness side** button, if you want to reverse the thickness side of the wall.
9. Click the **Relief** tab and select the type of relief to be provided to a bend. The options available in this tab are given next.

Rip: This option rips off the bend extremes.

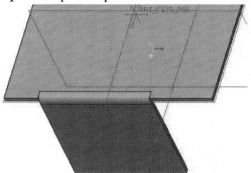

Rectangular: A rectangular relief is applied to bend extremes.

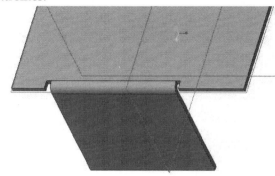

Obround: A round relief is applied to bend extremes.

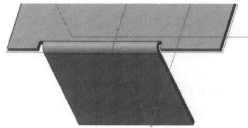

Stretch: The end faces of the bend are stretched at an angle.

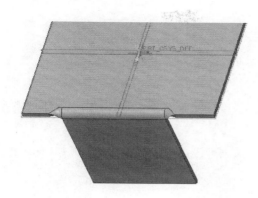

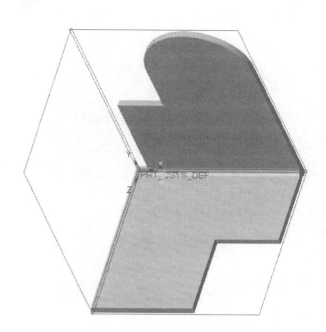

10. Click the green check to complete the flat wall.

Sketch Based Fall Wall on Edge

1. Activate the **Flat** command and select the edge to add a flat wall.
2. Click the **Shape** tab on the dashboard, and then click the **Sketch** button.
3. Delete unwanted entities of the sketch.
4. Draw the profile of the wall and exit the sketch.

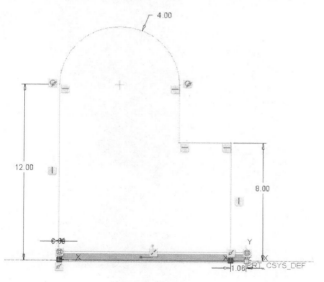

5. Type-in a value in the **Rotation Angle** box, if you want to create an inclined wall.
6. Click the green check to create the wall.

Extrude

The **Extrude** command extrudes an open sketch.

1. Create a sketch on the side face of the sheetmetal as shown.

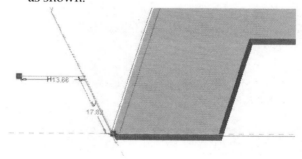

2. Click **OK**.
3. On the ribbon, click **Model > Shapes > Extrude**.
4. On the **Extrude** dashboard, click the **Extrude as wall** icon.
5. Click the **Depth direction** icon to change the extrude direction.
6. Type-in the extrusion distance on the dashboard or drag the extrude handle.
7. Click the **Change material direction** icon to change the thickness side.

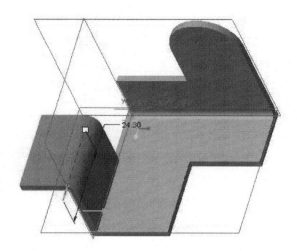

8. Click the **Options** tab on the dashboard.

The **Add bends on sharp edges** option creates bends at the intersections between the sketch elements.

9. Click **OK** to complete the extrusion feature.

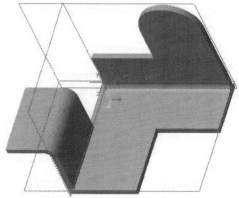

You will notice that there is no bend between the extrusion and the base wall.

 Flange

This command creates a flange by sweeping a parametric profile along the selected edge.

1. On the ribbon, click **Model > Shapes > Flange**.
2. Click on an edge of the planar wall.

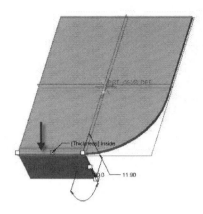

3. Click the **Placement** tab on the dashboard and click **Details**.
4. On the **Chain** dialog, select **Rule-based** and set the **Rule** to **Tangent**.
5. Click **OK** to select the tangentially connected edges. The preview of the flange appears.

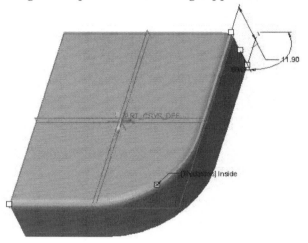

6. On the Dashboard, click the **Shape** tab and modify the **Height** and **Angle** values.
7. Click the **Length** tab and select **Blind** from the first drop-down.

8. Drag the length handle as shown.

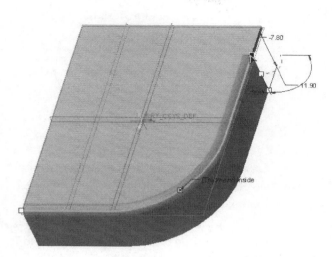

9. On the **Length** tab, select **To selected** from the second drop-down.

10. Select a plane to define the flange end.

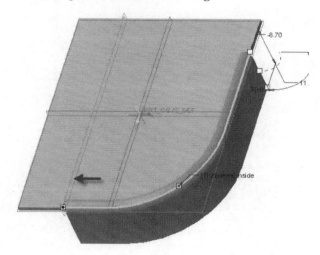

11. On the Dashboard, click the **Offset** tab and check the **Offset wall with respect to attachment edge** option.

12. Select **Type > By Value** and drag the offset handle.

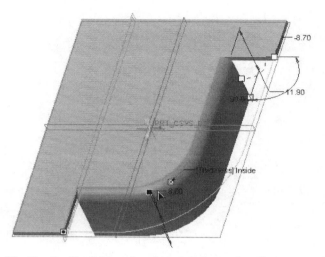

13. On the Dashboard, select **Arc** from the **Shape** drop-down.

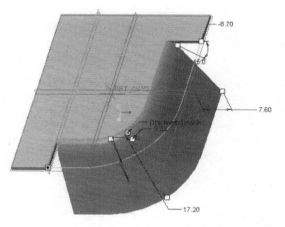

Likewise, you can select other shapes for creating a flange as shown.

I

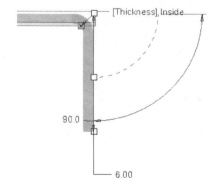

S

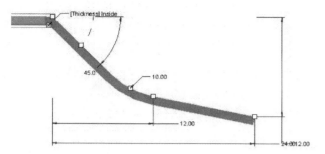

Open

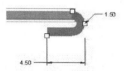

Flushed

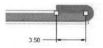

Joggle

Duck

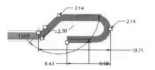

C

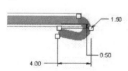

Z

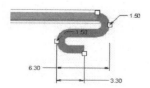

You can also create a user-defined flange by clicking the **Sketch** button on the **Shape** tab.

14. Click the green check on the dashboard to complete the feature.

Corner Relief

The **Corner Relief** command allows you to control the appearance of sheet metal seams. For example, when two flanges meet at a corner, this command allows you to add corner treatment between them.

1. Activate this command (On ribbon, click **Model > Engineering > Corner Relief**). The corner point is selected, automatically.
2. On the **Corner Relief** dashboard, select the required corner relief. For example, select the **Circular** corner relief from the drop-down and click the **Placement** tab. The corner relief types available in the drop-down are:

V-notch

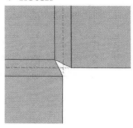

Circular

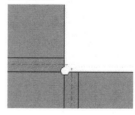

Rectangular

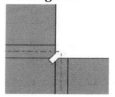

Obround

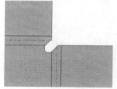

No relief

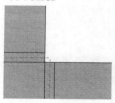

3. On the **Placement** tab, set the **Relief anchor point** type. You can position the anchor point at the Intersection of bend edges or Intersection of bend lines.

Intersection of bend edges

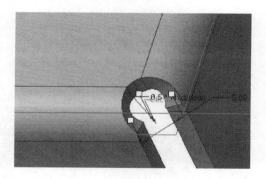

Intersection of bend lines

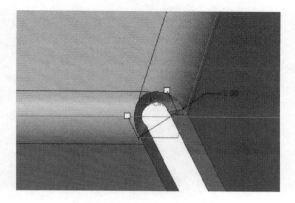

4. Select the Corner relief depth type. You can specify the depth by using the **Blind**, **Up to bend**, **Tangent to bend** options.
5. Type-in the relief width value.

You can offset the corner relief by checking the **Offset perpendicular to bisector** option and rotate the corner relief by checking the **Rotate by origin** option.

6. Click the green check to complete the corner relief.

Bend

In addition to adding flanges and user flanges, you can also bend a flat sheet using the **Bend** command.

1. Draw a sketched line on the flat sheet and click **OK**.

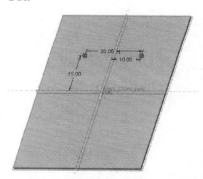

2. On the ribbon, click **Model > Bends > Bend**.
3. Select the sketched line.
4. Click the **Reverse Direction** icon located next to the **Fixed side** icon (or) the horizontal arrow to change the portion to be fixed.

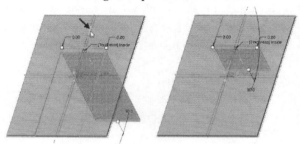

5. Click the vertical arrow that appears on the bend, if you want to reverse the bend direction.
6. Type-in a value in the **Angle** box to change the

folding angle.

7. Select the option to define the material side of the bend feature. These options are given next.

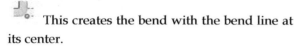 This creates the bend with the bend line at its center.

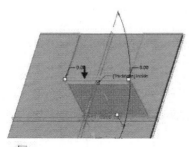

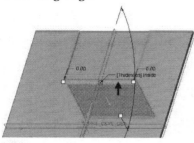 This creates the bend with the bend line at its starting edge.

This creates the bend with the bend line at the intersection of outer faces.

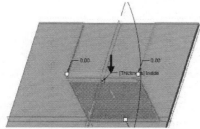

8. Click the **Placement** tab on the dashboard, and then check the **Offset bend line** option. Now, you can drag the bend to offset it from the sketched line.

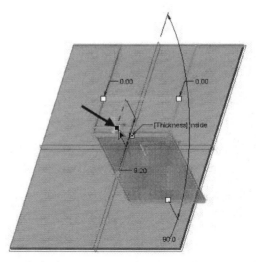

9. Click the green check to complete the bend feature.

Angled Bend

The **Bend** command can also create angled bend without using any sketched line.

1. Activate the **Bend** command and click on the face to bend.
2. Drag the placement handle on to the side edges of the flat sheet.

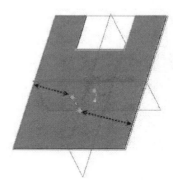

3. Drag the offset handles onto the front edge of the flat sheet.

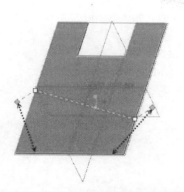

4. Modify the offset dimensions and angle value.

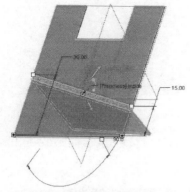

5. On the Dashboard, click the **Relief** tab and select **Type > No relief**.
6. Click the green check to complete the bend feature.

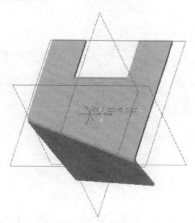

Rolled Bend

The **Bend** command can also bend a sheet by rolling it about a line.

1. Activate the **Bend** command.
2. Click on the flat sheet to be rolled.

3. On the dashboard, click the **Bend Line** tab, and then click the **Sketch** button.
4. Sketch a straight line as shown. Make sure that the end points of the line coincide with the adjacent edges of the sheet. Next, click **OK** on the ribbon.

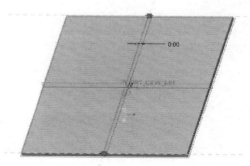

5. On the Dashboard, click the **Bend to end surface** icon (or) right-click and select **Rolled Bend**.
6. On the Dashboard, type-in the **Bend Radius** value.

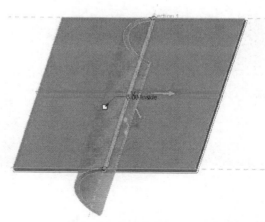

7. On the Dashboard, click the **Bend material up to Bend line** icon.

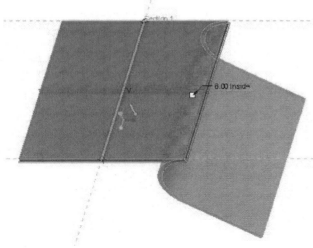

8. Click the **Bend material on Both sides of Bend line** icon.

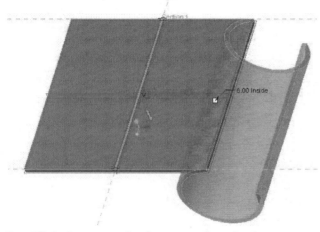

9. Click the green check to complete the feature.

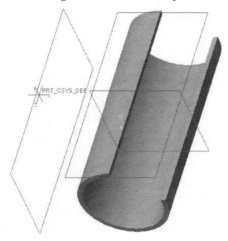

Transition Bend

The **Bend** command allows you to create a transition

between the rolled and flat portions of a sheet metal part.

1. Activate the **Bend** command.
2. Select the sketched line to define the bend.

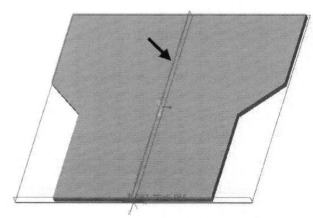

3. On the Dashboard, click the **Bend to end surface** icon (or) right-click and select **Rolled Bend**.

4. On the Dashboard, type-in the Bend Radius .
5. Click the **Bend material on Both sides of Bend line** icon.

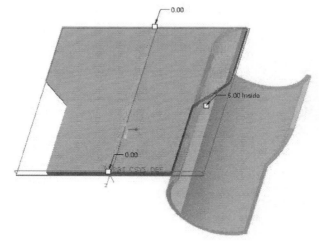

6. On the Dashboard, click the **Transitions** tab and select **Add transition**.
7. Click the **Sketch** button.
8. Sketch the start and end transition line perpendicular to the bend line, and then click **OK** on the ribbon.

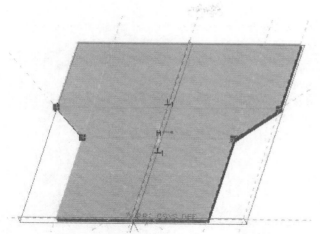

10. Click the green check to complete the feature.

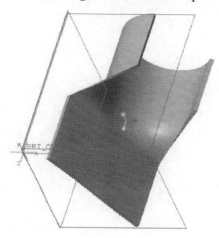

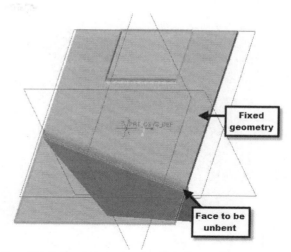

Fixed geometry

Face to be unbent

5. Click the green check to unbend the bent faces.

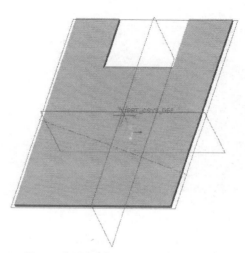

Unbend

This command unfolds a bend to its original position.

1. On the ribbon, click **Model > Bends > Unbend**. The preview of the unbent sheet appears.

Notice that the **Reference selected automatically** icon is active. As a result, the horizontal portion of the sheet is selected as the fixed geometry, automatically.

2. Activate the **Reference selected manually** icon on the Dashboard.
3. Select the edges or bends to be unbend.
4. Click in the **Fixed geometry** collector on the Dashboard and select the face to be fixed.

Bend Back

This command refolds the unfolded bend.

1. Create a bend feature, and then unbend it using the **Unbend** command.

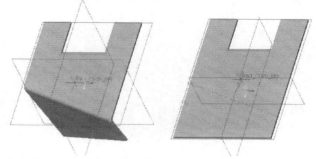

2. Create a sketch on the top face of the flat sheet.

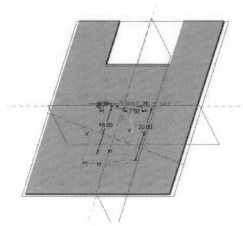

3. Activate the **Extrude** command and create a cutout.

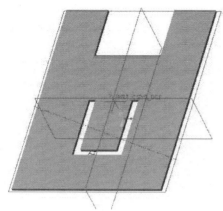

4. On the ribbon, click **Model > Bends > Bend Back**. The references are selected automatically.
5. Click the **Preview** icon on the Dashboard.

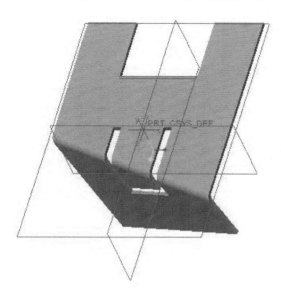

6. Click the **Resume** icon to disable the preview mode.
7. On the Dashboard, click the **Bend Control** tab and select Contour 1.
8. Select **Keep flat** to flatten the contour 1.
9. Click the green check to refold the unfolded bend.

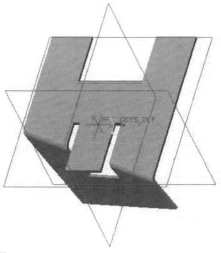

Punch Form

The **Punch Form** command molds a flat sheet using the shape of a reference part. The external surface of the reference part is used mold a flat sheet. For example, the following figure shows a punch and shape created on the sheet metal part.

1. On the ribbon, click **Model > Engineering > Form > Punch Form**.
2. On the **Punch Form** Dashboard, select

CLOSE_FLAT_LOUVER_FORM_MM from the drop-down.

3. Click on the bottom face of the flat sheet to be formed.

4. Drag the offset handles on to the side edges of the sheet.

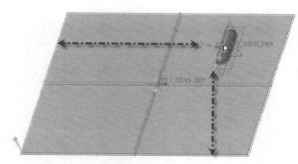

5. Modify the offset dimensions.

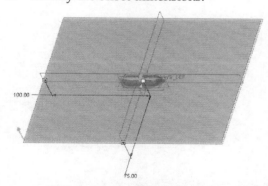

6. On the dashboard, click the **Placement** tab and check the **Add rotation about the first axis** option.

7. Type-in 90 in the **Rotation value** box.

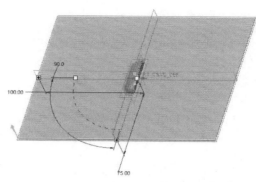

8. On the Dashboard, click the **Copy form model using independent inheritance** icon.

9. On the Dashboard, click the **Shape** tab and click the **Vary Punch Model** button.

10. On the **Varied Items** dialog, click the **Dimensions** tab and select the + button located at the bottom.

11. In the preview window, select the revolve feature of the reference model as shown.

12. Select the dimension as shown.

13. On the **Varied Items** dialog, click in the **New value** box and type-in 50.

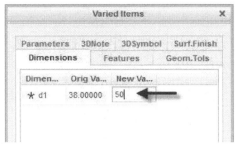

14. Click **OK**.
15. Click the green check to complete the feature.

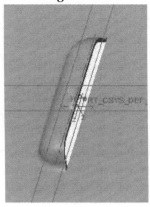

⩗ Die Form

The **Die Form** command (on the ribbon, click **Model > Engineering > Form > Die Form**) adds a form to a flat sheet using the shape of a reference part. The internal surface of the reference part is used to mould a flat sheet. For example, the following figure shows a die and shape created on the sheet metal part. The procedure to create a die form is same as that of punch.

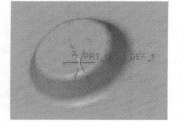

⩗ Sketched Form

The **Sketched Form** command adds a form to a flat sheet by using sketch profile.

1. On the ribbon, click **Model >Engineering > Form > Sketched Form**.
2. On the dashboard, click the **Create Punch** icon located at left side.
3. Click on the sketch profile as shown.

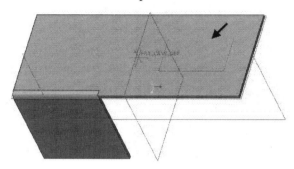

4. Type-in the depth value (or) the handle to define the depth.

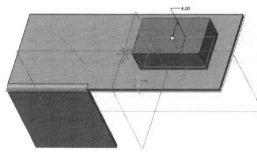

5. On the Dashboard, click the **Options** tab and check the **Add taper** option.
6. Drag the taper handle (or) type a value in the taper box.

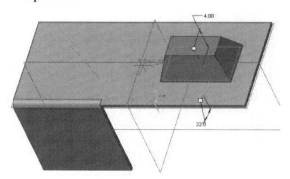

7. On the **Options** tab, check the **Nonplacement edges** option. The side edges are rounded.

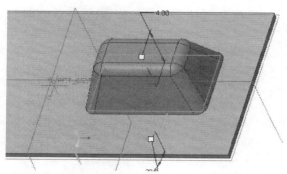

8. On the **Options** tab, check the **Placement edges** option. The placement edges are rounded.

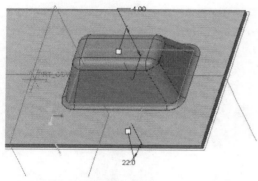

11. On the **Options** tab, click in the **Exclude Surfaces** box and click on the front face of the form. The selected face is removed.

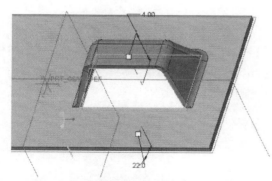

12. Click the right mouse button in the **Exclude Surface** box and select **Remove**.
13. Uncheck the **Capped ends** options to remove the end surface of the form.

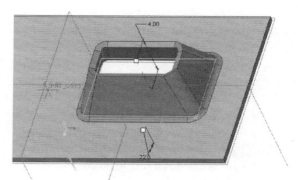

14. On the Dashboard, click the **Change Form Direction** icon next to the depth value box. The form direction is reversed.

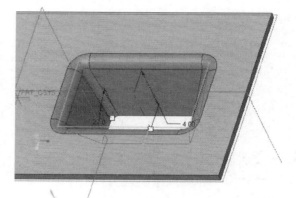

15. On the Dashboard, click the **Change Material Direction** icon next to the **Pause** icon. The material direction is reversed.

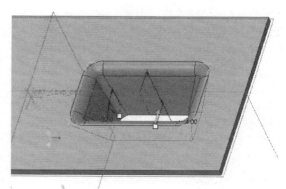

16. Click the green check to complete the feature.

Creating the Pierced Sketched Form

If you click **Create a piercing** icon on the dashboard, the height of the stamp will be half of the sheet metal thickness. You can increase the height value up to the sheet metal thickness.

1. Activate the **Sketched Form** command and click on the sheet to add the form.
2. Draw the profile of the form feature and click **OK**.

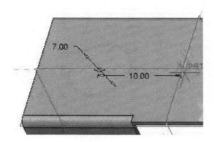

3. On the Dashboard, click the **Create a piercing** ⬇ icon.
4. Click the **Change Form Direction** icon.
5. Click the green check.

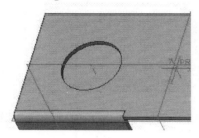

Flat Pattern Preview

The **Flat Pattern Preview** command lets you to preview the flattened view in a separate window.

1. On the **Graphics** toolbar, click **Flat Pattern Preview**. A separate window appears with the flattened view.

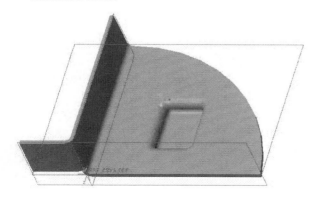

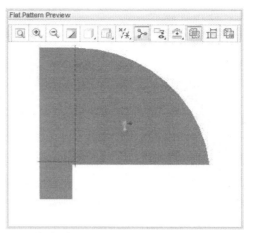

2. Click the **Bounding Box** icon in the **Flat Pattern Preview** window. The program displays the bounding dimensions.

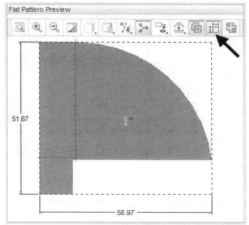

3. Click the **Form Geometry** icon and uncheck the **Flatten Forms** option. The forms are not flattened.

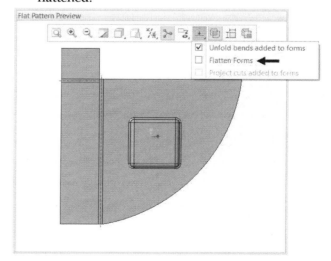

4. On the **Graphics** toolbar, click **Flat Pattern Preview** to close the preview window.

Flat Pattern

The **Flat Pattern** command flattens the part so that you can easily display the manufacturing information. Before creating a flat pattern, you need to configure the settings on the **Flat Pattern Preview** window.

1. On the ribbon, click **Model > Bends > Flat Pattern**.

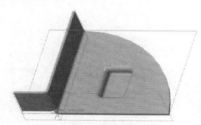

2. Click the green check on the Dashboard. The program flattens the entire sheet metal part. In addition, the bend annotations appear on the bends.

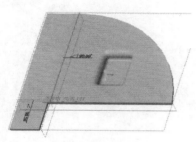

Notice that the form geometry is not flattened as the **Flatten Forms** option is unchecked in the **Flat Pattern Preview** window.

3. Activate a sheetmetal command from the ribbon and notice that the flat pattern mode is disabled.

Extruded Cuts

When it is necessary to remove material from a sheet metal part, you must use the **Extrude** command.

1. Draw a sketch, and then click the **Extrude** icon on the **Shapes** panel.
2. Select the sketch, if not selected.

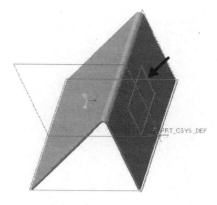

3. On the dashboard, set the depth type to **Through All**.
4. Click the **Preview** icon on the Dashboard.

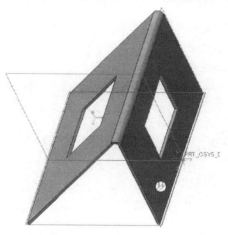

5. Change the **Display Style** to **Wireframe** and **Orientation** to **Front**. Notice that the cut is created normal to the sheet metal surface.

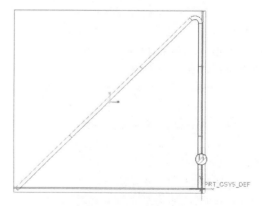

6. Click the **Resume** icon on the Dashboard.

7. On the Dashboard, deactivate the **Remove material normal to surface** icon. Notice that the cut is created normal to the sketch plane.

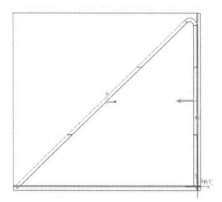

8. Click the green check to complete the feature.

Revolve

This command creates a sheetmetal by revolving a profile about an axis.

1. Create an open sketch along with an axis.

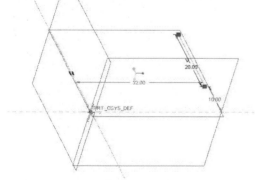

2. On the ribbon, expand the **Shapes** panel and click the **Revolve** icon.
3. On the Dashboard, click the **Revolve a wall** icon.
4. Type-in the revolution angle and sheetmetal thickness on the Dashboard. Note that the revolution angle should be less than 360 so that you can create a flat pattern.
5. Click the green check to complete the feature.

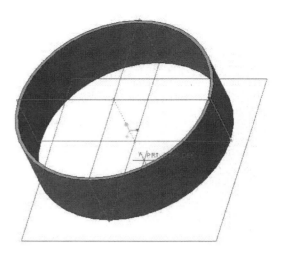

6. Activate the **Flat Pattern** command (on the ribbon, click **Model > Bends > Flat Pattern**).
7. Select an edge on the end face of the revolved sheetmetal to define the fixed end.

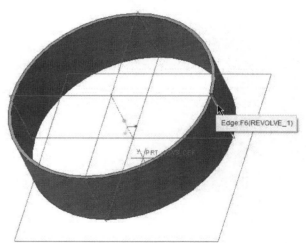

8. Click the green check to create the flat pattern.

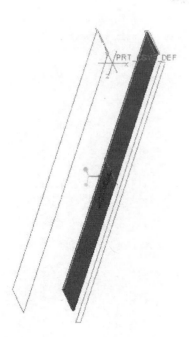

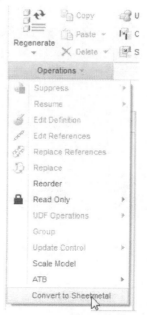

Conversion

Creo Parametric has a special command called **Conversion**, which automates the process of converting an already existing solid part into a sheet metal part.

1. Create a part in the solid **Part** environment.

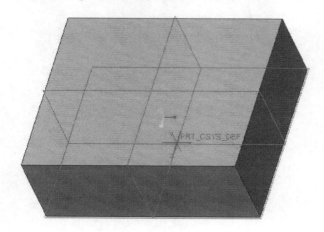

2. On the ribbon, expand the **Operations** panel and select **Convert to Sheetmetal**.

3. On the **First Wall** Dashboard, click the **Shell** icon and select a face to remove.

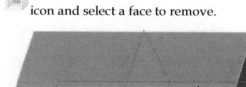

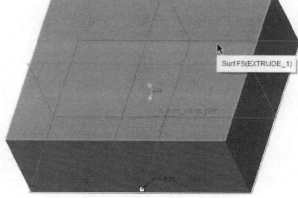

4. Type the thickness value on the Dashboard and click the green check. The solid part is converted into sheetmetal part. Now, you need to make this part developable by using the **Conversion** command.

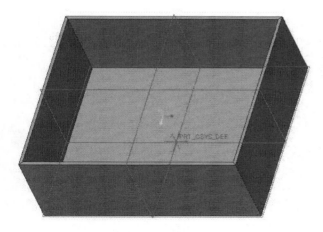

5. On the ribbon, click **Model > Engineering > Conversion**.

6. On the **Conversion** Dashboard, click the **Edge Rip** [M].

7. Click the edges to be ripped.

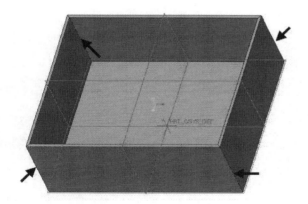

8. On the Dashboard, click the **Placement** tab and select the edge treatment **Type** for each edge.

9. Define the edge treatment parameters on the **Placement** tab and click the green check.

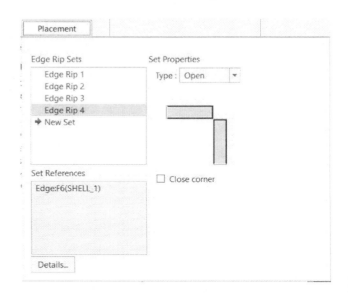

10. Click the green check on the **Conversion** Dashboard. Now, you can perform other sheet metal operations.

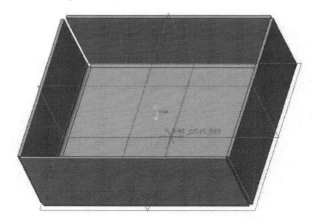

Examples

Example 1

In this example, you will construct the sheet metal part shown below.

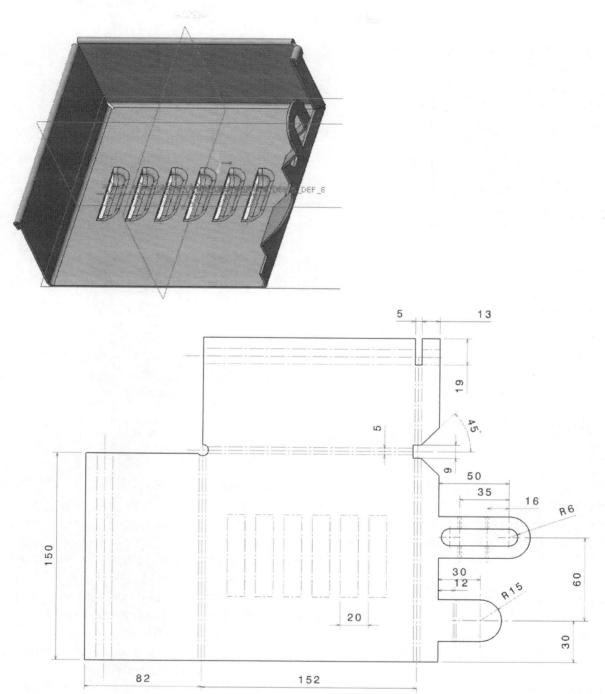

Unfolded view
Scale: 2:3

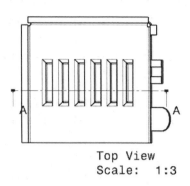

Top View
Scale: 1:3

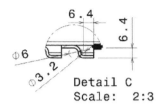

Detail C
Scale: 2:3

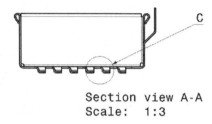

Section view A-A
Scale: 1:3

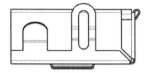

Auxiliary view B
Scale: 1:3

1. Start **Creo Parametric 4.0**.
2. Create a folder with the name *Sheet Metal Design* and set it as current working folder.
3. On the Quick Access Toolbar, click the **New** button.
4. On the **New** dialog, select **Type > Part**.
5. Select **Sub-Type > Sheetmetal**.
6. Type-in *Example1* in the **Name** box and uncheck the **Use default template** option.
7. Click **OK**.
8. On the **New File Options** dialog, select **mmns_part_sheetmetal** option and click **OK**.
9. Click **File > Prepare > Model Properties**.
10. On the **Model Properties** dialog, click the **change** option next to **Thickness**.
11. Type-in 1.6 in the **Material Thickness** box and click **Regenerate**.
12. Click the **change** option next to **Bend allowance**.

13. On the **Sheetmetal Preferences** dialog, select the **K factor** option and type-in 0.33 in the **Factor value** box.
14. Click the **Bends** option from the left side of the dialog and type-in 2.4 in the **Bend radius** box.
15. Click the **Reliefs** option from the left side of the dialog and select **Rip** from the **Type** drop-down under the **Bend relief settings** section.
16. Leave the other default values, click **OK**, and close the **Model Properties** dialog.
17. Create a sketch on the XY plane and exit the sketch mode.

Sheet Metal Design

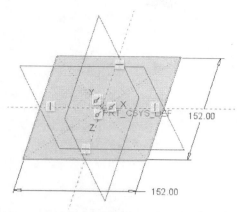

18. On the ribbon, click **Model** tab > **Shapes** panel > **Planar** .
19. Select the sketch.
20. Click the green check to create the sheet metal wall.

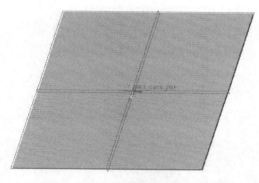

21. On the ribbon, click **Model** tab > **Shapes** panel > **Flange** .
22. Click on the bottom back edge of the sheet metal wall.

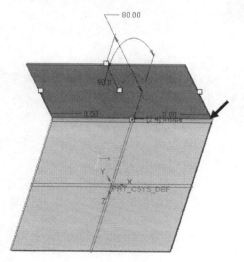

23. On the **Flange** dashboard, click the **Placement** tab, and then click **Details**.
24. On the **Chain** dialog, click the **References** tab.
25. Select the **Rule-based** option, and the select **Partial Loop** from the **Rule** section.
26. Select the bottom edge of the left side face.

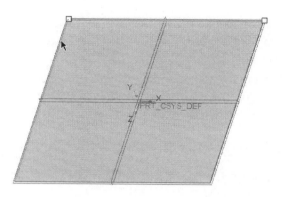

27. Click **OK** on the **Chain** dialog.

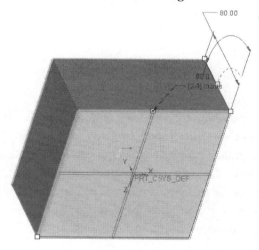

28. On the **Flange** dashboard, click the **Offset** tab.
29. On the **Offset** tab, check the **Offset wall with respect to attachment edge** option.
30. Select **By value** from the **Type** drop-down.
31. Select **Origin** from the **Measure** to drop-down.
32. Type 1.6 in the **Offset** box.

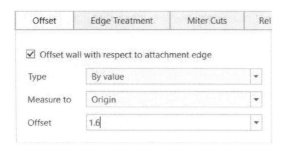

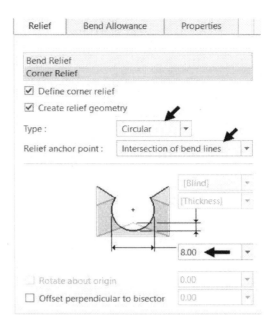

33. On the **Flange** dashboard, click the **Edge Treatment** tab.
34. On the **Edge Treatment** tab, select **Open** from the **Type** drop-down.
35. Check the **Closer corner** option.

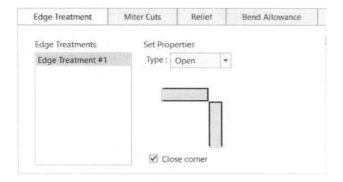

36. On the **Flange** dashboard, click the **Relief** tab.
37. Select the **Corner Relief** option from the list.
38. Select the **Circular** option from the **Type** drop-down.
39. Select the **Intersection of bend lines** option from the **Relief anchor point** drop-down.
40. Type **8** in the **Relief width** box.

41. Double-click on the length dimension of the flange and type 65. Next, press Enter.

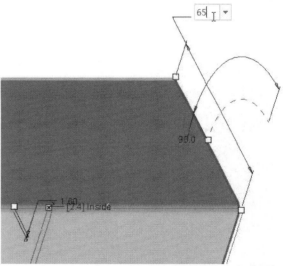

42. Click the green check to create the flange on the selected edges.

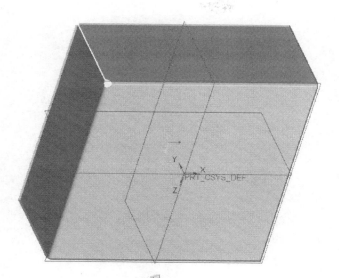

43. Activate the **Flat** command and click on the right bottom edge of the sheet metal.
44. On the **Flat** dashboard, select **User Defined** from the drop-down located at the left side.
45. On the **Flat** dashboard, click the **Shape** tab, and then click the **Sketch** button.
46. Leave the default settings on the **Sketch** dialog, and then click the **Sketch** button.
47. Click the **Sketch View** icon on the **Graphics** toolbar.
48. Create the sketch, as shown.

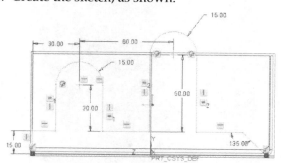

49. Click **OK** on the **Sketch** tab of the ribbon.
50. Click the **Offset** tab on the dashboard.
51. On the **Offset** tab, check the **Offset wall with respect to attachment edge** option.
52. Select **Add to part edge** from **Type** the drop-down.
53. Click the green check on the dashboard to create the flat wall.

54. Set the height of the flat wall to **65** and click the green check.

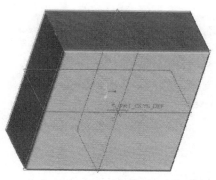

55. On the ribbon, click **Model** tab > **Shapes** panel > **Flat** .
56. Select the right edge of the flange.

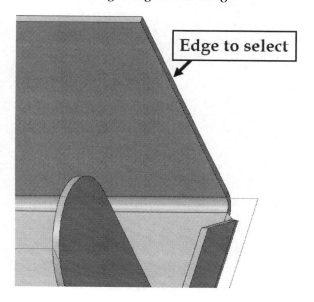

Edge to select

57. On the **Flat** dashboard, select **User Defined** from the drop-down located at the left side.
58. On the **Flat** dashboard, click the **Shape** tab, and select the **Sketch** button.
59. Leave the default settings on the **Sketch** dialog, and then click the **Sketch** button.
60. Click the **Sketch View** icon on the **Graphics** toolbar.
61. Create the sketch, as shown.

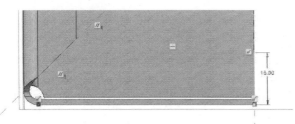

62. Click **OK** on the **Sketch** tab of the ribbon.
63. Click the **Offset** tab on the dashboard.
64. On the **Offset** tab, check the **Offset wall with respect to attachment edge** option.
65. Select **Add to part edge** from **Type** the drop-down.
66. Click the green check on the dashboard to create the flat wall.

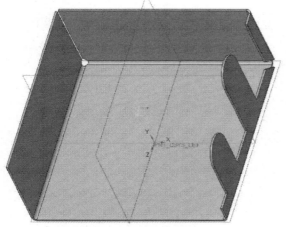

67. Create a sketched line on the outer face of the flat wall, as shown.

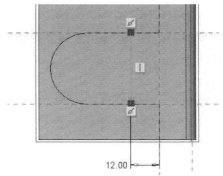

68. On the ribbon, click **Model** tab > **Bends** panel > **Bend** drop-down > **Bend** .
69. On the Dashboard, click the **Bend On Other Side** icon.
70. Type-in **45** in the **Angle** box.
71. Click the **Change bend direction** icon next to the **Angle** box.
72. Select **Bend Angle From Straight** from the **Bend angle type** drop-down.
73. Click the green check to complete the feature.

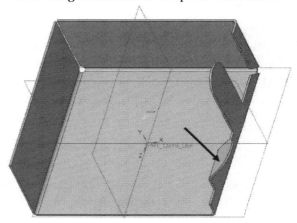

74. Sketch a horizontal line on the vertical wall exit the sketch.

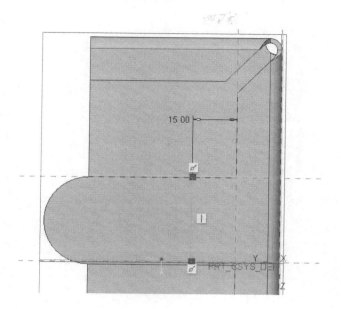

75. Activate the **Bend** command and bend the wall using the sketched line. The bend angle is 45 degrees. Use the **Change bend direction** ⟋ icon, if required.

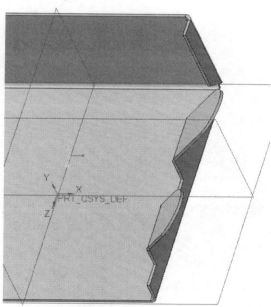

76. Sketch another horizontal line on the inclined face of the wall and bend it in the reverse direction. The bend angle is 45 degrees. Use the **Change location of fixed side** ⟋ icon, if required.

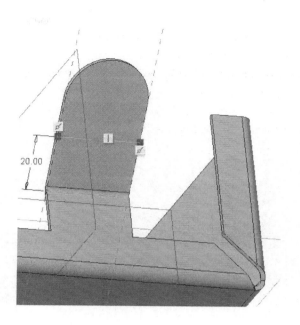

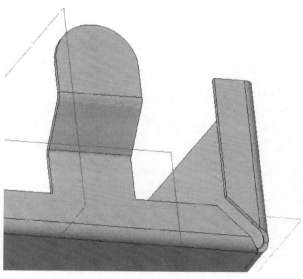

77. On the ribbon, click **Model** tab > **Bends** panel > **Unbend** .

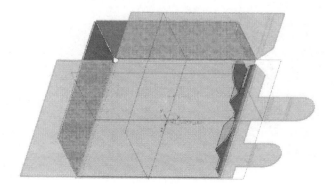

78. Click the green check to unbend the sheetmetal part.

79. Draw a sketch on the sheet metal part, as shown below.

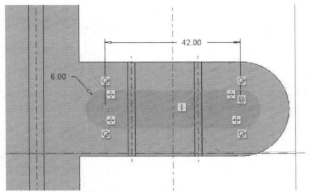

80. Exit the sketch and activate the **Extrude** command (on the ribbon, click **Model** tab > **Shapes** > **Extrude**).

81. Create an extruded cut, as shown below.

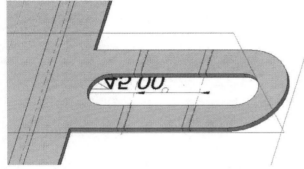

82. On the ribbon, click **Model** tab > **Bends** panel > **Bend Back** .

83. Click the green check to unbend the sheetmetal part.

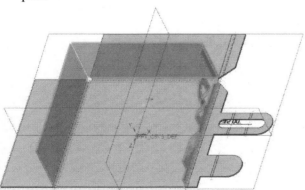

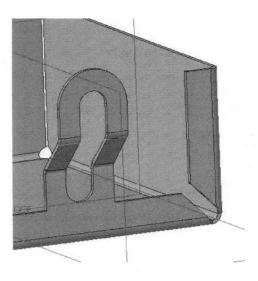

84. On the ribbon, click **Model** tab > **Shapes** panel > **Flange** .

85. On the Dashboard, select the C option from the drop-down located at the left side.

86. Click on the inner edge of the left-side wall.

87. Double-click on the length dimension of the flange and enter 8.

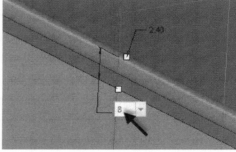

88. Click the green check to create the C-flange.

89. Likewise, create C-flanges on other vertical walls.

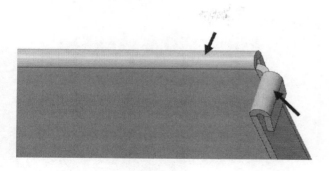

90. On the ribbon, click **Model** tab > **Engineering** panel > **Form** drop-down > **Punch Form** icon.
91. On the Dashboard, select CLOSE_FLAT_LOUVER_FORM_MM from the drop-down located at the left side.
92. Click on the top face of the horizontal planar wall.
93. Drag and align the placement handles to the left-side wall and front plane.
94. Click the **Placement** tab and specify the settings, as shown.

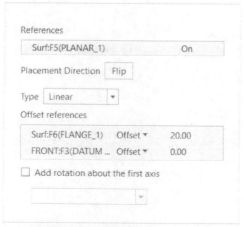

95. Position the punch tool, as shown below.

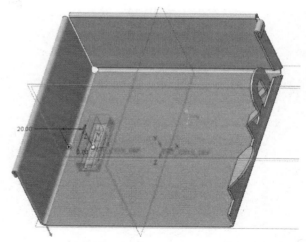

96. On the dashboard, click the **Copy form model using independent inheritance** option.
97. Click the **Shape** tab, and then click the **Vary Punch Model** button.
98. On the **Varied Items** dialog, click the **Dimensions** tab.
99. In the preview window, click on the features, as shown.

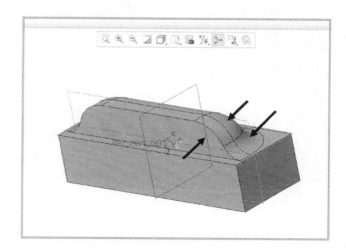

100. Click the plus icon, and then select the dimensions, as shown.

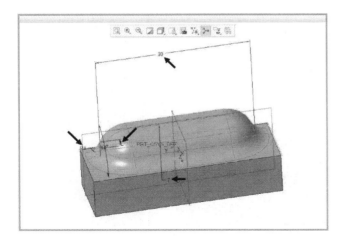

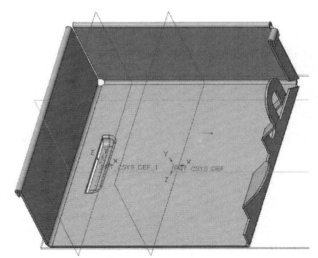

101. Click in the **New Value** box of the first d1 dimension.
102. Type 50 and press Enter.
103. Likewise, change the other values, as shown.

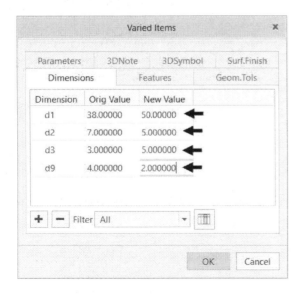

104. Click **OK** on the **Varied Items** dialog.
105. Click the green check to create the louver punch.

106. Select the louver punch.
107. On the ribbon, click **Model** tab > **Editing** panel > **Pattern** drop-down > **Pattern**.
108. On the Dashboard, select the **Dimension** option from the drop-down located at the left side.
109. Select the dimension displayed along the x-axis.

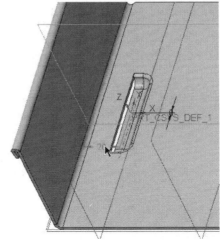

110. Type-in 20 in the value box and press Enter.

111. Type-in 6 as the Pattern member count in the first direction box.

112. Click the green check to create the pattern.

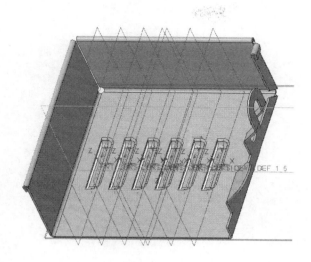

113. On the **Graphics** toolbar, click **Flat Pattern Preview** . This displays the flat pattern preview of the sheet metal part.

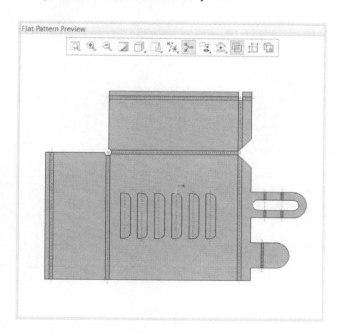

114. In the **Flat Pattern Preview** window, click the **Bounding box** icon to display the dimensions of the bounding box.

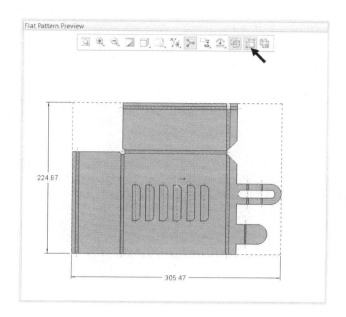

115. On the **Graphics** toolbar, click **Flat Pattern Preview** to close the **Flat Pattern Preview** window.
116. On the ribbon, click **Model > Bends** panel > **Flat Pattern**.
117. Click the green check on the dashboard to create the flash pattern.
118. Save and close the sheet metal part.

Questions

1. Describe parameters that can be specified on the **Model Properties** dialog.
2. Define the term 'K Factor'.
3. List any two sheet metal part parameters that can be overridden when creating a feature.
4. What is the use of the **Corner Relief** command?
5. List the types of flange walls that can be created in Creo Parametric?
6. How is the **Conversion** command useful?
7. What are the corner relief types available?
8. What is the difference between a punch and die form?

Exercises

Exercise 1

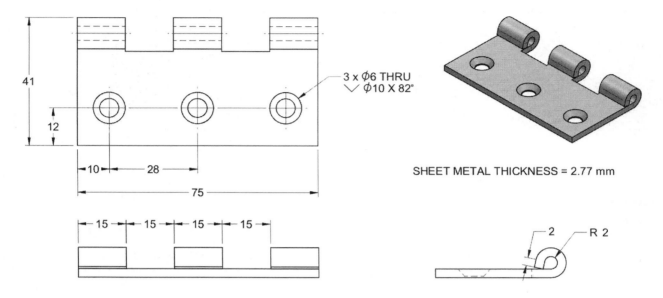

3 x ⌀6 THRU
⌵ ⌀10 X 82°

41

12

10

28

75

15 — 15 — 15 — 15

SHEET METAL THICKNESS = 2.77 mm

2 — R 2

Exercise 2

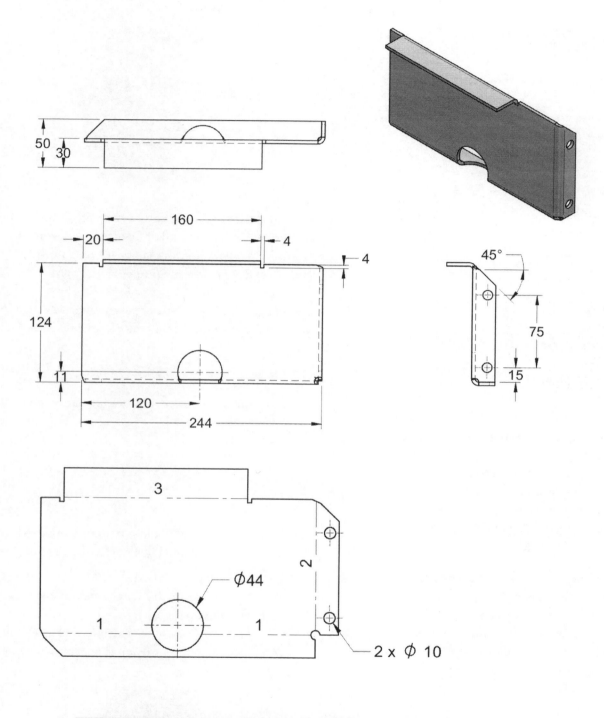

Sequence	Feature	Radius	Angle	Direction	Included Angle
1	Bend 1	3.58 mm	90.00 deg	Down	90.00 deg
2	Bend 2	3.58 mm	90.00 deg	Down	90.00 deg
3	Bend 3	3.58 mm	90.00 deg	Up	90.00 deg

Chapter 12: Surface Design

The topics covered in this chapter are:

- *Basic surfaces*
- *Datum Geometry*
- *Curves*
- *Splines*
- *Boundary Blend*
- *Fill surfaces*
- *Offset Surfaces*
- *Trim*
- *Merge*
- *Solidify*
- *Extend*
- *Mirror*
- *Copy and Paste Surfaces*
- *Mirror*
- *Thicken Surface*

Creo Parametric Surfacing commands can be used to create complex geometries that are very difficult to create using standard extrudes, revolve features, and so on. Surface modeling can also be used to edit and fix the broken imported parts. In this chapter, you learn the basics of surfacing commands that are mostly used. The surfacing commands are available in the **Part** environment.

Creo Parametric offers a rich set of surface design commands. A surface is an infinitely thin piece of geometry. For example, consider a cube shown in figure. It has six faces. Each of these faces is a surface, an infinitely thin piece of geometry that acts as a boundary in 3D space. Surfaces can be simple or complex shapes.

In solid modeling, when you have created solid features such as an extruded feature or a Revolved feature, Creo Parametric creates a set of features (surfaces) that enclose a volume. The airtight enclosure is considered as a solid body. The advantage of using the surfacing commands is that you can design a model with more flexibility.

Extrude

1. To create an extruded surface, first create an open or closed sketch.

2. On the ribbon, click **Model > Shapes > Extrude**.
3. Select the sketch and click the **Extrude as surface** icon on the dashboard.
4. Type-in a value in the **Depth** box available or drag the Depth handle.
5. Click **Preview** to view the extruded surface. You will notice that the extrusion is not capped at the ends.

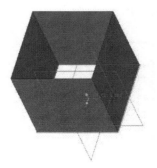

6. Click the **Resume** on the Dashboard.
7. Click the **Options** tab on the Dashboard and check the **Capped ends** option. The ends are capped.
8. Click the green check to complete the feature.

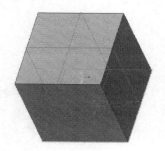

Even if you create an enclosed surface, Creo Parametric will not recognize it as a solid body. You will learn to convert a surface body into a solid later in this chapter.

Revolve

1. To create a revolved surface, first create an open or closed profile and the axis of revolution.

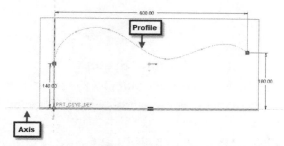

2. On the ribbon, click **Model > Shapes > Revolve**.
3. On the Dashboard, click the **Revolve as surface** icon.
4. Select the sketch.
5. Type-in the angle of revolution in the **Angle 1** box and click the green check.

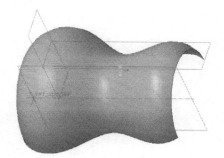

Likewise, you can create surface using other solid modeling commands such as **Sweep, Helical Sweep, Swept Blend, Blend,** and **Rotational Blend**. These commands are already covered in earlier chapters.

Datum Geometry

Creo Parametric has commands to create three dimensional curves and datum elements. They help you to create complex surfaces.

Point

This command creates a point in the 3D space.

1. On the ribbon, click **Model > Datum > Point**.
2. Click on a supporting plane or surface.

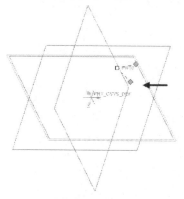

3. Click the right mouse button and select **Offset References**.
4. Press the Ctrl key and select the offset references.

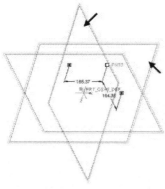

5. Modify the offset reference values on the **Datum Point** dialog, and click **OK**.

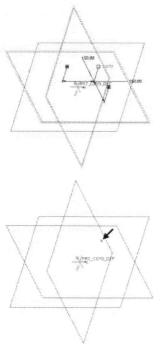

6. Create a new datum plane offset from the Top plane.

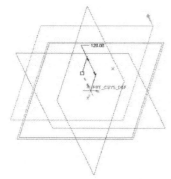

7. Press the Ctrl key and select offset, front and right plane.

8. Activate the **Point** command (On the ribbon, click **Model > Datum > Point**). A new datum point appears at the intersection of the selected planes.

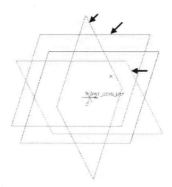

9. Click **OK**.

*⁂ Offset Coordinate System

This command creates a point by using the offset values from an existing coordinate system. You can specify these values in the Cartesian, Cylindrical, or Spherical coordinate system.

1. On the ribbon, click **Model > Datum > Point > Offset Coordinate System**.
2. Select an existing coordinate system from the graphics window.

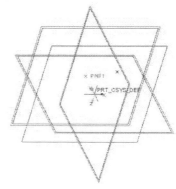

3. On the **Datum Point** dialog, select **Type > Cartesian**.
4. On the **Datum Point** dialog, click in the table

and enter the X, Y, and Z values.

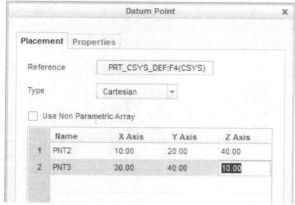

5. Click **OK**.

~ Curve through Points

This command creates a three dimensional curve through selected points.

1. On the **Model** tab of the ribbon, expand the **Datum** panel and click **Curve > Curve through Points**.
2. Select a point.
3. Likewise, select other points one-by-one.

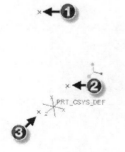

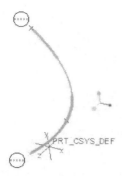

4. On the dashboard, click the **Placement** tab and select **Point 2** from the list.
5. On the **Placement** tab, select the **Straight line** option. A straight line is created between the **Point 2** and **Point 1**.

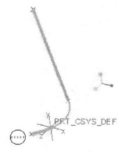

6. Select **Point 3** from the list and select **Straight line**.

7. Select **Point 2** from the list and check the **Add fillet** option.
8. Type-in a value in the **Radius** box.

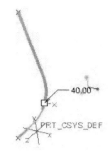

9. Click the green check to complete the curve.

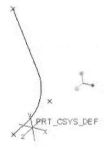

Project

This command projects an element on to a supporting surface.

1. On the ribbon, click **Model > Editing > Project**.
2. Select the element to project.
3. On the dashboard, click in the **Surfaces** box and select the supporting surface.
4. Select **Direction > Normal to surface**. This projects the element in the direction normal to the supporting surface. You can select the **Along direction** option to define the direction of projection. You can use a line or plane to define the direction.

Normal to surface

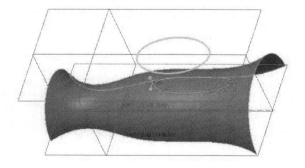

Along direction

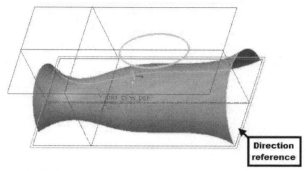

5. Click the green check.

Intersect

This command creates curve at the intersection of two elements.

1. Press the Ctrl key and select two intersecting elements.

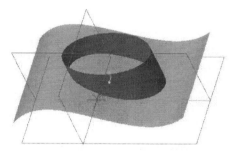

2. On the ribbon, click **Model > Editing > Intersect**. A curve appears at the intersection of the two surfaces.

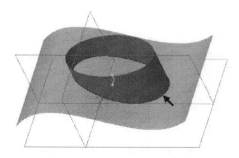

Splines

Splines are non-uniform curves, which are used to create smooth and ergonomic shapes. You have learnt to create splines earlier in Chapter 2. Now, you will learn to modify splines.

1. Start a sketch and create a spline as shown.

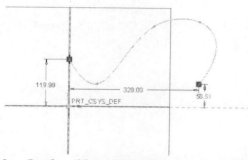

2. On the ribbon, click **Sketch > Operations > Select > One-by-One**.
3. Click on the Interpolation point as shown.

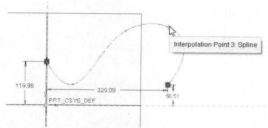

4. Drag the point and notice that the spline is changed.

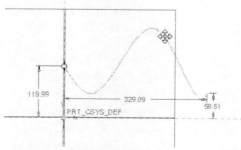

5. Click to release the point.
6. On the ribbon, click **Sketch > Dimension > Dimension** ↔.
7. Click on the Interpolation Point and select the vertical axis of the sketch.

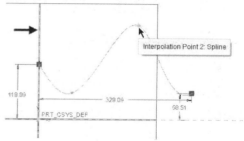

8. Middle-click to place the dimension.
9. On the ribbon, click **Sketch > Operations > Select > One-by-One**, and modify the dimensions.

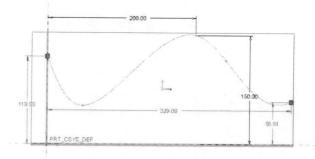

10. Double-click on the spline to activate the edit mode.
11. Select a point on the spline, click the right mouse button and select **Add Point**. A new point is added to the spline as shown. You can drag the point or add dimensions to position it.

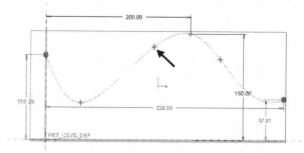

12. On the **Spline** dashboard, click the **Control Points** icon. The **Modify Spline** message appears.

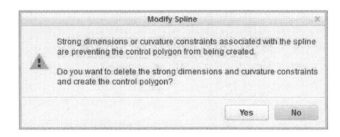

13. Click **Yes** to display control points.
14. Drag the control points of the spline to modify it.

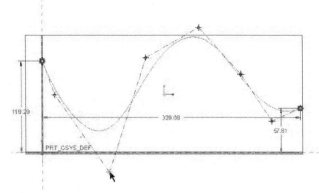

15. Click the right mouse button on a control point and select **Delete Point**. The control point is removed.

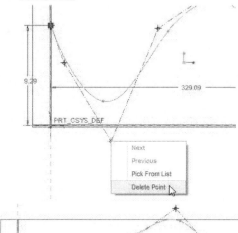

16. On the Dashboard, click the **Curvature analysis tools** ✎ icon.

17. On the Dashboard, type 15 in the **Scale** box and press Enter (or) drag the spinner to change the curvature line length.
18. On the Dashboard, type 2 in the **Density** box and press Enter (or) drag the spinner to change the number of curvature lines.

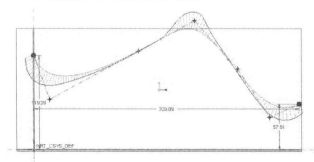

19. Drag the control point and notice the change in curvature length.

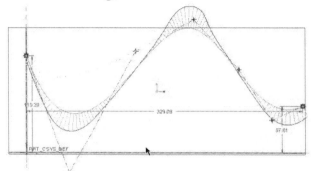

20. On the Dashboard, click the **Control Polygon** icon. Now, you can edit the spline by modifying the dimensions of the control polygon.
21. On the ribbon, click **Sketch > Dimension > Normal**. The dimensions of the control polygon appear.
22. Change a dimension of the control polygon and notice the change.

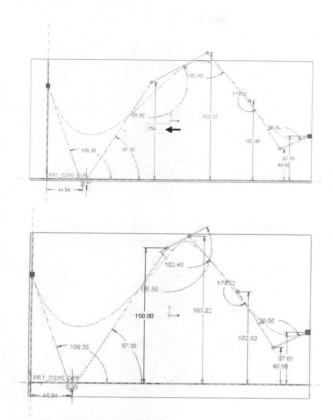

23. Click **OK** on the ribbon.

Boundary Blend

The **Boundary Blend** command creates a surface by using boundary curves in one or two directions. This is a multi-purpose tool, which can be used to achieve a variety of the results.

1. Create three boundary curves on different planes as shown.

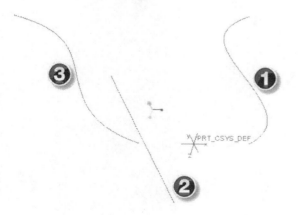

2. On the ribbon, click **Model > Surfaces > Boundary Blend**.
3. Press the Ctrl key and select the first, second, and third boundary curves.

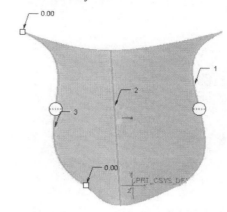

4. On the Dashboard, click the **Constraints** tab. Notice that there are different boundary conditions.

Tangent

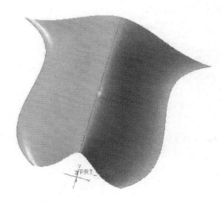

Curvature

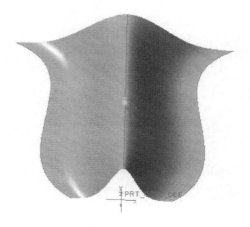

Normal

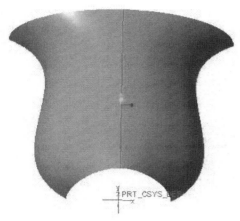

You can adjust the continuity by changing the **Stretch value** on the **Constraints** tab (or) check the **Display drag handles** option and adjust the stretch value.

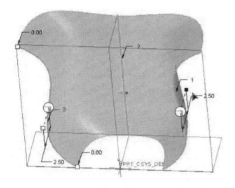

5.   Click **Cancel** on the Dashboard.
6.   Create three curves as shown.

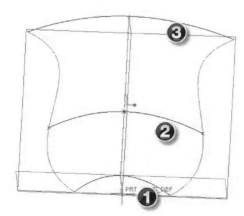

7.   Activate the **Boundary Blend** command.
8.   Press the Ctrl key and select the three curves as shown.

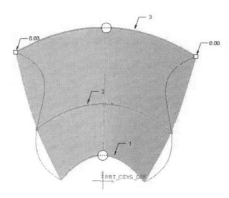

9.   On the Dashboard, click in the **Second direction** box and select the curves as shown.

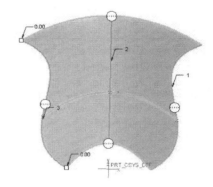

10. Click the green check.

11. Create a sketch as shown.

12. In the **Model Tree**, click and drag the sketch above the boundary blend.

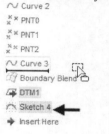

13. Click the right mouse button on the Boundary Blend and select **Edit definition**.
14. On the Dashboard, click the **Options** tab, and then click in the **Influencing curves** box.
15. Select the new sketch and click the green check.

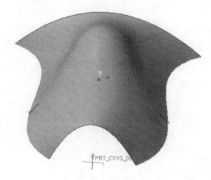

The **Boundary Blend** command creates a surface blending two surfaces. This can be tangent, or curvature continuous in both the directions.

1. On the ribbon, click **Model > Surfaces > Boundary Blend**.
2. Select the edge of the first surface.
3. Press the Ctrl key and select the edge of the second surface.

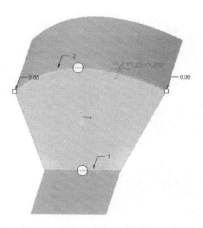

4. Drag the end handles on the second curve as shown.

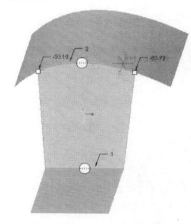

5. Click the right mouse button on the left handle and select **Extend To**.
6. Select the left edge of the surface.

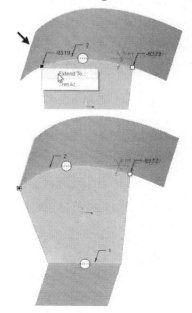

7. Likewise, extend the right edge of the blend surface up to the right edge of the supporting surface.
8. On the Dashboard, click the **Constraints** tab and set the boundary conditions to **Tangent**.
9. Check the **Display drag handles** option.
10. Drag the handles to stretch the surface as shown.

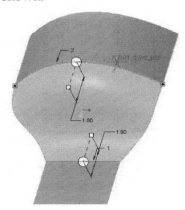

11. Click the green check.

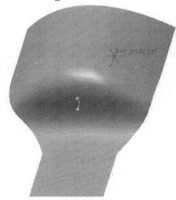

12. Set the **First Continuity** and **Second Continuity** type.
13. Click **OK** to blend the two surfaces.

Fill

The **Fill** command can be used to fill the region enclosed by a sketch.

1. On the ribbon, click **Model > Surfaces > Fill**.
2. Click on the closed sketch.

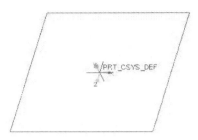

3. Click the green check to fill the sketch.

Offset

To create an offset surface, follow the steps given next.

1. Select the surface to offset from the Model Tree.
2. On the ribbon, click **Model > Editing > Offset**.
3. Type-in a value in the **Offset** box (or) drag the handle to change the offset distance.
4. Click the arrow attached to the surface to reverse the offset direction.

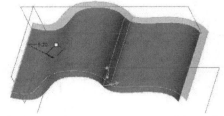

5. Click the **Options** tab on the Dashboard and click in the **Special Handling** box.
6. Select the portion of the surface as shown.

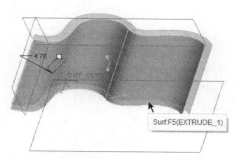

The surface is excluded from the selection.

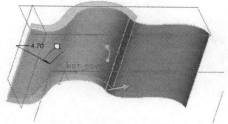

7. On the **Options** tab, select **Automatic Fit** from the drop-down.
8. Change the view orientation to Front.
9. Drag the offset handle and notice the change.

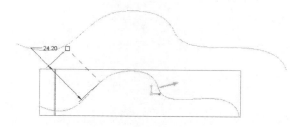

10. Select **Controlled Fit** from the drop-down.
11. Uncheck the **X** option and drag the offset handle. Notice that there is no transition in the X direction.

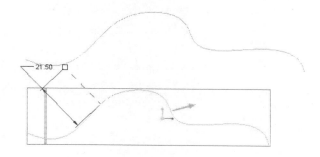

7. Change the view orientation to Default.

8. Check the **Create side surface** option to create side surfaces.

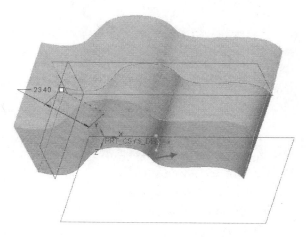

9. Click the green check to complete the feature.

Likewise, you can offset a curve. Select a curve and click the **Offset** icon the **Editing** panel. Select a plane/surface to define the offset direction.

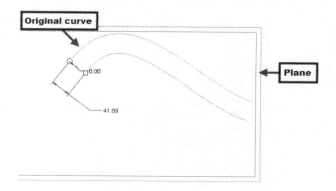

Trim

This command trims a surface using an intersecting element such as plane, curve, and surface.

1. Select the surface to trim.

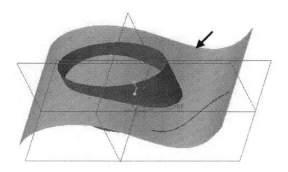

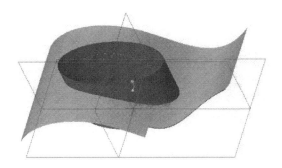

2. On the ribbon, click **Model > Editing > Trim**.
3. Click on the trimming surface.
4. Click the arrow that appears on the trimming surface to change the side to be trimmed.

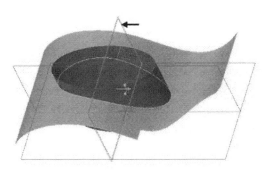

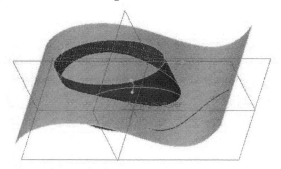

5. Click the green check.

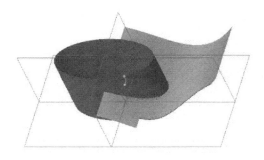

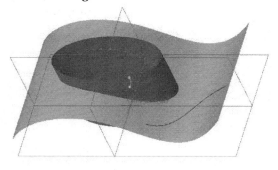

Merge

This command trims and assembles two intersecting surfaces.

1. Press the Ctrl key and select the surfaces to merge
2. On the ribbon, click **Model > Editing > Merge**.

You can also use an intersecting curve or plane to trim the surface.

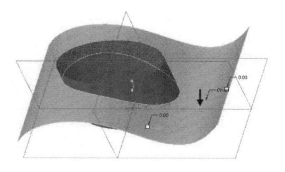

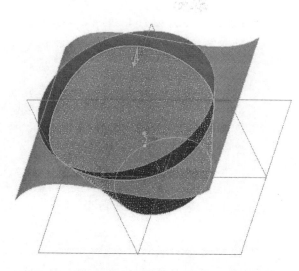

3. Click on the arrows to change the portions to keep.
4. Click the green check.

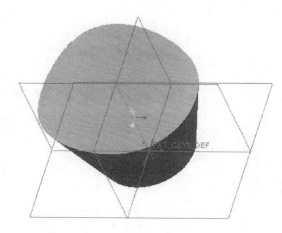

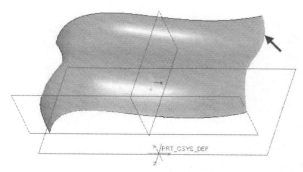 Extend

During the design process, you may sometimes need to extend a surface. You can extend a surface using the **Extend** command.

1. Select the surface to extend and click the right edge

2. On the ribbon, click **Model > Editing > Extend**.
3. Type-in a value in the **Length** box or click and drag the limit handle to define the length of the extended portion.

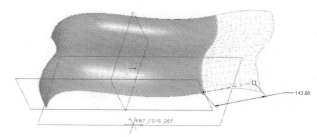

4. Click the **Options** tab and set the extension method. You can extend the surface using three methods: **Same**, **Tangent**, and **Approximate**.

Same

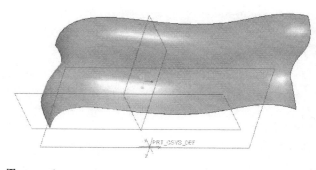

Tangent

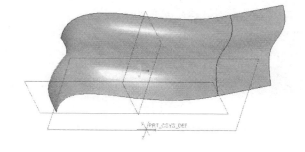

Approximate

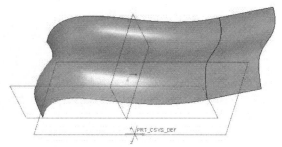

5. On the Dashboard, click the **Extend Surface To Plane**  icon.
6. Select the horizontal plane.
7. Click **Preview**.

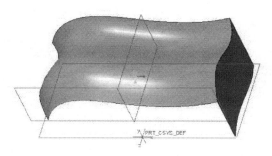

8. Click **Resume**, and then click **Extend along the original surface** .
9. Click the **Measurements** tab and notice that the **Measure in surface** option is selected. The extension distance is measured along the surface.

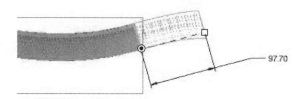

10. Select **Measure in plane** option and select the horizontal plane. Notice that the distance is measured along the selected plane.

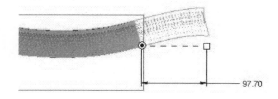

11. On the **Measurements** tab, click the right mouse button on the table and select **Add**. A new measurement point is added to the surface.

12. Drag the limit handle to define the length of the extended surface at the new point.

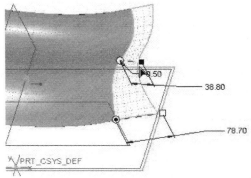

13. Drag the measurement point to change its position.

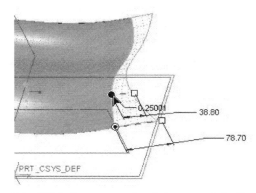

14. Click the green check to complete the feature.

Moving a Surface Copy

The **Paste Special** command moves and copies a surface.

1. Select the surface/element to move.

Creo Parametric 4.0 Basics

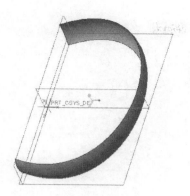

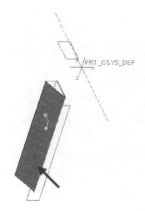

2. On the ribbon, click **Model > Operations > Copy** .

3. On the ribbon, click **Model > Operations > Paste > Paste Special** .

4. On the dashboard, click the **Options** tab, and uncheck the **Hide original geometry** option.

5. On the dashboard, click **Move** .

6. Select a line, axis, or plane to define the translation direction.

7. Type-in a value in the **Distance** box or drag the distance handle (white square).

8. Click the green check to complete the feature.

2. On the ribbon, click **Model > Operations > Copy** .

3. On the ribbon, click **Model > Operations > Paste > Paste Special** .

4. On the dashboard, click the **Options** tab, and uncheck the **Hide original geometry** option.

5. On the dashboard, click **Rotate** .

6. Select a line or axis to define the rotation axis.

7. Type-in a value in the **Angle** box.

8. Click the green check.

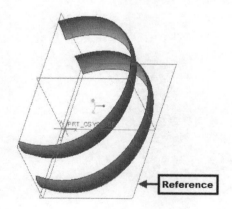

Rotating Surfaces

Creo Parametric allows you to rotate an element about an axis.

1. Select the surface/element to rotate.

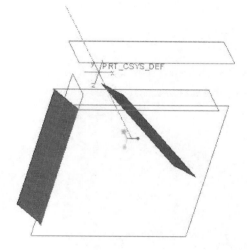

Solidify

This command uses a surface to modify the shape of a solid geometry. You can use a surface to add or remove geometry.

1. Create a solid body and a surface as shown.

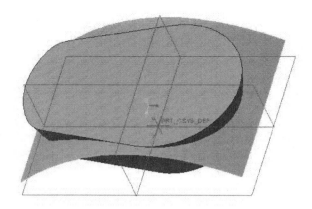

2. Select the surface used to modify the geometry.
3. On the ribbon, click **Model > Editing > Solidify**.
4. On the dashboard, click the **Remove** ◹ icon.

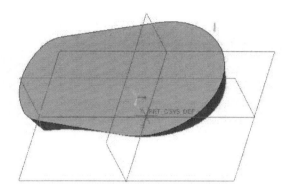

5. Click the arrow that appears in the graphics window to reverse the side to be removed.

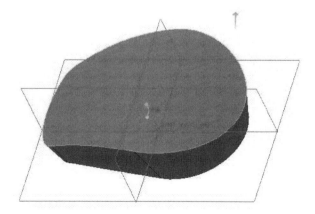

6. Click the green check.

Adding geometry using a surface

1. Create a solid body and an intersecting surface forming a closed volume.

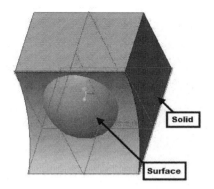

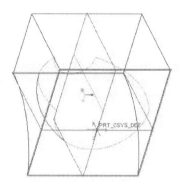

2. Select the surface and activate the **Solidify** command.
3. On the Dashboard, click the **Fill volume** ⬚ icon.
4. Click the green check.

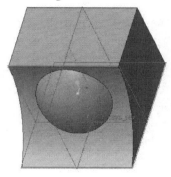

⊏ Thicken

Creating a solid from a surface can be accomplished by simply thickening a surface. To add thickness to a surface, follow the steps given next.

1. Select the surface to thicken.

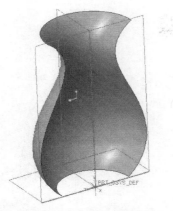

2. On the ribbon, click **Model > Editing > Thicken**.
3. Enter the thickness value in the **Offset** box (or) drag the offset handle.
4. Click the arrow that appears on the geometry to reverse the side of material addition.
5. Click the **Options** tab and select a method to add thickness. These methods are same as that available in the **Offset** commend.
6. Click the green check.

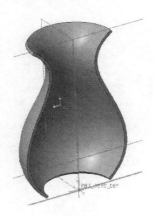

Example

In this example, you will construct the model shown below.

Creating the Layout Curves

1. Start **Creo Parametric 4.0**.
2. Create a folder with the name *Surface Design* and set it as current working folder.
3. On the Quick Access Toolbar, click the **New** button.
4. On the **New** dialog, select **Type > Part**.
5. Select **Sub-Type > Solid**.
6. Type-in *Example1* in the **Name** box and uncheck the **Use default template** option.
7. Click **OK**.
8. On the **New File Options** dialog, select **solid_part _mmks** option and click **OK**.
9. On the ribbon, click **Model > Datum > Point > Offset Coordinate System** ⁎.
10. Select the default coordinate system.
11. On the **Datum Point** dialog, select **Type > Cartesian**.
12. Click in the table and enter the point coordinates as shown. Click **OK**.

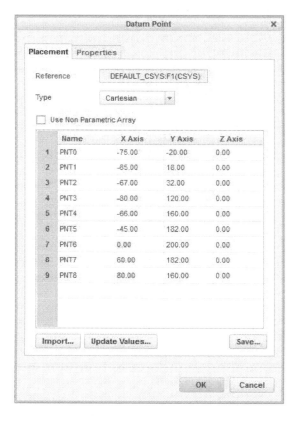

	Name	X Axis	Y Axis	Z Axis
1	PNT0	-75.00	-20.00	0.00
2	PNT1	-65.00	18.00	0.00
3	PNT2	-67.00	32.00	0.00
4	PNT3	-80.00	120.00	0.00
5	PNT4	-66.00	160.00	0.00
6	PNT5	-45.00	182.00	0.00
7	PNT6	0.00	200.00	0.00
8	PNT7	60.00	182.00	0.00
9	PNT8	80.00	160.00	0.00

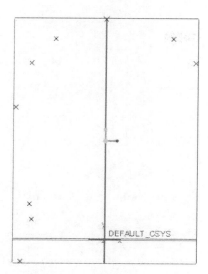

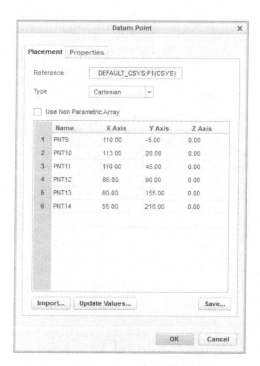

13. On the **Model** tab of the ribbon, expand the **Datum** panel and click **Curve > Curve through point** ∿ .

14. Select the points one-by-one and click the green check.

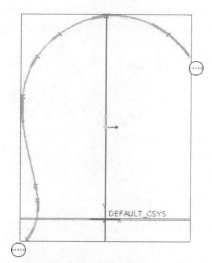

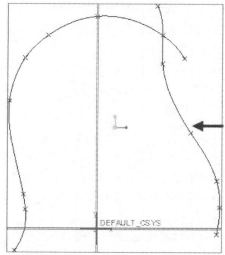

15. Likewise, create the second and third curves as shown.

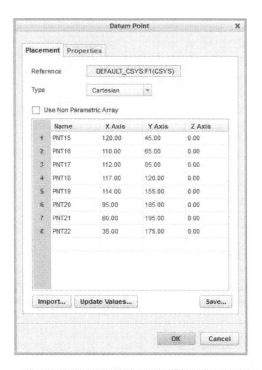

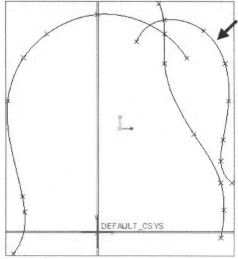

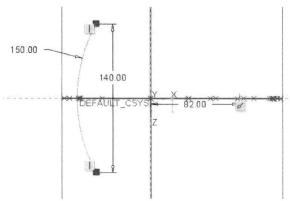

2. Create an arc on the Right Plane and add dimensions to it. Finish the sketch.

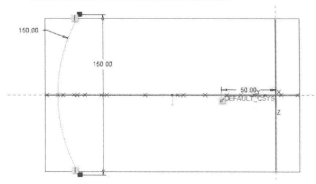

3. Create a datum plane normal to the first curve.

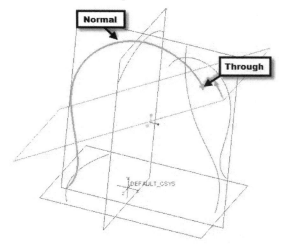

Creating the Front Surface

1. Create an arc on the Top Plane and add dimensions to it. Exit the sketch.

4. Create an arc on the plane normal to curve. Finish the sketch. Maintain a coincident constraint between the arc and the end point of the curve.

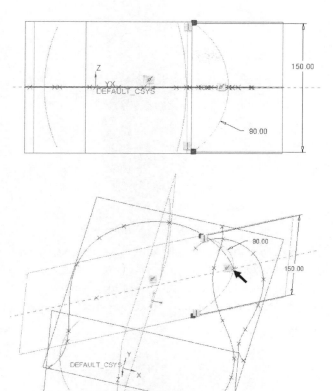

9. Select the lower most arc.

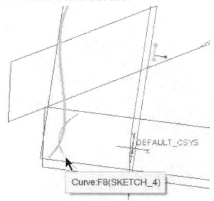

5. On the ribbon, click **Model** tab > **Shapes** panel > **Swept Blend** .

6. On the Dashboard, click the **Surface** icon.

7. Select the first curve to define the trajectory.

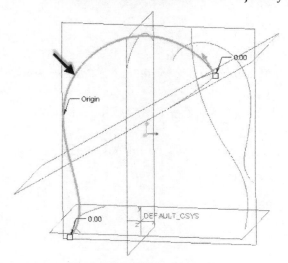

10. Click the **Insert** button on the **Section** tab, and then select second arc.

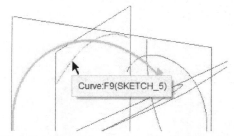

11. Click the **Insert** button and select the third arc.

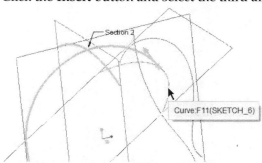

12. Make sure that the arrows point in the same direction. Double-click the arrow to change its direction, if they point in the opposite direction.

8. On the Dashboard, click the **Sections** tab and select the **Selected Sections** option.

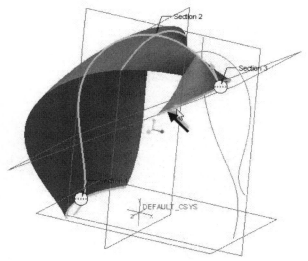

13. Click the green check to complete the swept bend surface.

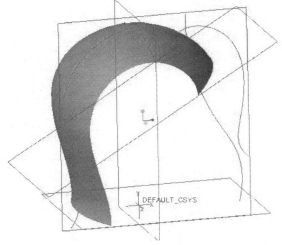

14. Save the file. As you are creating a complex geometry, it is advisable that you save the model after each operation.

Creating the Label surface

1. Create an arc on the top plane. Exit the sketch.

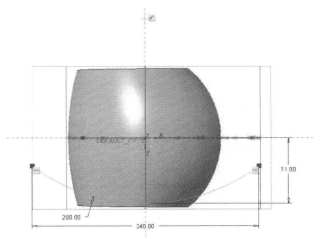

2. On the ribbon, click **Model** tab > **Shapes** panel > **Extrude**.
3. On the Dashboard, click the **Surface** icon.
4. Extrude the sketch up to 220 distance.

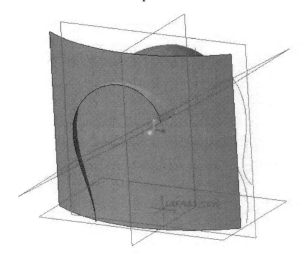

5. Select the extruded surface.
6. On the ribbon, click **Model** tab > **Editing** panel > **Mirror** .
7. Select the front plane to define the mirroring plane.
8. Click the green check on the dashboard.

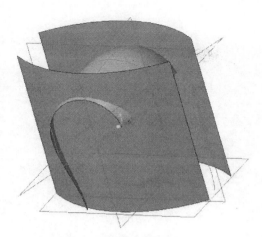

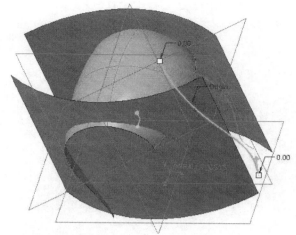

Creating the Back surface

1. On the ribbon, click **Model** tab > **Shapes** panel > **Sweep** .

2. On the Dashboard, click the **Surface** icon.

3. Select the curve, as shown below.

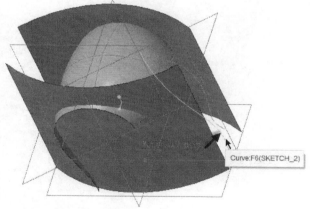

4. Double-click on the arrow displayed on the curve such that the origin point is located at the bottom end of the curve.

5. On the Dashboard, click the **Create edit sweep section** icon.

6. Create an arc and exit the sketch.

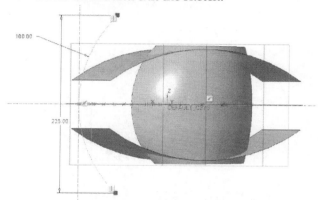

7. Click the green check to create the surface.

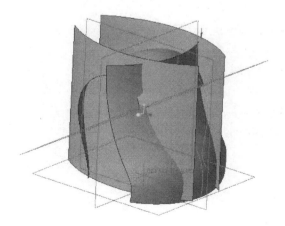

Trimming the Unwanted Portions

1. Press the Ctrl key, select the swept blend and
   front extruded surface, and click the **Merge** icon on the **Editing** panel.

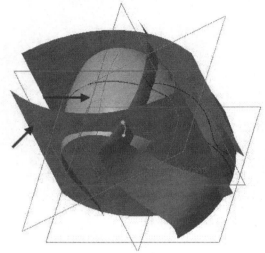

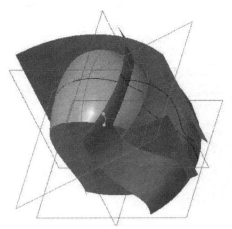

2. Make sure that the arrows point inwards. You can click on them to change the direction.

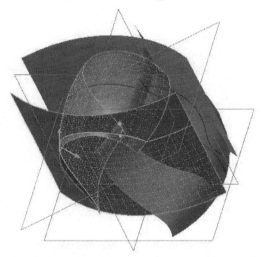

4. Likewise, merge the swept blend and mirror surfaces as shown.

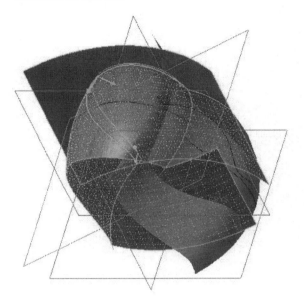

3. Click the green check to merge and trim the swept blend and extrude surfaces.

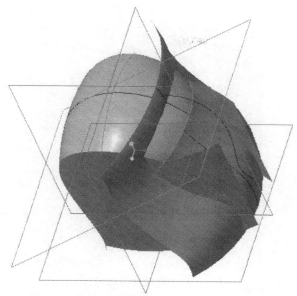

5. Press the Ctrl key and select swept blend and sweep surfaces.

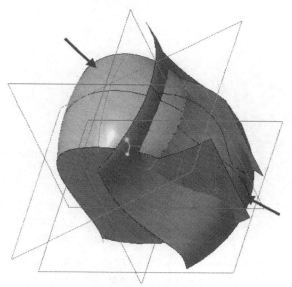

6. On the ribbon, click the **Merge** icon and make sure that the arrows point in the direction as shown.

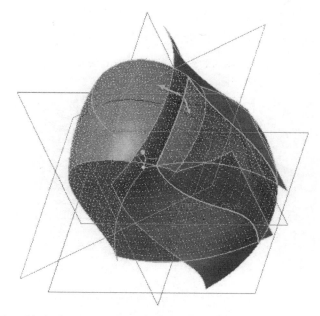

7. Click the green check to merge the surfaces.

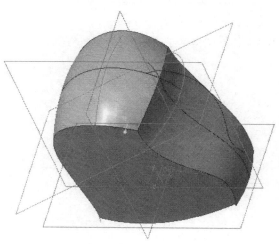

8. Select the sweep surface and click the **Trim** 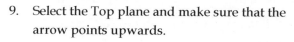 icon.

9. Select the Top plane and make sure that the arrow points upwards.

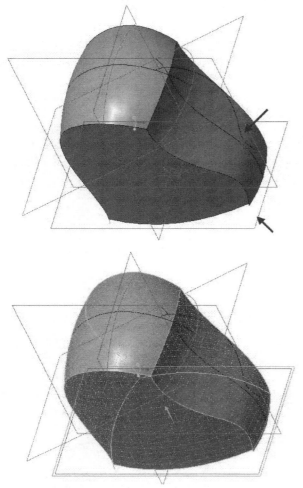

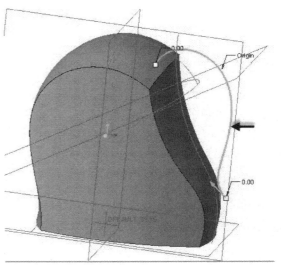

10. Click the green check to trim the unwanted portion of the sweep surface at the bottom.

Creating the Handle Surface

1. Activate the **Sweep** command and select the third curve.
2. Make sure that the origin is located at the bottom.

8. On the Dashboard, click the **Create edit sweep section** icon.
9. Create an ellipse and make sure that the top quadrant point is coincident with the end point of the curve.
10. Add dimensions and click **OK** on the ribbon.

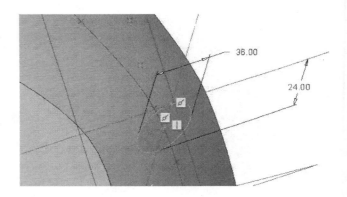

11. On the Dashboard, click the **Surface** icon.
12. Click the green check to complete the swept surface.

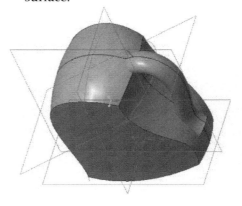

Rounding the intersecting edge

1. On the ribbon, click **Model** tab > **Engineering** panel > **Round** .

2. Click on the edge connecting the front and back faces.

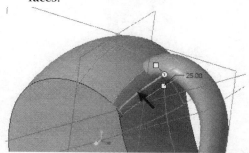

3. On the Dashboard, type-in 25 in the **Radius** box, and then click the green check.

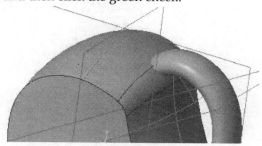

Blending the Bottom handle

1. Start a sketch on the Front plane and select the third layout curve as the sketch reference.

2. Draw a line tangent to the third layout curve, as shown below.

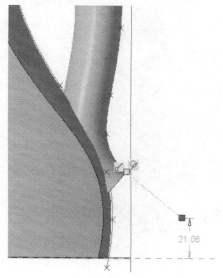

3. Exit the sketch.
4. Activate the **Plane** command.
5. Press and hold the Ctrl key and select the tangent line and Front plane. A new plane appears.
6. Make the plane normal to the Front plane and pass through the tangent line.

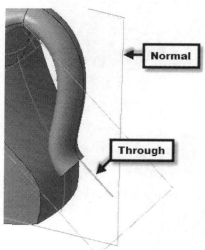

7. Click **OK** to create the datum plane.
8. Draw an ellipse and trim it by half.

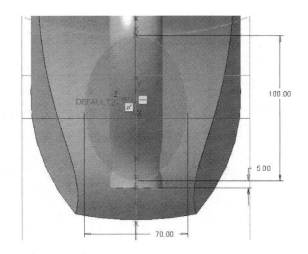

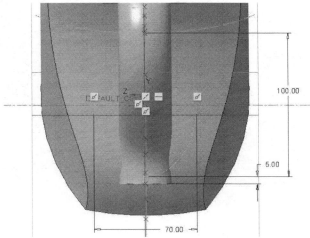

9. Exit the sketch and extrude it in both the directions up to an arbitrary distance.

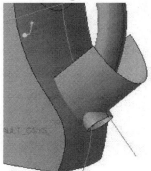

10. Press hold the Ctrl key, and then select the handle and extruded surfaces.

11. Click the **Merge** ⬡ icon on the **Editing** panel.

12. Make sure that the arrows point in the direction as shown.

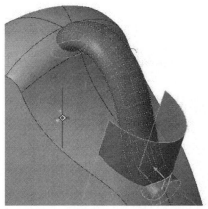

13. Click the green check to merge the two surfaces.

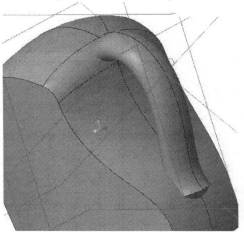

14. Press Ctrl and select the handle surface and main surface body.

15. On the **Editing** panel of the ribbon, click the **Merge** icon.

16. Make sure that the arrows point outward.

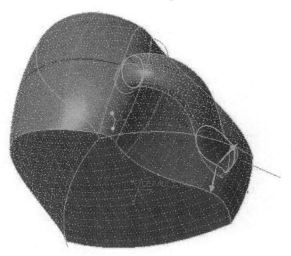

17. Activate the **Round** command and round the edge of the handle. The round radius is 6 mm.

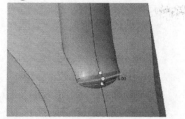

18. Round the intersection between the main surface and handle. The fillet radius is 5 mm.

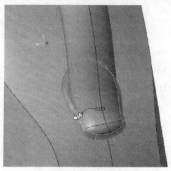

Trimming the Handle

1. Create a vertical line on the Front Plane and finish the sketch.

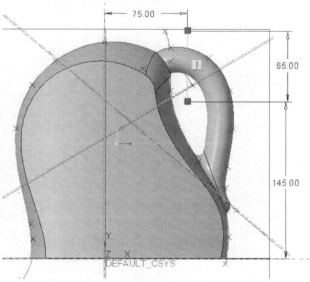

2. Activate the **Project** command (on the ribbon, click **Model** tab > **Editing** panel > **Project**) and click on the sketched line.
3. On the dashboard, click in the **Surface** selection box, and then click on the handle surface.

4. On the dashboard, **Direction > Along Direction**.
5. Click in the selection box next to the **Direction** drop-down, and then select the Front plane.

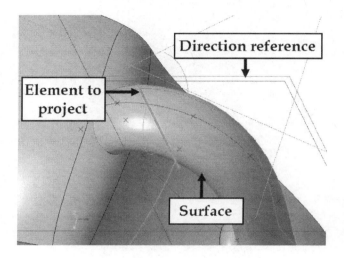

6. Click the green check on the dashboard.
7. Press Esc to deselect the projected curve.
8. Click on the handle surface, and then activate the **Trim** command.
9. Click on the projected curve.

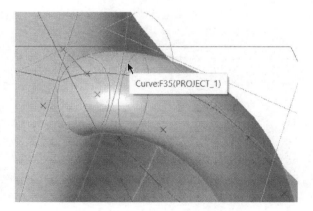

10. Make sure that the arrow points toward right. Use the **Flip** icon, if required.

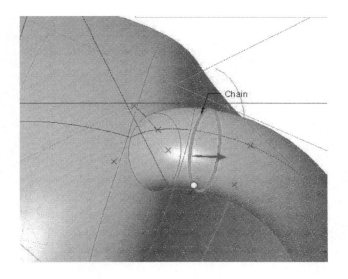

11. Click the green check on the dashboard.

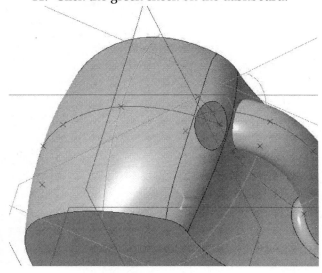

12. On the ribbon, click **Model** tab > **Datum panel** > **Plane**.
13. Press hold the Ctrl key, and then click on the curve of the handle surface and its top end point.
14. On the **Datum Plane** dialog, click on the drop-down located next to the selected curve.
15. Select **Normal** from the drop-down.
16. Likewise, select **Through** from the drop-down located next to the selected point, and then click **OK**.

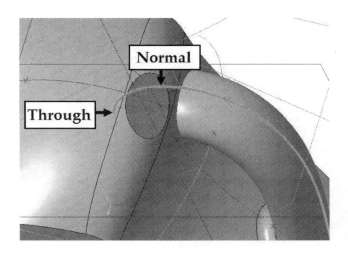

17. Start a sketch on the plane normal to the spline and draw an ellipse. Add dimensions to position the ellipse, and then finish the sketch.

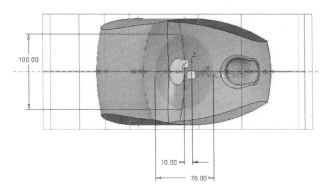

18. Activate the **Project** ✎ command (on the ribbon, click **Model** tab > **Editing** panel > **Project**) and click on the sketched ellipse.
19. On the dashboard, click in the **Surface** selection box.
20. Press hold the Ctrl key, and then click on the three surfaces, as shown.
21. On the dashboard, **Direction** > **Along Direction**.
22. Click in the selection box next to the **Direction** drop-down, and then select the plane normal to the handle curve.

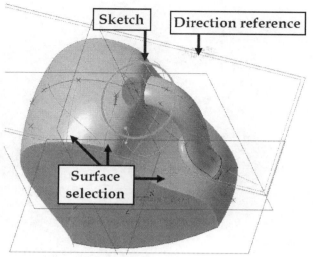

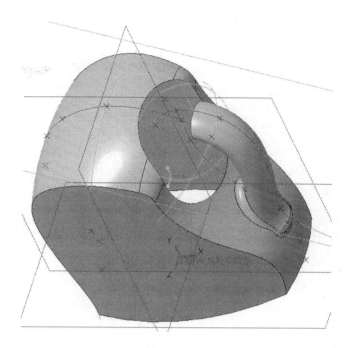

23. Click the green check on the dashboard to project the sketch.
24. Select the surface, as shown.
25. Activate the **Trim** command (on the ribbon, click **Model > Editing > Trim**).
26. Select the projected curve.
27. Make sure that the arrow points toward left.

Blending the Top handle

1. Activate the **Boundary Blend** command (on the ribbon, click **Model > Surfaces > Boundary Blend**).
2. Press hold the Ctrl key and click on the edges of the trimmed openings.

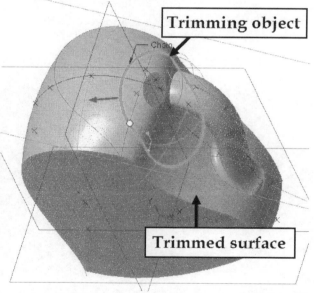

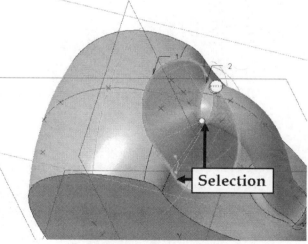

28. Click the green check on the dashboard to trim the surface.

3. On the **Boundary Blend** dashboard, on the **Curves** tab, click **Details** under the **First direction** section.
4. On the **Chain** dialog, select the first chain from the list box located at the top.
5. Click on the **Options** tab.

6. Click in the **Start Point** box located at the bottom.
7. Select the point on the first chain, as shown.

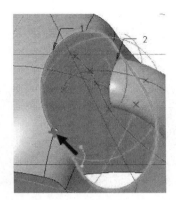

8. On the **Chain** dialog, select the second chain from the list box located at the top.
9. Click on the **Options** tab.
10. Click in the **Start Point** box located at the bottom.
11. Select the point on the second chain, as shown.

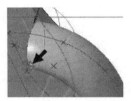

12. Click **OK** on the **Chain** dialog.
13. On the **Boundary Blend** dashboard, click the **Constraints** tab.
14. On the set the **Condition** of the two boundaries to **Tangent**.
15. Select the **Direction 1-First Chain** and change the **Stretch value** to 1.
16. Select the **Direction 1-Last Chain** and change the **Stretch value** to 2.

Boundary	Condition
Direction 1-First chain	Tangent
Direction 1-Last chain	Tangent

☐ Display drag handles

Entities	Surfaces
1	Default Surf:F24(SWEEP_2)
2	Default Surf:F24(SWEEP_2)

Stretch value | 0.50 | ▼

☐ Add side curve influence
☑ Add inner edge tangency
☐ Optimize surface shape

17. Click the **Control Points** tab on the dashboard.
18. Select **Fit > Natural**.
19. Right click in the **Sets** list box, and then select **Add**; the Set 1 is added to the list.
20. Set Set 1 from the Sets list box.
21. Select the points, as shown.

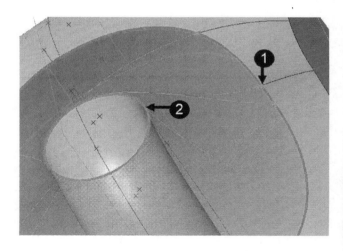

22. Right click in the **Sets** list box, and then select **Add**; Set 2 is added to the list.
23. Select **Set 2** from the **Sets** list box.
24. Select the points from the first and last chain, as shown.

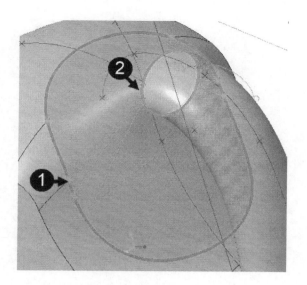

25. Click the green check on the dashboard to blend the handle surface.

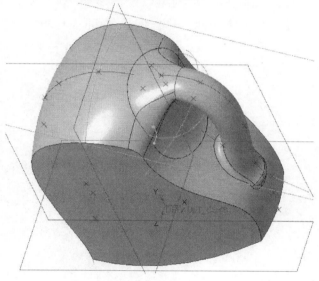

Creating the Neck and Spout

1. Start a sketch on the Front Plane and draw the sketch for the revolved surface. Exit the sketch.

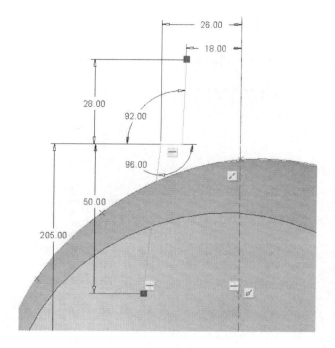

15. On the ribbon, click **Model** tab > **Shapes** panel > **Revolve**.
16. Type-in 360 in the **Angle** box and click the green check.

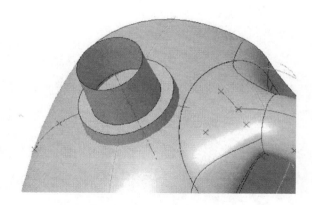

17. Press and hold the Ctrl key and select the main body and boundary blend.
18. Activate the **Merge** command.
19. Click the green check on the dashboard.

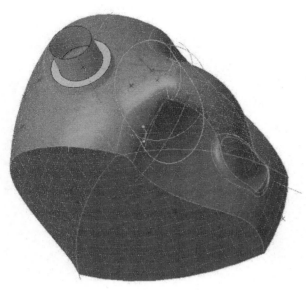

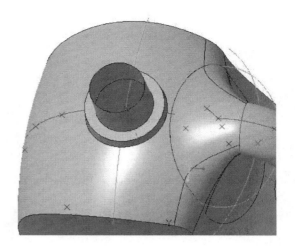

Creating the Variable Radius Round

1. On the **Engineering** panel of the ribbon, click the **Round** icon.

2. Click on the edge of the label surface, as shown below.

20. Press and hold the Ctrl key and select the main body and neck.

21. Activate the **Merge** command.

22. Make sure that the arrows point in the direction shown below.

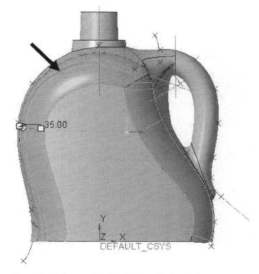

3. On the Dashboard, click the **Sets** tab.

4. In the **Radius** section, click the right mouse button and select **Add Radius**. This adds a radius point at the end of the selected edge chain.

23. Click the green check to trim the unwanted portion.

5. Likewise, add another radius point.
6. In the **Radius** section, select the third radius point and set the location type to **Reference**.

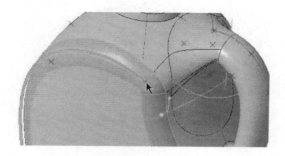

7. Select the vertex point, as shown below.

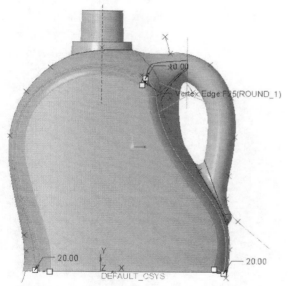

8. In the **Radius** section, set the first and second radius values to 20, and third one to 10.

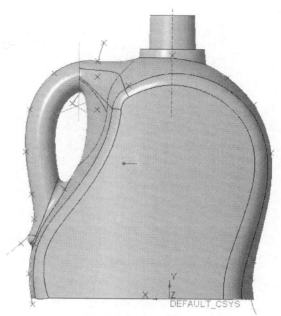

9. Click the green check to complete the variable round.
10. Likewise, create the variable radius round on the other side of the bottle.

Creating a bump at the bottom

1. Start a sketch on the Top datum plane and project the edge chain at the bottom (refer to the **Project** section in **Chapter 3** to learn how to project edges).

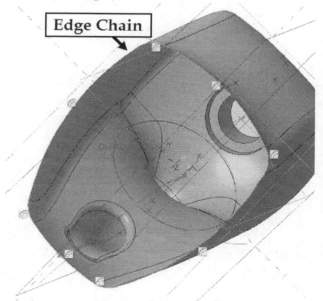

2. Click **OK** on the **Sketch** tab of the ribbon.
3. Create an offset plane from the Top Plane. The offset distance is 10 mm.

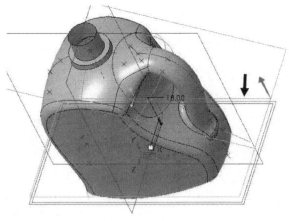

4. Start a sketch on the offset plane.

5. Offset the project edges up to -40 distance (refer to **The Offset Command** section of Chapter 2 to learn how to offset entities).

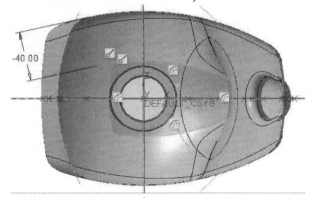

6. Round the corners of the offset sketch using the **Circular Trim** command. The corner radius is 10 (refer to **The Circular Trim command** section in **Chapter 2** to learn how round corners).

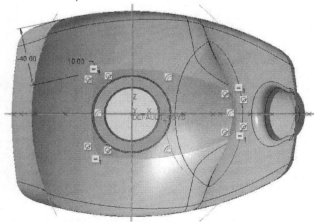

7. Click **OK** on the ribbon and deselect any sketch, if selected.

8. Expand the **Shapes** panel of the ribbon and click the **Blend** icon.

9. On the Dashboard, click the **Surface** icon.

10. Click the **Sections** tab and select the **Selected sections** option.

11. Select the outer loop and click the **Details** button.

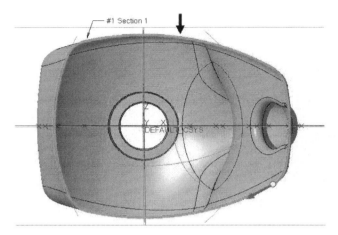

12. On the **Chain** dialog, click the **Options** tab.

13. Click in the **Start Point** selection box and select the end point of the curve, as shown below. Make sure that the arrow points towards right.

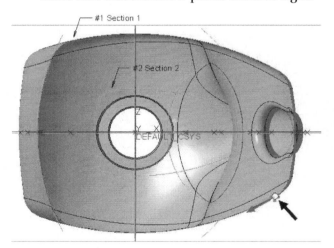

14. Click **OK** on the **Chain** dialog.

15. Click the **Sections** tab on the Dashboard, and then click the **Insert** button.

16. Select the inner loop and click the **Details** button.

17. On the **Chain** dialog, click the **Options** tab.

18. Click in the **Start Point** selection box and select the endpoint, as shown below. Make sure that

the arrow points towards right.

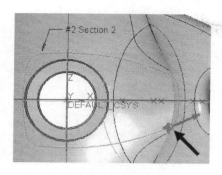

19. Click **OK**.
20. Click the green check to complete the blend.

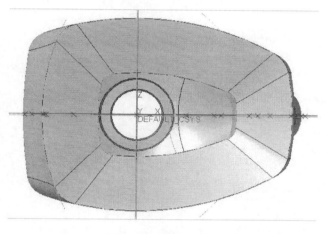

21. On the **Surfaces** panel of the ribbon, click the
    Fill ▢ icon.
22. Click on the inner loop, and then click the green
    check.

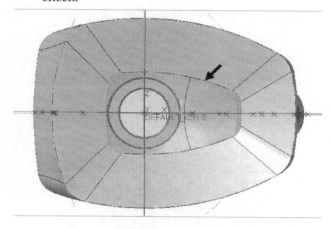

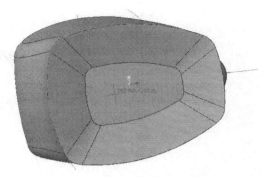

23. Merge the blend and fill surfaces.

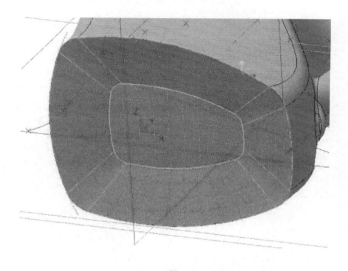

24. Activate the **Round** ⌐ command.
25. Press and hold the Ctrl key and select the Fill
    and blend surfaces.
26. Type-in 30 in the **Radius** box, and click the
    green check.

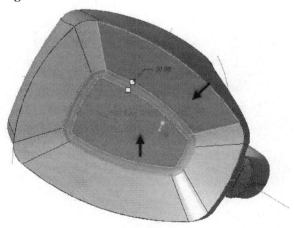

27. Merge the bottom surface with the main surface
    body.

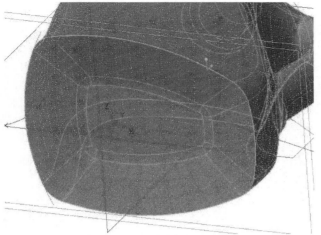

28. Activate the **Round** command.
29. Press and hold the Ctrl key and click on the bottom surface and main body.

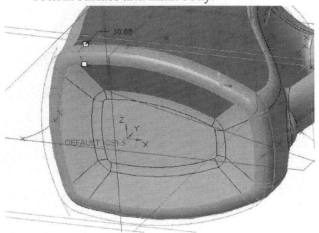

30. Type-in **10** in the **Radius** box and click the green check.

Adding thickness to the model

1. Select the surface model and click the **Thicken** icon on the **Editing** panel.
2. On the Dashboard, type 2 in the **Offset** box.
3. Make sure that the arrow points outwards.
4. Click the green check to thicken the surface.

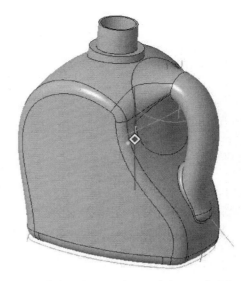

5. Round the sharp edges of the neck. The round radius is 1 mm.

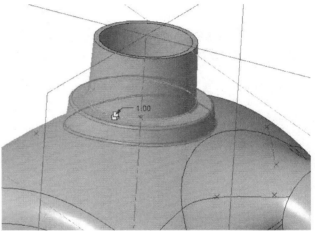

Creating the thread

1. Activate the **Plane** command, and then create a plane offset from the neck surface. The offset distance is 20 mm.

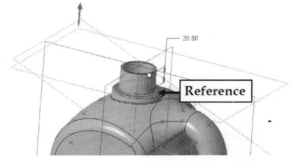

2. On the **Shapes** panel of the ribbon, click **Sweep**

drop-down > **Helical Sweep** .

3. On the Dashboard, click the **References** tab, and then click the **Define** button.
4. Select the front plane. Click the **Sketch** button to activate the sketch.
5. On the **Setup** panel of the ribbon, click the **References** icon.
6. Select the offset plane and silhouette edge of the sprout.

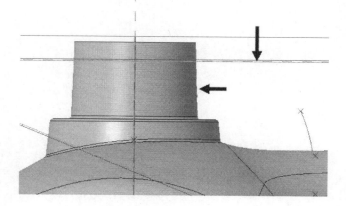

7. Draw a line coinciding with the reference silhouette edge.

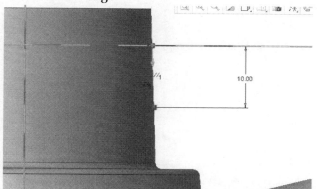

8. Draw a centerline passing through the center of the neck, and then click **OK**.
9. On the Dashboard, click the **Create or edit sweep section** icon.
10. Draw the section, as shown below. Click **OK**.

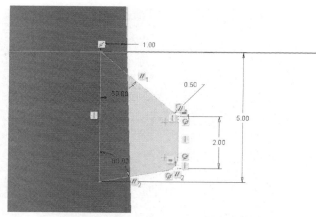

11. On the Dashboard, type-in 5 in the **Pitch Value** box and click the green check.

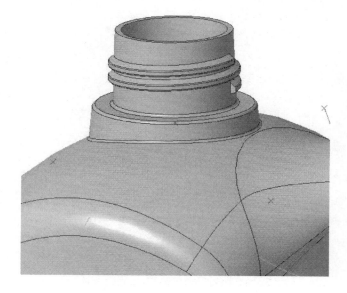

12. Save and close the file.

Questions

1. What is the use of the **Merge** command?
2. Why do we use the **Fill** command?
3. What are the commands that can be used to fill the openings on a surface?
4. Which command can be used to bridge the gap between two surfaces?
5. Name the command that can be used to trim and join the surfaces.
6. How do you add thicknesses to a surface body?
7. Which command is used to extend surfaces from an edge?
8. How do you split a solid body?

9. Which command is used to offset a face?

Index

Made in the USA
Lexington, KY
11 July 2018